# How to Do Theory

# How to Study Literature

The books in this series – all written by eminent scholars renowned for their teaching abilities – show students how to read, understand, write, and criticize literature. They provide the key skills which every student of literature must master, as well as offering a comprehensive introduction to the field itself.

**Published**

| | |
|---|---|
| *How to Do Theory* | Wolfgang Iser |
| *How to Write a Poem* | John Redmond |

# How to Do Theory

*Wolfgang Iser*

Blackwell
Publishing

BLACKWELL PUBLISHING
350 Main Street, Malden, MA 02148-5020, USA
9600 Garsington Road, Oxford OX4 2DQ, UK
550 Swanston Street, Carlton, Victoria 3053, Australia

First published 2006 by Blackwell Publishing Ltd

1 2006

*Library of Congress Cataloging-in-Publication Data*

Iser, Wolfgang.
    How to do theory / Wolfgang Iser.
        p. cm. — (How to study literature)
    Includes bibliographical references and index.
    ISBN-13: 978-1-4051-1579-7 (hardcover: alk. paper)
    ISBN-10: 1-4051-1579-3 (hardcover: alk. paper)
    ISBN-13: 978-1-4051-1580-3 (pbk.: alk. paper)
    ISBN-10: 1-4051-1580-7 (pbk.: alk. paper)
    1. Literature—Philosophy. 2. Criticism. 3. Literature—History and
criticism—Theory, etc. I. Title. II. Series.
    PN49.I77 2006
    801'.95—dc22

                                                            2005004140

A catalogue record for this title is available from the British Library.

Set in 10$^1$/$_2$/13pt Minion
by Graphicraft Limited, Hong Kong
Printed and bound in the United Kingdom
by TJ International Ltd, Padstow, Cornwall

The publisher's policy is to use permanent paper from mills that operate a
sustainable forestry policy, and which has been manufactured from pulp
processed using acid-free and elementary chlorine-free practices. Furthermore,
the publisher ensures that the text paper and cover board used have met
acceptable environmental accreditation standards.

For further information on
Blackwell Publishing, visit our website:
www.blackwellpublishing.com

# Contents

Contents

# Preface and Acknowledgments

This exposition of modern theories of literature and the arts has been conceived as an introduction to theory-building primarily, but not exclusively, for students in the humanities. I have therefore chosen a fairly wide variety of theories in order to highlight the many different ways in which works of art have been conceptualized.

Each theory translates art into cognition, for which a scaffolding is required. This starts out from a presupposition, on which are built certain structures that serve a particular function, the fulfillment of which is organized through specific modes of operation. In trying to make the theories sufficiently transparent, I have confined myself to a bare outline of their components. Since the aim of this handbook is to acquaint interested students with the architecture of theory-building, I have presented the theories as dispassionately as possible, and have refrained from judging, let alone criticizing, them. It is for readers to voice their own likes and dislikes. Indeed, there is no need to subscribe to any of the theories outlined, since the object of this book is simply to elucidate both the arguments and the achievements.

With a few exceptions, I have chosen only one representative of the theory concerned in order to explain the procedure according to which the cognitive framework was built. It would not have made sense to piece together concepts from different theorists, even of the same camp, as this would have distracted from the consistency of theory-building. I have tried to let the authors speak for themselves by quoting them extensively, and in this respect the book is an anthology of key theoretical statements. It must be said that not all of the theories assembled are heavyweights, but in order to assess what they are able to accomplish, their difference in range and depth is in itself a relevant factor.

Some readers may wonder why there is hardly any mention of structuralism, poststructuralism, postmodernism, and intertextuality. No doubt these phenomena are important, and they are often hotly debated in the humanities. However, they are not theories; they may have inspired certain theories, slanted their arguments, and shaped their objectives, but in themselves they are movements, preoccupations, period concepts, and forces that jostle for prominence, at best raising the hue and cry "against theory." In order to provide an overview of theory formation, I chose to stay clear of all these "isms."

Some might advance the same arguments against my inclusion of feminism, and I must confess that I found only a few essays that head toward a genuine theory of literature without ever coming up with something fully fledged. However, I would take this as a justification, for while other theories set out from a basic premise in search of elucidation, feminism sets out from a basic premise in search of theory.

As regards the theories that I have chosen, I agree beforehand with all those potential critics who will object to the omissions. If I had been given more space, I would certainly have expanded the repertoire. It was a hard decision, for instance, to leave out general systems theory, sociological theories of art, analytical language theories, and theories of symbolic logic. I did so mainly because they have a highly elaborate technical structure. This applies to Arnold Gehlen's sociological approach to art, and even more to Nelson Goodman's *Languages of Art*. Apart from the logical intricacies of their frameworks, their appeal is limited to students in the humanities, whereas a handbook should focus on what is widely debated.

It may be expedient to say a few words about why I have chosen Anton Ehrenzweig to represent a psychoanalytical theory of art, and Eric Gans to represent an anthropological theory. Ehrenzweig was both an analyst and a historian of fine arts. Instead of using works of art in order to corroborate findings or to illustrate tenets of psychoanalytical theory, Ehrenzweig proceeded in the opposite direction by putting psychoanalytical theory to work in order to elucidate the creative process of the artist. One would be hard put to find a psychoanalytical theory of art comparable to that which Ehrenzweig proposed. Although it was eclipsed for a while, it is now resurfacing even in professional circles of psychoanalysis.

There are several reasons for my choice of Gans. First of all, he created a new discipline, generative anthropology, single-handedly. In order to accomplish his end, the theory had to be global and rigorously reasoned. This makes it an interesting case of theory-building, since it had to embrace the rise of humankind, the development of human culture, the necessity of the arts, and the history of literature from the Greeks to postmodernism. Needless to say, such a theory requires a framework that was bound to be reductive, if the welter of phenomena was to be marshaled into an overall explanatory pattern. Regardless of whether this pattern is convincing or not, the theory itself is unique in that it is based entirely on a construct, whereas the others arise from realities such as perception, consciousness, sign usage, etc. Gans has fulfilled in his own way what other anthropologists have striven for: "a functional aesthetics."

It was one of the publisher's stipulations that the skeletal exposition of a theory should be followed by an example, intended to add flesh to the bones. As theories are not merely methods of interpretation, the examples provided are not applications. If one were to apply a theory to such a purpose, a much more extensive elaboration of the example would be necessary. Furthermore, the examples are not meant to corroborate the validity of the theory concerned, not least because – as the reader will see – theories themselves often resort to examples in order to underpin basic arguments at the point where explanation leaves off. The example then functions as a compensation for what the concepts are unable to grasp, and thus is meant to furnish the generalizations which the cognitive frameworks can no longer provide. This is a practice by no means confined to theories of art but one which is widespread in a great many theoretical discourses today. Therefore, the examples are simply meant to show what a work of art would look like if viewed in terms of the theory concerned.

Also in accordance with the publisher's wishes, I have provided a glossary of technical terms. All the terms that appear in the glossary are printed in bold on their first occurrence in order to distinguish them from those explained in the text.

Finally, I should like to thank Andrew McNeillie, who commissioned this book and persuaded me to write it. I am equally grateful to my friend David Henry Wilson for his astute and penetrating criticism, as well as for polishing my English. Last but not least my thanks are due to Barbara Caldwell for compiling the index.

# 1

# Introduction

## Why Theory?

Literary theory is of recent vintage. Since entering the scene after World War II, it has had a considerable impact on the main concern of the humanities: the interpretation of texts. Interpretation had long been understood as an activity that did not seem to require analysis of its own procedures. There was a tacit assumption that it was a natural process, not least because human beings live by constantly interpreting. We continually emit a mass of signs and signals in response to the bombardment of signs and signals that we receive from outside ourselves. But while such a basic human disposition makes interpretation appear to come naturally, the forms it takes do not.[1] Literary theory created an awareness of the variety and changing validity of interpretation, thereby changing interpretive practice in the humanities altogether.

Theory became a necessity at a critical juncture in literary studies, and as there is no simple explanation for this development we must look to history for possible reasons. Obviously, time-honored approaches to art were no longer capable of dealing with modernity, and it is no exaggeration to maintain that the rise of theory marks a shift in the history of criticism equal to the replacement of Aristotelian poetics by philosophical aesthetics at the threshold of the nineteenth century. The rule-governed Aristotelian poetics offered a recipe for making works of art, whereas the triumphantly emerging aesthetics proclaimed art to be knowable. "Making" versus "cognizing" art articulates the change wrought by aesthetics.

1

Such a turnabout had more or less invalidated a central eighteenth-century preoccupation, namely, the tracing of distinctions between the "sister arts," as exemplified by Lessing's *Laokoön*. Lessing contrasted the verbal and the pictorial arts, with poetry as the temporality of verbal sequence and painting as the spatiality of the pictorial instant. This distinction – though differently evaluated and at times even understood hierarchically, as evinced by Addison – was also meant to pin down the respective impacts of the arts on the recipient. More often than not the verbal arts were privileged, because they spurred the imagination into more comprehensive action than painting or sculpture. Poetry, according to Murray Krieger, "works on the 'soul' or mind," and its "virtue is its capacity to function just where mere picturing leaves off."[2] In other words, poetry is a spiritual experience, whereas painting engages only the senses. Thus the individual arts were marked off from one another according to their operation, medium, and effect.

This neatly distinguished plurality of the "sister arts" was displaced by philosophical aesthetics, which strove to determine the nature of art by means of definitions which – though continually changing from Hegel to Adorno – gave art an ontological basis. Pluralism gave way to holism. It all began with the Romantics, who elevated aesthetics to the be-all and end-all and entrenched it as a philosophy of art. This identification of aesthetics with the work of art gained such dominance throughout the nineteenth century that the great philosophical systems felt compelled to extend their speculations to the realm of art by giving the latter a systematic exposition, and hence an ontological root.

Aesthetics, then, became a philosophical discipline, ranking alongside metaphysics and ethics, and was basically concerned with cognition of art in relation to the dominant tenets of the system. Hegel, for instance, exemplifies the ontological definition of art by conceiving aesthetics as the study of how the "spirit" on its way to self-consciousness assumes ever new trappings embodied in works of art, which provide the "sensuous appearance of the idea."[3] In other words, the work of art gives sensory expression to the direction in which the "spirit" is destined to move. Aesthetics turns into a study of representation, conceiving art as a medium for the appearance of truth. Powered by the conviction that art is knowable, such an assumption, however, is less concerned with the work of art for its own sake than with something other than the work, for which art serves as an indicator. This holds true from Hegel up to Adorno, irrespective of what they considered the basic definition of aesthetics to be.

A genuine work of art, Adorno maintains, is permeated by a rift, which indicates that it has cut itself loose from the world within which it was produced. By imitating the beautiful in nature, the work creates an appearance which in turn features the presence of something nonexistent, and by giving outward form to something inconceivable, the work endows a figment with illusory reality.[4] The latter, however, is not so much a deception as a foreshadowing of perfection in an imperfect world.

Aesthetics, which had elevated art to the highest pinnacle of human achievement, declined in the twentieth century because the holistic conception of art was no longer tenable. When it became apparent that the work of art could not be pinned to any metaphysical basis, let alone have a definable essence, a host of new questions arose. What are the functions of the work, what are its modalities, how do they operate, and what accounts for their differences? Even reflection on approaches to art became a major preoccupation. Consequently, theory found itself tackling not art but issues such as the language and structure of the work, its message, the organization of its sign relationships, its patterns and their communication, the inroads made into its contextual realities, the processing and reception of texts, and the exposure of assumptions inherent in the work.

Theory liberated art from the umbrella concepts that had been superimposed on it by philosophical aesthetics, thus opening up a vast array of facets inherent in the individual work. Instead of formulating an overriding definition of what art is, theories provided an ever-expanding exhibition of art's multifariousness; the ontological monolith of the work became pluralized.

Another important historical reason for the rise of theory was triggered by the state in which literary criticism found itself in the 1940s and 1950s. Theory counteracted the prevailing impressionistic approach to art and literature, which was highly personalized, appealing only to the initiated. The postwar generation of critics began to query the validity of what was regarded as "the great adventure of the soul among masterpieces." Hence it became necessary to find ways to access art and literature that would objectify insights and separate comprehension from subjective taste. Theory became a means of preventing and unraveling the confusion created by impressionistic criticism. The success of this approach became apparent from the degree to which various disciplines of the humanities, e.g., semiotics, gestalt theory, psychoanalysis, hermeneutics, information theory, sociology, and pragmatism, felt called upon to develop their own theories

3

of art and literature. The very fact that the latter were based on empirical findings made them all the more persuasive.

Furthermore, the impasse in which impressionistic criticism found itself was highlighted by a growing conflict of interpretation. The cultural heritage no longer served as an unquestioned means of promoting what was called *Bildung*, because there were no uniform guidelines for such an education any more, as there had been in the past. Initially, though, there did not seem to be a problem if an individual work generated very different and, at times, controversial interpretations. The professor was a kind of feudal lord or at least an arbiter in the existing hierarchy, and he decided what a work had to mean. The fact that works had a content, which was considered a carrier of meaning, was taken for granted. Therefore interpretation had to uncover the work's meaning, which legitimized the whole process because meanings represented values to be employed for the purpose of education. Thus excavation of meaning became a prime concern, but in due course this raised the question of why the meaning had been concealed within the work and why authors should indulge in such a game of hide-and-seek with their interpreters. What turned out to be even more puzzling was why the meaning – once found – should change again with a different reader, even though the letters, the words, and the sentences of the work remained the same. Eventually this created an awareness of the fact that the presuppositions governing interpretation were to a large extent responsible for what the work was supposed to mean. Therefore the claim to have found *the* meaning of the text implied justification of one's assumptions and presuppositions, and this triggered what has since become known as the conflict of interpretation. What the latter revealed, however, and what made it really interesting was the inherent limitation of all presuppositions, and hence their restricted applicability to the tasks they were meant to perform.

This situation cried out for investigation, and theory addressed itself to the task. Presuppositions came under scrutiny, not least as the theories implicitly reflected on the premises in order to find out what they were able to master. No doubt there are additional reasons for the rise of theory, such as the proliferation of the media and a growing interest in culture and intercultural relationships, but the main driving forces were a declining belief in the ontology of art, the growing confusion spread by impressionistic criticism, and the quest for meaning that generated the conflict of interpretation.

## Hard-Core and Soft Theory

Theories are first and foremost intellectual tools. There is, however, a difference between hard-core theory and soft theory. The former – as practiced in physics, for instance – makes predictions, whereas the latter – as practiced in the humanities – is an attempt at mapping. These objectives require different forms of theory. "Physical theories," writes Norwood Russell Hanson, "provide patterns within which data appear intelligible. [ ... ] A theory is not pieced together from observed phenomena; it is rather what makes it possible to observe phenomena as being of a certain sort [ ... ] Theories put phenomena into systems. [ ... ] A theory is a cluster of conclusions in search of a premiss. From the observed properties of the phenomena the physicist reasons his way towards a key-stone idea from which the properties are explicable as a matter of course."[5] Such "keystone ideas," when found, are considered laws: Karl Popper maintains that it is the task of the natural scientist "to search for laws which will enable him to deduce predictions. [ ... ] he must try to advance hypotheses about frequencies, that is, laws asserting probabilities, in order to deduce frequency predictions."[6]

Soft theory is almost the reverse. First of all, it actually "pieces together" observed data, elements drawn from different frameworks, and even combines presuppositions in order to gain access to the domain to be charted. This *bricolage*[7] is adapted to what is scrutinized, and augmented by new viewpoints when required. This is in keeping with the objective of soft theory, as it would be meaningless for theoretical inquiries in the humanities to make predictions. Art and literature can be assessed, but not predicted, and one cannot even anticipate the multiple relationships they contain. Prediction aims ultimately at mastering something, whereas mapping strives to discern something.

Furthermore, soft theory is not governed by laws, let alone driven to establish or even discover them – again in contrast to the procedures of hard-core theory. Instead of moving toward a general principle, it starts out from a basic presupposition, which can be modified in view of observed data that are to be incorporated into the framework.

This accounts for a conspicuous feature of soft theory. All theories assume their plausibility through the closure of the framework; closure is, of course, perfect when a law for making predictions is discovered. Soft theories, especially when focusing on art, aspire to closure through the introduction of metaphors or what has been called "open concepts," i.e., those marked by equivocalness owing to conflicting references. For instance, "polyphonic harmony" (the strata of the work merging together) is the favorite metaphor of phenomenological theory; the "fusion of horizons" (between the past experience embodied in the work and the disposition of the recipient) is integral to hermeneutics; and the inter-relation between making and matching (adapting "inherited schemata" [Gombrich] to the world perceived) is favored by gestalt theory. The metaphor performs the necessary function of finishing off the system, for only if the system is closed can it put on the mantle of theory.

Metaphor versus law, as the respective "keystone idea" of soft and hard-core theory, highlights a vital difference between the sciences and the humanities. A law has to be applied, whereas a metaphor triggers asso-ciations. The former establishes realities, and the latter outlines patterns.

There are two further distinctions between the two types of theory, relat-ing to their efficacy and to the task they must perform. If predictions are to be deduced from a theory, its various statements must be tested in order to find out which are the most efficient for ensuring prediction. "If this decision is positive," according to Popper, "that is, if the singular con-clusions turn out to be acceptable, or *verified*, then the theory has, for the time being, passed its test: [ . . . ] So long as theory withstands detailed and severe tests and is not superseded by another theory in the course of scientific progress, we may say that it has 'proved its mettle' or that it is '*corroborated*.' "[8]

Such testing procedures do not apply to soft theory. Its ability to map and chart can be neither verified nor falsified, as there is no objective and measurable reference – like a prediction that has come true. Consequently, humanistic theories cannot be discarded if their intended function is not fulfilled; at best they compete with one another. Yet even such competition is not governed by an overarching idea to which all the different theories feel themselves beholden. On the contrary, it is due to changing interests and fashions that certain theories at times dominate their "rivals," while others move out of orbit, as currently witnessed by the waning of Marxist theory and the rise of general systems theory. The very fact that humanistic theories – in contradistinction to scientific ones – are not judged by being put to the test may account for the multiplicity of soft theories, as each of them starts out from a different presupposition, pursues a specific objective, has a limited scope, and yields something its competitors do not. Soft theories gain their acceptance by assent and not through tests, and for such an acceptance their relative persuasiveness is more often than not decisive.

The second major distinction between the two types of theory is closely connected with the testing procedure. Physical theories are discarded when they no longer stand the test, whereas humanistic theories move in and out of focus, depending on changing interests. Why are physical theories discarded? Because predictions are not made for their own sake but are meant to solve problems. Thomas Kuhn has described "normal science" as working within a paradigm, defining it as follows: "Normal science, the activity in which most scientists spend almost all their time, is predicated on the assumption that the scientific community knows what the world is like. Much of the success of the enterprise derives from the community's willingness to defend that assumption, if necessary at considerable cost."[9]

This does not apply to the humanities. Although the scholarly community may work for a certain period of time within the parameters of a dominant theory, this does not mean – as is the case with a scientific paradigm – that the basic assumptions of the theory in question must be defended. This is due to the fact that the humanities are not a problem-solving undertaking. Instead, their prime concern is to achieve understanding, to assess context-relatedness, to investigate meaning and function, and to evaluate art and literature, as well as to address the question of why we need them. In the sciences we witness a succession of theories, judged according to their achievements in predicting natural phenomena, whereas in the humanities we have an assembly of theories each seeking to grasp or even exploit the inexhaustible potential of art and literature. Consequently, there is no need for "retooling" theory in the humanities, because multiple theories are their hallmark in view of what they intend to conceptualize. Things are different in the sciences, however. "So long as the tools a paradigm supplies continue to prove capable of solving the problems it defines, science moves fastest and penetrates most deeply through confident employment of those tools. The reason is clear. As in manufacture so in science – retooling is an extravagance to be reserved for the occasion that demands it. The significance of crises is the indication they provide that an occasion for retooling has arrived."[10] Retooling as a consequence of failure as opposed to a multiplicity of competing tools – this again marks the difference between the sciences and the humanities.

## Modes of Theory

Why do we have so many different theories? Each one subjects art to a cognitive framework, which is bound to impose limits on the work. Whatever aspects one concept fails to cover will more often than not be taken up by another approach, which will of course be subject to its own restrictions, and so on ad infinitum. However, this not only accounts for the multiplicity of theories, but also allows us to experience the ultimate unknowability of art. In the final analysis, it refuses to be translated into cognition, because it transcends all boundaries, references, and expectations. Thus it simultaneously provokes cognitive attempts at understanding, and exceeds the limits of the cognitive frameworks applied. This duality transforms art into an experiential reality for which, however, the cognitive quest is indispensable.

How do theories operate and what are their distinguishing features? To answer this question we need to examine a great variety of theories: phenomenological, hermeneutical, gestalt, reception, semiotic, psychoanalytical, Marxist, deconstructionist, and pragmatist theories. These will form the bulk of our detailed investigation. But we shall also have a cursory glance at feminist theories. The presuppositions of these are differently applied. They may be heuristic, i.e., the assumptions made are tentative, and hence subject to revisions; prescriptive, i.e., the assumptions have to be followed, and hence rules are to be obeyed; exploratory, i.e., the assumptions are probes, and hence to be changed in the event of failure; dogmatic, i.e., the assumptions are taken as realities; or the assumptions may even become equated with what is to be elucidated, and hence are superimposed on the object of investigation.

Basically all modern theories of art and literature replace the question formerly asked by aesthetics, but instead of defining what art is, their concern is how art comes about, or when it is art, or what function is exercised by art, or what are its modalities. There is also a switch to be observed from a semantics to a pragmatics of art, and from thematics to operations of art. Furthermore, modern theories do not lay claim any longer to universal application of their basic principles.

There are three key concepts that govern the intentions of modern theories: structure, function, and communication, which more or less dovetail within the theories concerned. Structure allows classification of the work's components and a description of how meaning is produced.

Meaning, however, remains an abstraction, and only function gives it concrete form, as this concerns itself with the relationship between art and the world. The relationship in turn remains an abstraction that is to be made concrete by communication, through which the recipient can conceive what the interaction is meant to convey.

Modern theories have broadened the focus, as the work of art is no longer conceived as something given in isolation but is always viewed in relation to its interaction with its context and with its recipient. Hence the human subject, and the various human faculties upon which art begins to work, must always be taken into consideration. The work of art is never independent of these faculties, which it activates and mobilizes into a possible reformulation of our knowledge, and reorganization of our stored experience. The work also impinges on the context within which it was produced. It encapsulates cultural norms, prevailing attitudes, and other texts, and in doing so recodes their structures and semantics.

Generally speaking, the emphasis of modern theories is on relationships between the work of art, the dispositions of its recipients, and the realities of its context. Theories translate the experience of art into cognition which – being criterion-governed – provides an opportunity for a heightening of awareness, a refining of perceptive faculties, and a conveying of unfalsifiable knowledge. Furthermore, theories set out to explain the social and anthropological function of art, and finally, they serve as tools for charting the human imagination, which is after all the last resort human beings have for sustaining themselves.

The frameworks of modern theories of art are derived from philosophies, or disciplines, or ideologies, or critical practices, or even political stances. Phenomenological theory hails from Husserl, and deconstruction from Heidegger; the theory of meaning from modern language philosophy; hermeneutical theory from the exegesis of the Bible as a critical practice; gestalt theory from psychology; psychoanalytical and semiotic from their respective disciplines; Marxist theory from ideology, reception theory from history and phenomenology; feminist theory from a political stance. The diversity of provenance accounts for the different focal points of these theories, and for the different tasks they set out to tackle, which we shall inspect in detail when dealing with each of them. In contradistinction to aesthetics, then, theories of art derive their components from sources outside themselves, thus obtaining a more reliable basis than the contrived speculations of aesthetics could ever provide.

## Theory and Method

"Scientists," Thomas Kuhn writes, "never learn concepts, laws, and theories in the abstract and by themselves. Instead, these intellectual tools are from the start encountered in a historically and pedagogically prior unit that displays them with and through applications. A new theory is always announced together with applications to some concrete range of natural phenomena; without them it would not have been even a candidate for acceptance."[11] This practice differs from the use and function of theory in the humanities. Sometimes theories have been learned "in the abstract," especially when interest in theory was booming during the 1970s and 1980s. They were more often than not read as texts not unlike those that they were actually intended to open up. Thus the current talk of the decline of theory refers to its misreading rather than to its obsolescence, because there is no doubt that even cultural studies rampant today cannot dispense with theory if it wants to communicate the cultural phenomena which it has conceptualized in the first place.

Within the humanities one must distinguish between theories that can be more or less directly applied (these will also differ from one another) and those that have to be converted into a method before they are able to function. What are the reasons for such a distinction?

Every theory embodies an abstraction of the material it seeks to categorize. The degree of abstraction is a precondition for the success of categorization, and so the theory screens off the individuality of the material, whereas it is the central function of interpretive methods to focus on and elucidate this very individuality. Thus theory provides the framework of general categories, while method, through individual analysis, makes it possible to differentiate retrospectively between the assumptions underlying theory because of the material that is not covered by the categories.

This feedback loop accounts for the variations to be observed in a great many modern theories. Marxist theory is a case in point, where the original concept of mirror reflection is differentiated by such attempts as the reappropriation of the literary past for the enrichment of the present. But even if not all specifications are as far reaching, basic categories are often diffracted when applied as interpretive instruments. In some of these cases the impact of what interpretation has yielded has led to changes of emphasis. Here semiotic theory is a case in point. Morris privileged the semantic aspect of the sign (i.e., the meaning of signs) over the syntactic (i.e., the relationships between signs) and the pragmatic aspect (i.e., responses elicited by signs), whereas Ritchie emphasized the syntactic, and Creed-Hungerland the pragmatic predominance of the sign. Eco finally considered the interplay between the semantic, syntactic, and pragmatic sign-function as a basic prerequisite for creating the *idiolect* of the work concerned. We shall detail these differences later on.

There are, however, theories that are not as directly applied as those mentioned above. Theories generally lay the foundation for the framework of categories, whereas methods provide the tools for processes of interpretation. Thus phenomenological theory, for instance, explores the work's mode of existence; hermeneutical theory is concerned with the observer's or reader's self-understanding when confronted with the work; gestalt theory focuses on the perceptive faculties of the observer as brought into play by the work. All three theories are based on different premises: descriptive for the phenomenological theory, historical for the hermeneutical, and operational for the gestalt. Distinctive assumptions are made which reveal a particular mode of access to the work, although they do not represent a technique of interpretation. Hence these theories must undergo a transformation if they are to function as interpretive techniques. For instance, the basis laid down by these three theories must be transformed into (1) the strata model, (2) question-and-answer logic, and (3) the interaction between schema and correction. Again we shall look at these in more detail later.

Furthermore, these three theories – as mentioned earlier – strive to attain closure through central metaphors: i.e., polyphonic harmony of the strata, fusions of horizon between past and present, and the correction of inherited schemata through a newly perceived reality. As methods need not trouble themselves with basic premises – for these are laid down by theory – their close attention to the work serves to elucidate the concrete significance of the central metaphors. By translating these metaphors into concrete terms of individual perception, methods lend stability to theories at precisely those points where the efficacy of the latter reaches its limit. In other words, method clears up the individual problems arising from theory's generalizations, thereby utilizing the explanatory potential of the theory to chart the territory which it has signposted.

Hence there are two types of theory in the humanities: those that have to be transformed into a method in order to function, and those that are applied directly, retroactively undergoing a diffraction of their categories.

## Theory and Discourse

There are certain similarities between theory and discourse, although they are distinctly separate from one another as regards their intentions and achievements. Both of them are criterion-governed and launch their operations from underlying assumptions. In contradistinction to theory, however, discourse has a long history, in the course of which some of its features have changed. Jeremy Bentham defined it as a way of transmitting thoughts through signs, leading to a linguistically conceived social action. George Boole spoke of a universe of discourse, stating that the reality we live in is nothing but an assembly of discourses. Each individual discourse organizes a realm of meaning, and their sum total patterns our world. This holds true all the way through to Foucault, for whom discourse is "the power of constituting domains of objects, in relation to which one can affirm or deny true or false propositions."[12]

Although the boundaries are somewhat contingent, and thus changeable, discourse nevertheless features a definitive view of the world we live in, irrespective of whether it is meant to describe this world or is identified with it. Thus discourse is deterministic, whereas theory is explorative. Determination versus exploration marks the essential difference between the two, and it may well be that humans need these contrasting ways of dealing with their reality. Discourse draws boundaries, and theory lifts them, thereby opening up new territories of anthropological significance. It is important to register this distinction because the two are sometimes bracketed together as if they were the same thing. Although what is to follow will be basically confined to spotlighting how theory is "done," and what one can do with it, I have added a postscript to elucidate the difference between theory and discourse and to outline the basic features of a discourse that is widely debated nowadays: namely, postcolonial discourse.

## Notes

1   For details see Wolfgang Iser, *The Range of Interpretation*, New York: Columbia University Press, 2000.
2   Murray Krieger, *Ekphrasis: The Illusion of the Natural Sign*, Baltimore: Johns Hopkins University Press, 1992, pp. 150 and 159.

3   G. W. F. Hegel, *Aesthetics: Lecture on Fine Art I*, trans. T. H. Knox, Oxford: Oxford University Press, 1975, p. 111.

4   See Theodor W. Adorno, *Ästhetische Theorie* (Gesammelte Schriften 7), Frankfurt/Main: Suhrkamp, 1970, p. 131.

5   Norwood Russell Hanson, *Patterns of Discovery: An Inquiry into the Conceptual Foundations of Science*. Cambridge: Cambridge University Press, 1965, p. 90.

6   Karl R. Popper, *The Logic of Scientific Discovery*, New York: Harper Torchbooks, 1965, p. 246.

7   Claude Lévi-Strauss, *The Savage Mind*, Chicago: Chicago University Press, 1966, p. 26, has introduced this term for conceptualizing the workings of both myth and art. "Art thus proceeds from a set (object + event) to the *discovery* of its structure. Myth starts from a structure by means of which it *constructs* a set (object + event). [ . . . ] The first aspect of bricolage is thus to construct a system of paradigms with the fragments of syntagmatic chains" (150).

8   Popper, *Logic of Scientific Discovery*, p. 33.

9   Thomas S. Kuhn, *The Structure of Scientific Revolution*, Chicago: Chicago University Press, 1970, p. 5.

10  Ibid., p. 76.

11  Ibid., p. 46.

12  Michel Foucault, *The Archaeology of Knowledge*, trans. A. M. Sheridan Smith, New York: Pantheon Books, 1972, p. 234.

# 2

# Phenomenological Theory: Ingarden

Phenomenology was conceived by Edmund Husserl (1865–1937) as a form of scientific research. Its basic operation consisted in a "transcendental reduction" of phenomena in order to ascertain their "essence" and to understand how the latter is given in unmediated perception to consciousness. This required a "bracketing" of the phenomena, i.e., separating them from one another and from their contextual relations. Phenomenology was a reaction against metaphysics and, especially at the end of the nineteenth century, against a rampant psychologism whose assumptions were beyond proof. It intended to provide verifiable knowledge and intersubjectively controllable processes of cognition, in contradistinction to philosophical speculation. It started out from two presuppositions on which consensus could be easily reached: (1) we live in a world in which we are confronted with given realities, leading to Husserl's exhortation, "Let us go back to things" ("Zurück zu den Sachen"); (2) we relate to what is independent of ourselves through acts of consciousness, which are intentional in directing themselves to something outside themselves. In so doing, they also fashion the mode of **apperception** of things given, and so phenomenology focuses basically on intentional acts for the purpose of gaining insight into the way in which we relate to the world.

## The Layered Structure of the Work

How is a literary work of art conceived within this framework? Just as the author perceives given (even imaginary) things and fashions them into the work, the work in turn is given to the reader, who has to fashion the author's communication of the world perceived. This is the basis for a phenomenological theory of art. Roman Ingarden (1893–1970) fleshed out this pattern in his two books, *The Literary Work of Art*[1] and *The Cognition of the Literary Work of Art*.[2] He delineates the basic components of the literary text and confronts them with the ways in which it can be *concretized* (realized). The text is given as a layered structure through which the subject matter of the work can come to light, but the actual bringing to light occurs in an act of **concretization**. Thus the literary work has two poles, which we might call the artistic and the aesthetic: the artistic refers to the text created by the author, and the aesthetic to the realization accomplished by the reader. From this polarity it follows that the literary work cannot be completely identical with the text, or with the realization of the text, but in fact must lie halfway between the two. The work is the point of convergence, since it is located neither in the author's psyche nor in the reader's experience. This is the minimal hypothesis for a phenomenological theory.

What kind of object is the literary work? It is not an ideal object, because it has no ontological foundation, having originated in time and being subject to change in each of its realizations. However, it is not a real object either, as the words on the page do not mean themselves but denote something "other" that does not exist. Hence, according to Ingarden, it is an intentional object, whose component parts function as instructions, the execution of which will bring the work to fruition.

How is an intentional object given to us? The answer is as "a stratified formation" (29) and the strata are the following: "(1) the stratum of *word sounds* and the *phonetic formation* of higher order built on them; (2) the stratum of *meaning units* of various orders; (3) the stratum of manifold schematized *aspects* and aspect continua and series, and, finally, (4) the stratum of *represented objectivities* and their vicissitudes" (30). Each stratum has a role to play in the general makeup of the literary work (56), but each has to be focused on separately in order to ascertain what it contributes to the final shape of the work. What distinguishes Ingarden's model of the layered structure is an almost total avoidance of presuppositions, since he sticks to what is given, i.e., sounds, words, sentences, and the sequence of sentences.

We must look at these layers individually in order to highlight how they function. "The stratum of linguistic sound formations" (36ff.) is the elementary layer consisting of "*phonic material*," i.e., sounds and letters, which we do not scan separately but constantly group into units. The material is neither there for its own sake nor does it represent itself; instead, it functions as a carrier for something else. The units thus formed are not unchangeable entities but act upon each other, and in so doing influence and alter the nature of the "**correlate**" that they produce. The correlates that arise out of "sound arrangements" are rhythm, tempo, melody. The phonetic stratum forms the base, on which "all of the remaining strata find their external point of support" (59).

"The stratum of meaning units" is unfolded in a graduated sequence of layers: the sentence level, the sequence of sentences, the state of affairs, the schematized aspects, and the represented object. What do they entail and what kind of operations do they perform?

*The sentence level*: Each word in a sentence functions – in Ingarden's sometimes unwieldy terminology – as an "intentional directional factor," which means that the word points beyond itself, thus helping to bring about a unit of which the words are component parts, though none of them can be identified with the unit as such. The pointer is basically variable, and is used to shape the content of the unit. It is a guideline for projecting features of the intentional object. For instance, in Keats's *Ode on a Grecian Urn* (Appendix A), when the urn is called a "foster-child" and "sylvan historian" different projections will occur: as a foster-child it turns into a human being who has survived the ravages of time and who is now acted upon by the following pointer, "sylvan historian." The latter turns the foster-child into a narrator, allowing the personified urn to tell its own story. Simultaneously, the two pointers keep switching within a background–foreground relationship in which the history told is authenticated by the experience of the foster-child, who in the role of sylvan historian marshals this experience into a higher order. Thus a richly orchestrated correlate emerges from the interaction of these intentional pointers, which function as instructions for the correlate to be built. None of the pointers is identical with the correlate. This holds true even if one makes a statement about a real object; the statement is not part of the object but is a correlate of the way in which the object is referred to or is to be constituted by an act of consciousness. Consequently, the meaning of a sentence is the product of intentional pointers and manifests itself in the correlate that arises out of verbal arrangements. The correlate slants the mode of perception (the urn is to be conceived as a person) and it is open-ended, as it cannot be related to real objects. "In comparison with the existence of the real, the ideal, and, finally, the purely conscious, what is created is analogous to 'illusion,'

16

to something which only pretends to be something though it is not this something in an ontically autonomous sense" (101).

*The sentence sequence*: The semantic pointers of individual sentences always imply an expectation of some kind. As this structure is inherent in all intentional sentence correlates, it follows that their interplay will lead not so much to the fulfillment of expectations as to their modification. Each individual sentence correlate prefigures a particular horizon, but this is immediately transformed into the background for the next correlate and must therefore necessarily be modified. Since each sentence correlate aims at things to come, the prefigured horizon will offer a view which – however concrete it may be – must contain indeterminacies, and so arouse expectations as to the manner in which these are to be resolved. Each new correlate, then, will answer expectations (either positively or negatively) and, at the same time, will arouse new expectations.

As far as the sequence of sentences is concerned, there are two fundamentally different possibilities. If the new correlate begins to confirm the expectations aroused by its predecessor, the range of possible semantic horizons will be narrowed correspondingly. This is normally the case with texts that are to describe a particular object, for their concern is to narrow the range in order to bring out the individuality of that object. In most literary texts, however, the sequence of sentences is so structured that the correlates serve to modify and even frustrate the expectations they have aroused. In so doing, they automatically have a retroactive effect on what has gone before, which now appears quite different.

When Ingarden speaks of intentional sentence correlates, the statement and information are already qualified in a certain sense, because each sentence can achieve its end only by aiming at something beyond itself. Since this is true of all sentences in a literary work, the correlates constantly intersect, ultimately giving rise to the semantic fulfillment at which they have aimed. The fulfillment, however, takes place not in the work but in the reader, who must "activate" the interplay of the correlates prestructured by the sequence of sentences. In brief, the sentences set in motion a process which will lead to the formation of the intentional object of the work in the reader's mind.

The question now arises as to the nature of the sentences in a literary work. Are they of a different grammatical category from sentences used in ordinary language? Ingarden's answer is as follows:

> If we were to compare the declarative sentences (affirmative propositions) appearing in a literary work, we would immediately observe that, despite

the same form and despite at times also a seemingly identical content, they are essentially different: those appearing in a scientific work are genuine *judgments* in a logical sense, in which something is seriously asserted and which not only lay claim to truth but *are* true or false, while those appearing in a literary work are not pure affirmative propositions, nor, on the other hand, can they be considered to be seriously intended assertive propositions or judgments. In order adequately to grasp the essence of the stratum of the meaning units and their role in the literary work, it is indispensable to clarify this special modification of the declarative sentences and [ . . . ] of all sentences appearing in a literary work. (160f.)

How can we differentiate between the seemingly identical – namely, the declarative sentence in the literary work and in the scientific paper? The answer is simply that declarative sentences in a literary work do not mean what they say. They "bracket" what they designate, and so they suspend judgment, which makes them into "quasi-judgmental sentences."

This apparent deficiency, however, has a twofold advantage. (1) With judgment suspended, the declarative sentence is open for recoding in order to make it mean something which it does not say. For instance, Percy Hotspur's dying words, "Time must have a stop," are not a statement about time but designate what is not said – namely, the futility of his own life. In this respect the declarative sentence in a literary work creates an individual "state of affairs," which is not matched by any individually existing object. (2) "Since in a literary work there are only quasi-judgmental assertive propositions of various types, they are not [ . . . ] pure affirmative propositions. Thus, by virtue of their described properties, they are capable of invoking, to a greater or lesser degree, the illusion of reality; this pure affirmative proposition cannot do" (171f.).

There is, however, a major omission in Ingarden's argument. How do we know whether the text in front of us consists either of assertive propositions or quasi-judgmental sentences? The linguistic signs themselves do not allow us to spot the difference. At this juncture of the argument Ingarden keeps conspicuously silent. The recoding of declarative sentences in the literary work comes about because of the "contract" between author and reader, for the linguistic signs can become significant only through particular, historically varying conventions shared by authors and public. The linguistic signs themselves do not invoke the fictional nature of literature, but shared conventions do. Among the most obvious and the most durable of such conventions are literary genres, which have provided a wide variety of contractual terms between author and reader. Even such

recent inventions as the nonfiction novel reveal the same contractual function, since they must invoke the convention before renouncing it in order
to highlight the fact that the text is not discourse but "staged discourse."[3]

*State of affairs:* Basically, sentences project intentional meaning units, which
are subject to modifications by the sequence, thus producing the state of
affairs as a new stratum of the layered structure. States of affairs are standpoints that arise out of the interconnected sentence correlates and form a
guideline for viewing the intentional object. Ingarden called the states of
affairs windows, through which the intentional object is revealed. "[T]he
same object can be revealed in various differently constructed states of affairs – [ . . . ] the states of affairs are like many windows through which we
can look into one and the same house, each time from a different standpoint and from a different side, into another part" (190).

Referring to Keats's Ode again we might specify the windows as follows:
the urn is not a vessel but an "unravish'd bride of quietness" and is thus
to be seen as a living being, which is a viewpoint sustained throughout the
whole poem. Endowing the urn with life transforms it into a personification that is seen from somewhere by someone. Figuring the urn as
"foster-child of silence and slow time" allows us to witness an extraordinary event, as the urn has transgressed all human boundaries. Such a
description illuminates Ingarden's basic types of window through which
the intentional object is displayed for perception – namely, essence,
appearance, and occurrence.

*Schematized aspects:* The states of affairs are the windows through
which we view the intentional object; the schematized aspects are patterns
for exhibiting it. They are schematic insofar as they are reduced to those
features that are considered important. This holds true even for a story which
can never be told in its entirety and is confined to those components that
allow it to make its point. The sequence of schematized aspects results in
the assembly of the intentional object. For instance, characters in a novel
are schematized aspects, just like the narrator or the plot line. None of them
is fully fleshed out, apart from the fact that even a character portrayal could
never be brought to completion, but all of them have the function of exhibiting the intentional object of the novel.

Furthermore, the sequence of aspects is sometimes disconnected, the continuity of which can be established only in the reading process. Therefore
Ingarden maintains: "But the jumpiness of the succession of aspects can
never be entirely removed. Even when it is overcome to a certain degree,
that which causes the overcoming, and the overcoming itself, do not

19

belong to the literary work itself but to one of its concretizations, which in their essence relate to a given reading and a given reader" (269). This very disconnectedness, however, also indicates that there has been a selection, thereby revealing the blueprint according to which the intentional object has been shaped.

Just like the states of affairs, the schematized aspects exercise a dual function. The states of affairs organize the viewing of the intentional object, and in doing so, they have to constitute viewpoints. The schematized aspects exhibit the intentional object in a sequence of segments, thus allowing the intentional object to be built up for perception.

*The sequence of the strata*: Let us summarize what we have seen so far. Each stratum has a dual quality: (1) it has its foundation in another stratum; (2) it yields something that the other does not contain. The level of the *phonic material* is the only exception insofar as it provides the launch pad for all the others, but it already shows a patterning, as the arrangement of "sounds" and "words" gives rise to rhythm, rhyme, and melody. The *sentence level* is based on the phonic one. The sentence activates the semantic potential of each word by a mutual backgrounding and foregrounding, and by adumbrating what the words point to, thus producing the correlate of a meaning unit. The level of *states of affairs* starts out from and molds these meaning units through which a slanting and viewing of the intentional object is produced. The level of *schematized aspects* takes up the link between the object and the stance from which it is perceived, and produces schematic sections of the intentional object. The level of the *intentional object* is based on the schematized aspects through which it is exhibited and brought into view. It functions as a carrier for the self-presentation of what Ingarden called "metaphysical qualities" (290–9).

This sums up the various pre-aesthetic reflections on the literary work as a schematic formation which is basically incomplete and will gain its completion through the act of concretization. Pre-aesthetic means that the layered structure provides only a skeleton, as the layers are nothing but guidelines to elucidate the operations that may be observed in each individual work of art.

So far we have outlined the steps that build up the intentional object. As we have seen, the latter is neither an ideal nor a real object but a projection mapped out by the different layers of its verbal structure. If Ingarden had left it at that, the stratified model would be highly persuasive, because it structures what the language of a work of art is able to achieve, and how the work is given to human consciousness. What appears to be the crux of Ingarden's theory, however, consists in the qualification of the intentional object as a representative of metaphysical qualities, which marks a break in the logic of his argument. The stratified model is a frame for observation and thus strictly formal by nature, whereas the intentional object is content-laden. What are the metaphysical qualities to which the intentional object gives expression? Ingarden enumerates some of them:

> for example the sublime, the tragic, the dreadful, the shocking, the inexplic-able, the demonic, the holy, the sinful, the sorrowful, the indescribable bright-ness of good fortune, as well as the grotesque, the charming, the light, the peaceful, etc. These qualities are not "properties" of *objects* in the usual sense of the term, nor are they, in general "features" of some psychic state, but instead they are usually revealed, in complex and often very disparate *situations* or *events*, as an atmosphere which, hovering over the men and the things contained in these situations, penetrates and illumines everything with its light. (290f.)

Keats's Ode may again serve as an illustration of how an intentional object represents metaphysical qualities. The urn as a work of art exercises an over-powering impact on a potential observer, who is rendered almost speech-less, because the experience transcends all ordinary expectations. From this emerges the "metaphysical quality" of the sublime. Even if one can make a case for what Ingarden considered the capstone of the work of art, a final ambivalence still persists in his argument. The layered structure produces the intentional object as a correlate, which adumbrates something that hitherto did not exist. If the work of art brings something new into the world, how can it represent existing (we might even say "given") metaphysical qualities? At best, one may say that Ingarden succeeds in revealing how a work of art is able to produce the experience of what the sublime, the tragic, the grotesque, etc. entail.

## Method Derived from Theory

A theory is an abstraction from the material to be processed, whereas the method applies theory to interpretation, and in so doing has a retroactive effect on any underlying assumptions. Thus a kind of feedback loop is set in motion. Theory sets the parameters for the method of interpretation, and the latter feeds back into theory what the practice has yielded. In

Ingarden's case the starting-point was a basic phenomenological principle – namely, how the work of art is given to us. It appears as a layered structure whose different levels help to build the intentional object, which represents metaphysical qualities to be experienced in the act of concretization. In order to bring out the distinctness of the intentional object, the relationship between the layers is important, as each of them has to play its own role.

How are the layers geared to one another? Ingarden's answer is a metaphor: polyphonic harmony (58). This provides closure of the system, for only if the system is closed can it put on the mantle of theory. As long as polyphonic harmony provides the guideline for interpretation of the literary work, its application will be restricted to classical texts. Harmony was the hallmark of the latter through which truth gained its tangible appearance. This residue of classical aesthetics runs counter to Ingarden's basic question of how the work of art is given to consciousness, because polyphonic harmony decrees how the levels of the stratified model have to relate to one another. This limitation is the price that theory has to pay for obtaining closure.

The organization of the layered structure is at best polyphonic, but hardly ever harmonious. The method of interpretation derived from such a theory is bound to focus on the contrasts, the contradictions, the ambivalences, the ambiguities, the conflicts, the interplay between what is said and concealed, and finally on the drama that develops between the strata out of which the individuality of the intentional object arises.

The more disturbances there are between the relationships of the strata, the more protracted becomes the perception of the intentional object. Suspended harmony, then, prolongs the recipient's efforts to come to grips with what the intentional object is meant to be, and this leads to a more intimate relationship between the intentional object and the recipient. Instead of resolving a seeming lack of harmony we obtain an impression of the multifaceted relationship between the strata, and hence are given to experience kaleidoscopically changing views of the intentional object.

The method thus derived from theory has repercussions on the latter. In dissolving the metaphor of polyphonic harmony as the capstone of the theory, it stretches the applicability of the latter beyond the limitations of the governing norm. Focusing on the diversified relationships between the strata reveals the extent to which Ingarden's theory is historically conditioned. Classical aesthetics is the underlying blueprint, and the illusionist concept of art the overriding feature, because polyphonic harmony means the "good continuation" of the strata. Thus the method reveals the concept of art that has conditioned Ingarden's theory, but also – even more importantly – it switches the focus from what these levels represent to how they function. As long as polyphonic harmony is the overriding norm, the relationship between the strata remains unspecific, because the representation of the levels is of paramount concern. What the method spotlights, however, is precisely the specific link-up of the strata, thus allowing us to perceive the way in which the representative qualities function. Such a shift has a far-reaching consequence insofar as representation becomes subservient to communication. If the work of art, according to Ingarden, comes to fruition in the act of concretization, then the recipient has to work out what it is meant to communicate. The method reveals what the theory has glossed over, and in so doing gives the theory a different slant. Ingarden conceived the stratified model in terms of semantics, whereas the method – as the practice of theory – lays bare the way it functions.

## An Example

Adding flesh to the bone, we shall briefly and rather selectively outline how to focus on a work of art in terms of the stratified model. John Keats's *Ode on a Grecian Urn*,[4] to which reference has already been made, will serve our purpose. The stratum of the phonic material is already structured by the rhyming patterns of the stanzas. There is a match between the patterns 1 and 5 (ababcdedce) and between 3 and 4 (ababcdecde). Although there is a correspondence between 1 and 5, they do not follow one another as 3 and 4 do. As stanza 2 (ababcdeced) has no match in the sequence, we have the impression of a movement that peaks in 3. Hence the movement has an upswing and a downswing, and also appears to have a different speed. The gradual upward move is slower than the downward one. This patterning of the phonic level reveals a non-semantic intentionality, thus adumbrating the correlate produced by the stratum.

The correlate prefigures a striving towards something that is differently articulated. The identical patterns of 1 and 5 signal fulfillment, as the many questions (1) have been given an all-encompassing answer (5). The identical patterns of 3 and 4, however, signal a longing to hold together what irrevocably has fallen apart, as the ecstatic moment cannot be retained. The emerging correlate of the phonic level bears the inscription of a dramatic tension.

Furthermore, there is also a rhetorical structuring to be observed, for which stanza 3 is an illuminating case in point. We have a complete rhythmic balance in almost all of the lines, which is underpinned by the rhetorical figure of parallelisms ("Ah, happy, happy boughs," "And, happy melodist," "More happy love! more happy, happy love!"). Thus the stanza, marking the climax prepared by stanzas 1 and 2, presents ecstasy in total rhythmical and rhetorical control. This endows the outburst of happiness with a specific significance, because agitation is not mimetically depicted; instead of rhythmical irregularity and rhetorical paradoxes, ecstasy appears in perfect order.

These few observations highlight already the extent to which the correlate projected by the phonic level transforms representative qualities into communicatory functions. The level of sentences builds upon this tension, and the correlate projected gives salience to the drama.

(Stanza 1) The personified urn begins to interact with a potential observer without developing a relationship, as both urn and observer – though interlocked – are pulled apart again, which is indicated by the omission of the finite verb and the welter of question marks. Thus a gap opens up between the two, and the core of the drama appears to be suspended.

(Stanza 2) This tendency is enhanced by the arrangement of the word order; if "Heard melodies are sweet, but those unheard / Are sweeter," then a mutual cancellation of meaning occurs. This cancellation spreads to almost all observable phenomena. And as the meaning of a sentence arises out of a foregrounding and backgrounding of words through which the semantic features are selected, the mutual abrogation of what the words mean transforms them into signs of the unsayable.

(Stanza 3) The correlate built up so far is nuanced again. The distinction between urn and observer is blurred, as the sentences make no statement about what can be seen or about the perspective from which they are seen. Moreover, the sentences tend to become inconclusive, and are simultaneously strictly organized by parallelism and anaphoric patter900 patternings. This dual countering indicates a drift toward speechlessness, which signals the inability of words to grasp what happens.

(Stanza 4) The moment of bliss has evaporated, as anticipated by the last clause of the previous stanza, which is hypotactically construed, contrasting violently with the foregoing paratactical order. Now blank spaces open up again between the observer and what is to be seen, indicated by the frequency of the question marks. There are no answers as to why the procession leaves the little town, which makes it so desolate that nobody will return. And the procession itself, though clothed in precious ritual trappings, appears to move toward nowhere. Whatever is perceived remains disconnected, thus adumbrating a falling apart of what has been experienced.

(Stanza 5) The relationship of urn and observer reemerges, but the initially bewildered observer is now in full command and conveys to a potential audience the message to be obtained from the urn. The maxim, however, that "Beauty is truth, truth beauty" summarizes discursively what is to be learned from that which has eluded language.

What the correlate of the sentence level – based on the dramatic tension of the phonic stratum – communicates is the incapacity of words to translate the work of art into language, although it is through language that the work of art comes into being. Hence the correlate tries to articulate how the work of art inscribes itself into language by making language speechless.

The state of affairs arises out of slanting the meaning units by putting them in perspective. In so doing it works out the salient feature of the sentence correlate.

(S1) The speaking urn delivers a silent speech, which according to Ingarden's classification would be the theme. What it assembles are incompatibles which give the theme its appearance, and what it reveals are transgressions: time is turned into a preserver, and the frozen pictures are endowed with life. Such boundary-crossing is an event, because it outstrips all familiar demarcations.

(S2) Now the oxymoronic situation is turned around. Urn and observer gradually shade into each other, and the latter turns into a partner by commanding the musicians to go on and by consoling the lovers that they will enjoy their anticipated bliss forever.

(S3) The gradually unfolding relationship comes to fruition in the total merger between urn and observer. Such an interpenetration obliterates their individual contours, because the overwhelming happiness now experienced transcends the foregoing interaction. This eclipse highlights the fact that both have been lifted out of their natural form of existence, the work of art becoming the redeemer.

(S4) Again there is turnabout, as urn and observer are split apart. There is puzzlement and a loss of understanding. The images appear alien in view of what had previously been perceived. The boundary-lifting in stanzas 2 and 3 issues into a redrawing of boundaries.

(S5) The observer interprets the urn for an audience by subsuming it under a literary genre and by telling us what kind of knowledge the urn purveys.

25

The correlate thus projected by the state of affairs is a rapid interchange of perspectives, which continually blend into one another without losing their salience. Incompatibles turn into transgressions, bewilderment into empathy, rapture into exegesis, and all of them appear to be gestures that point up the linguistic unsayability of the work of art.

Schematized aspects, according to Ingarden, exhibit the intentional object to its potential reader.

(S1) The feature exhibited is one of an intriguing blank, which exercises a suction-effect on the as yet distant reader. The aspect presented of the intentional object features perplexity and astonishment.

(S2) Now distance is removed, as indicated by the imperatives and vocatives that fill the previous blank insofar as it is not the urn but the emotional reactions triggered by it that are represented, which, in turn, infuse life into the engraved images.

(S3) Now total empathy prevails. The union with the art object is represented as a means of self-transcendence, which eliminates the subject/object division and restores the lost unity between self and world. This pre-intellectual state in which the self is now engulfed radiates an unbounded happiness to which trees, love, and music give expression.

(S4) Unity gives way to separation. Religious rituals represent incomprehension in view of the experience enjoyed before, and obviously figure an otherworldliness that has become obsolete. It is a contrasting foil to empathy focusing on a completely different means of transcending oneself.

(S5) The urn is a teacher, and sums up what has gradually evolved in the encounter with the work of art.

What the schematized aspects thus exhibit as features of the intentional object is the relationship between the work of art and its readers. The states of affairs have portrayed the art object as eluding language. The schematized aspects build on what cannot be said. Hence art can only be given expression by the impact exercised on the recipient, resulting in an experience. It is the exhibition of such an experience that enables the schematized aspects to move the intentional object into focus. The latter arises out of a nesting of correlates produced by their interlocking sequence. The correlates projected by each of the levels turn into components of the intentional object, through which it obtains its multifacetedness. The intentional object, in turn, represents, in Ingarden's terminology, metaphysical qualities. If we refashion this quaint terminology, we might say the intentional object gives expression to what transcends ordinary circumstances and experiences. It thus conveys the surpassing of existing things, as is indicated by overawing the observer and recipient alike. Overpowering is the hallmark of the sublime, which the intentional object represents. Now the functions of the correlates projected by each stratum come fully into the open; the graduation of correlates orchestrates the sublime by endowing it with a multiplicity of countervailing features. The sublime is dual by nature: it exercises an overwhelming impact, and it triggers the desire for emulation.

The relationship of levels in this stratified model, derived from Ingarden's theory, is by no means one of polyphonic harmony. Instead, we have clashes, contrasts, and disharmony between levels, and even within levels there are many paradoxes, oxymora, negations, bewilderment, and inconsistencies. Furthermore, the sequence of stanzas is more often ruptured than ordered, not least as the sublime cannot be captured as polyphonic harmony. Dispensing with the latter as an umbrella concept for interpreting the work of art, the method derived from phenomenological theory has to focus on the diversity of relationships between the layers in order to translate the internal drama of each work into cognitive terms. What used to be the capstone of Ingarden's theory proves to be a severe limitation when it comes to interpretation. Transforming the stratified model into a method thus has repercussions on the theory insofar as polyphonic harmony – which Ingarden considered an ultimate value – now turns out to be a residue of classicism in a theory that claims to assess the work of art as it is given to consciousness. And yet the interpretive potential of the theory is far reaching and widely applicable if freed from the restrictions which a theory has to impose on itself in order to gain closure.

## Notes

1  Roman Ingarden, *The Literary Work of Art*, trans. George G. Grabowicz, Evanston: Northwestern University Press, 1973. The sources of all other quotations from this volume are given in the text with references to the appropriate pages.
2  Roman Ingarden, *The Cognition of the Literary Work of Art*, trans. Ruth Ann Crowley and Kenneth R. Olson, Evanston: Northwestern University Press, 1973.
3  See Rainer Warning, "Der inszenierte Diskurs: Bemerkungen zur pragmatischen Relation der Fiktion," in Dieter Henrich and Wolfgang Iser, eds., *Funktionen des Fiktiven* (Poetik und Hermeneutik X), Munich: Fink, 1983, pp. 183–206.
4  For certain observations, I am indebted to Earl R. Wasserman, *The Finer Tone: Keats' Major Poems*, Baltimore: Johns Hopkins University Press, 1953, pp. 11–62.

# 3

# Hermeneutical Theory: Gadamer

Modern hermeneutics has its roots in Protestant theology, as developed by Friedrich Daniel Ernst Schleiermacher (1768–1834) at the beginning of the nineteenth century. Schleiermacher started out from what he called "the quite limited purpose of interpreting the Holy Scripture," but with awareness that such an undertaking required a "rigorous practice [ . . . ] based on the assumption that misunderstanding occurs as a matter of course, and so understanding must be willed and sought at every point."[1] Why is this "rigor" necessary? There is a gap between the text and its recipient, which makes the text into a "foreign or strange speech" (175), the grasping of which is continually threatened by misunderstanding. Therefore it is essential to discover and elucidate the ramified conditions pertinent to understanding. Hermeneutics is conceived as a theory of understanding, which holds true from Schleiermacher through Heidegger to Gadamer. An analysis of understanding is no longer linked to any kind of authority that might bridge the gap between text and recipient. On the contrary, it has to be freed from traditional conceptualizations in order to ensure the transparency of what happens in understanding. Even the holy texts – for which hermeneutics was originally devised – have to be subjected to hermeneutical procedures in order to find out how they can be understood in relation to their original intention. Hence the "dogmatic point of view [ . . . ] proceeding from the conviction that the Holy Spirit as a definite personality is the author of the Scriptures" (138) had to be dispensed with, since "the dogmatic point of view goes beyond its own requirements when it rejects individual development [ . . . ] and thus destroys itself" (139). It has to be combined, as Schleiermacher contends,

28

with the "philological view" that takes into account the several authors of the New Testament, "because the individuality of the writers was itself a product of their relationship to Christ [ ... ] (Paul is distinctive because of his dialectics, John because of his sensitivity)" (139). As a consequence, there is no given schema according to which the Bible has to be understood, as claimed by the dogmatic view, not least since "the New Testament has to be constructed from a group of things that are not exactly known to us" (122).

There is no need to go into further detail regarding the method that Schleiermacher proposed, because the procedures laid down by him were to a large extent conditioned by the philological practice prevailing at the time. Yet understanding remained the overriding concern of all the different brands of hermeneutics, which had a dual objective: how the gaps between text and recipient as well as between past and present were to be negotiated. Why had the human past attained such importance? History was taken as humanity's knowledge of itself, and thus a resuscitation of the past allowed humans to look into a mirror, thereby becoming conscious of themselves. This interconnection, however, raised another problem: achieving understanding as a central objective of hermeneutics is dually coded insofar as it is always an understanding *of* something *for* something. This accounts for the fact that when understanding has been achieved, it has to be applied. Such a broadening of issues converted hermeneutics – originally conceived as a method of interpretation – into a philosophy of which Heidegger and Gadamer are the main proponents.

As a general theory of understanding, hermeneutics does not confine itself to understanding a work of art. However, the latter is taken as a paradigm for illuminating the process through which understanding emerges, thus assuming crucial significance for both Heidegger and Gadamer. Just as Schleiermacher, in devising hermeneutics, started out with a critique of the dogmatic view of the Bible by trying to explore the individual and historical conditions out of which the holy texts have arisen, so contemporary hermeneutics criticizes whatever lays claim to be normative by nature. This critique, however, only serves as a ground-clearing operation for the elucidation of understanding. It launched the hermeneutical theory of art, as exemplified by Hans-Georg Gadamer's (1900–2002) criticism of "aesthetic consciousness" in his widely acclaimed work *Truth and Method*.

## Understanding

Roman Ingarden, as we have seen, retained the classical norm of harmony as the hallmark of the work of art. He did, however, differentiate between the elements of harmony by means of the layered structure, maintaining that the strata were geared to one another so that polyphonic harmony would ensue. This marks Gadamer's starting-point insofar as he subverts a normative conception of the work of art, and in doing so has to go back to history in order to trace the conditionality out of which aesthetic norms have arisen. Simultaneously he reveals the salience of hermeneutical theory, which unfolds its framework primarily in terms of history.

The concept of "aesthetic consciousness" sets the parameters for the way in which art was conceived in the nineteenth century, thus eclipsing the issue of how encountering a work of art might illuminate the process of understanding. Why did such a concept come into being and what did it entail? Aesthetic consciousness, according to Gadamer, developed as an offshoot of Kantian ideas. In his *Critique of Judgment* Kant writes: "An aesthetic judgment is unique in kind and provides absolutely no cognition (not even a confused one) of the object; only a logical judgment does that. An aesthetic judgment instead refers to the presentation, by which an object is given, solely to the subject; it brings to our notice no characteristic of the object, but only the purposive form in the [way] the presentational powers are determined in their engagement with the object."[2] Hence what Kant called the aesthetic is not to be identified with objects of any kind, whether beautiful or sublime; instead it qualifies both the subject's involvement in what is given, and the way in which the given is refracted in the subject's "inner intuition."[3]

It was Schiller who put a different slant on this idea by demanding that everybody adopt an aesthetic attitude toward things. Why should we do so? The reason is twofold and follows more or less directly from Kantian presuppositions. (1) The inaccessibility of reality proper or things in themselves made it necessary to devise schemata for dealing with the world – a world which now became marked by a split between reality and appearance. (2) Imagination as a go-between for the faculties of reason and the senses made them play into one another, and it was play that Schiller elevated into the be-all and end-all of education.

"This had far-reaching consequences," writes Gadamer, for "now art, as the art of beautiful appearance, was contrasted with practical reality and understood in terms of this contrast [ . . . ] It is the prose of alienated reality against which the poetry of aesthetic reconciliation must seek its own self-consciousness. [ . . . ] Where art rules, it is the laws of beauty that are in force and the frontiers of reality are transcended."[4] This elevation of "appearance" over reality, an offshoot of Kantian thinking, was turned into a program of education by Schiller which proliferated throughout the nineteenth century, and still persists in its ossified form in the literature departments of many universities. What Schiller initially proclaimed as education through art eventually turned into education in art.

If art as beautiful semblance transcends reality, it can only be identified by what it is not, because semblance outstrips the realities upon which – as their opposite – it nevertheless depends. Therefore the work of art has to be separated from the connections it might have had with existing realities, the uprooting of which has turned it into an autonomous object. In Kantian terms, it now becomes a "**purposive**" structure **without** "**purposiveness**," and hence something existing for its own sake. Art, as distinguished from reality, is now defined through semblance, illusion, magic, dream, and even if all of these are meant as glorifications, they are nevertheless derived from what is considered substantially inferior.

What in actual fact is "aesthetic consciousness"? It poses as a transcendental vantage point that accords the work of art a dignity manifested by overstepping what it is not. As "aesthetic cultivation" is the overriding concern, whatever "the aesthetically-formed consciousness [ . . . ] acknowledges as having 'quality' belongs to it. It no longer chooses among it, because itself is nothing, nor seeks to be anything, against which choice could measure itself." It represents, Gadamer continues, "a total lack of definiteness. The connection of the work of art with its world is no longer of any importance to it but, on the contrary, the aesthetic consciousness is the experiencing centre from which everything considered to be art is measured" (76). This means no less than that aesthetic consciousness is basically a blank, as it cannot be substantiated, although it figures as the guiding light for education and decrees what and even why art is. Thus it becomes one of the supreme fictions of nineteenth-century cultural life, which needed a backing in order to vindicate its claim.

This predicament was further aggravated by the necessity to provide a concrete idea of what autonomous art meant. The mere impulse of abstracting art from the given world was not enough to convey an image of its autonomy. After all, Schiller had proclaimed art as the realm of freedom, which allowed humans to ennoble themselves. But if humans were to be led to true humanity by way of art, the latter could hardly remain an abstract idea. How could one concretize art that defines itself only through the transcendence of its direct opposite? The answer was: by collecting all the great artistic achievements of the past. Hence the emergence of that typically nineteenth-century institution, the museum. Originally, collections had grown from the personal tastes of individuals; but now the varieties of taste had to be unified into a single concept, which could take on normative authority. And so works of art were taken out of their sacred or profane settings and placed in the museum. As a representative of a normative taste, the work of art must exercise its effectiveness entirely through itself, and not through any purpose or function. It is scarcely surprising that Marcel Duchamp caused a scandal when putting a bottle rack in a museum, for the museum was the final triumph of autonomous art, as it endowed the works from different periods with contemporaneity, asserting that what had been assembled reflected the universally valid norm of taste. At long last, so it seemed, a judgment regarding taste was not only possible, but could also be visibly grasped by the pieces displayed in the museum. The latter gave aesthetic consciousness a tangible gestalt, since the rapidly growing collections bore evidence of what an otherwise unfathomable aesthetic consciousness might be like. The indefinable aura radiating from the assembled works of art became the hallmark of aesthetic consciousness. "Thus aesthetic consciousness," Gadamer writes, "has the character of simultaneity, because it claims that it contains everything of artistic value" (77).

Although aesthetic consciousness gained its visible presence through the museum, its embodiment was short-lived. There is no escaping the very problem that the museum was meant to dispose of, because the museum brings to light precisely the factor that the unified collection of works sought to overcome – namely, the historical relativity of taste, as evinced by the individual works and also by the historical functions, sacred or profane, that they had to fulfill in their original settings. Thus the contemporaneity with which the museum endows the works actually reveals their historical differences, and so the normative conception of taste evaporated, and aesthetic consciousness lost its backing. Gadamer therefore asks: "If a thing is *eigenbedeutsam* (significant in its own right) rather than *fremdbedeutsam* (significant in relation to something else), it seeks to break off any connection with everything that could determine its meaning. Can such an idea be a solid ground for aesthetics?" (81). Before this question could be answered, an alternative for the concept of autonomous art had to be dismantled, not least because aesthetic consciousness took over Kant's notion of art as the work of genius.

The genius vies with nature, and hence is able to create like nature. In order to define his terms, Kant distinguished between genius and craftsman. Gadamer writes:

> What is a work of art and how is it different from the product of a craftsman or even from some mechanical creation, i.e. something of aesthetically inferior value? For Kant and idealism the work of art was, by definition, the work of genius. Its characteristic, of being completely successful and exemplary, was proved by the fact that it offered to pleasure and contemplation an inexhaustible object of lingering attention and interpretation. That the genius of creation is matched by genius in appreciating was already part of Kant's theory of taste and genius. (84)

Such reciprocity, however, entailed a serious problem that eventually came out into the open – namely, if the genius creates like nature that has no finality, how can "the perfection of a work of art, its being finished, be conceived?" (84).

Things are different with the craftsman. In contradistinction to the work of genius, whatever else

> is made or produced takes the criterion of its perfection from its purpose, i.e. is determined by the use that is made of it. The work is finished if it answers to the purpose for which it is intended. How is one, then, to understand the criterion for the perfection of a work of art? However rationally and soberly one may consider artistic "production," much that we call works of art is not intended to be used, and none derives the measure of its completion from such a purpose. Does not, then, the work's existence appear to be the breaking-off of a formative process which actually points beyond it? Perhaps it is not all completable in itself? Paul Valéry, in fact, thought this was the case. (84)

Valéry radicalized the implications hidden in the concept of art as the work of genius, because the lack of inherent finality left it to the recipients to end the process they experienced. Such a closure runs counter to perfection which the genius is supposed to produce.

> A chance and random breaking-off of a formative process cannot contain anything binding. From this, then, it follows that what he makes of what he

finds must be left to the recipient. One way of understanding a work of art is then no less legitimate than another. There is no criterion of an appropriate reaction. Not only that the artist himself does not possess one – the aesthetics of genius would agree here. Rather, every encounter with the work has the rank and the justification of a new production. This seems to me an untenable hermeneutic nihilism. (84–5)

In order to corroborate this verdict, Gadamer invokes Kierkegaard as a witness, who had exposed "the destructive consequence of subjectivism" (85) already in the middle of the nineteenth century, and whose "criticism of the aesthetic consciousness is of fundamental importance because he shows the inner contradictions of aesthetic existence" (85). Gadamer brought to the fore what had remained unnoticed at the time, thus revealing the main thrust of hermeneutics and retrieving what normative concepts had eclipsed. For such an intent, criticism is an indispensable first step in order to highlight the process of understanding that arises out of abrogating aesthetic norms. Moreover, criticism becomes a mode of discovery insofar as new questions have to be asked, since the old answers have run into an impasse. This does not mean, however, discarding the old answers because, hermeneutically speaking, the now obsolete answers always condition new questions. Instead of decreeing what art is, the question now to be asked is how the work of art can be understood, and what such an understanding might entail.

The waning of aesthetic consciousness was caused mainly by disenchantment with what the ideas of museum and genius had promised. The museum revealed the historicity of taste, and involuntarily resuscitated the settings of the works from which they had been uprooted for the purpose of authenticating a unified taste. The concept of genius dispersed the work into ever-changing instances of closure by the recipient, thus making it fall apart to an array of incomplete realizations. What can we retrieve from the crumbling principles that underpinned aesthetic consciousness? Gadamer answers as follows:

The pantheon of art is not a timeless presence which offers itself to pure aesthetic consciousness but the assembled achievements of the human mind as it has realized itself historically. Aesthetic experience also is a mode of self-understanding. But all self-understanding takes place in relation to something else that is understood and includes the unity and sameness of this other. Inasmuch as we encounter the work of art in the world and a world in the individual work of art, this does not remain a strange universe

into which we are magically transported for a time. Rather, we learn to understand ourselves in it, and that means that we preserve the discontinuity of
the experience in the continuity of our existence. Therefore it is necessary
to adopt an attitude to the beautiful and to art that does not lay claim to
immediacy, but corresponds to the historical reality of man. The appeal
to immediacy, to the genius of the moment, to the significance of the
"experience," cannot withstand the claim of human existence to continuity
and unity of self-understanding. The experience of art must not be side-tracked
into the uncommittedness of the aesthetic awareness. (86–7)

Developing self-understanding through an encounter with art is the main
focus of Gadamer's hermeneutical theory. What are the guidelines that allow
a successful mediation between our freedom and the constraints the work
imposes on us? First of all we have to refrain from superimposing our standards and preferences onto the work, because such an attempt would make
the encounter abortive. By suspending our guidelines, we expose ourselves
to the work, which renders it impossible to determine what art is; it only
allows us to experience its otherness. Thus Gadamer concludes: "This
negative insight, expressed positively, means that art is knowledge and the
experience of the work of art is a sharing of this knowledge" (87). How is
this type of experience transformed into knowledge, and what does this
knowledge consist of or bring about? "[A]rtistic experience is a mode of
knowledge [ . . . ] certainly different from that sensory knowledge which
provides science with the data from which it constructs the knowledge
of nature, and certainly different from all moral rational knowledge and
indeed from all conceptual knowledge, but still knowledge, i.e. the
transmission of truth." What, then, is the truth transmitted by the artistic
experience? According to Gadamer, Hegel had already given the answer in
his lectures on the fine arts by unfolding "a history of truth, as it is seen
in the mirror of art" (87). Gadamer contends – in the wake of Hegelian
ideas – that art reveals the historic manifestations of what the human mind
had been trying to achieve. This is the knowledge to be obtained from the
work of art, and it engenders self-understanding through its experience.

In order to illuminate such a process Gadamer develops his concept
of tradition, because works of art have come down from the past to the
present. Encountering the past entails being confronted with otherness, which
gives hermeneutics an eminently modern touch, not least as understanding "the foreign and strange speech" (Schleiermacher) requires a responsive
commitment to what is beyond one's orbit. "Every encounter with tradition,"
Gadamer writes, "that takes place within historical consciousness involves

the experience of the tension between the text and the present. The hermeneutic task consists in not covering up this tension by attempting a naïve assimilation but consciously bringing it out. This is why it is part of the hermeneutic approach to project an historical horizon that is different from the horizon of the present. Historical consciousness is aware of its own otherness and hence distinguishes the horizon of tradition from its own" (273).

There are two terms in Gadamer's concept of tradition that have to be elaborated on: tension and horizon. Tension means primarily conflict, which Gerald Bruns in a brilliant exposition has described as follows. The

> idea that what has come down to us in tradition, what tradition preserves or rather entails, is not a deposit of familiar meanings, but something strange and refractory to interpretation, resistant to the present, uncontainable in the given world in which we find ourselves at home, the world that makes sense to us and promises us a future that has a place for us. In a critical theory of tradition, tradition is not the persistence of the same; on the contrary it is the disruption of the same by that which cannot be repressed or subsumed into a familiar category. The encounter with tradition, to borrow Gadamer's language, is always subversive of totalization or containment. For Gadamer, this means the openness of tradition to the future, its irreducibility to the library or museum or to institutions of interpretation, in its refusal of closure or of finite constructions. Tradition in this respect is infinite in Levinas's ethical sense of Infinity to the Other that discloses itself in conversation.[5]

But this conversation is marked by conflict, which Gadamer takes as the basis of hermeneutic experience out of which knowledge arises, because it is an experience of negation, or, in his own words, "the reversal of direction that consciousness undergoes when it recognizes itself in what is alien and different."[6] Thus otherness turns into a mirror for self-observation, and such a relationship sets the process of self-understanding in motion, because the alien that is to be grasped realizes itself to the extent to which one's own dispositions come under scrutiny. The knowledge thus obtained is twofold: by getting to know what is different, one begins to know oneself. Furthermore, aesthetic experience reveals the historicity of the knowledge that the work of art provides, just as it creates awareness that our own consciousness is habitually conditioned.

This intertwining is effected by Gadamer's second basic concept: that of the horizon, which epitomizes his whole approach. "The concept of the 'horizon' suggests itself because it expresses the wide, superior vision that the person who is seeking to understand must have. To acquire a horizon means that one learns to look beyond what is close at hand – not in order to look away from it, but to see it better within a larger whole and in truer proportion" (272). Horizon designates comprehensiveness albeit constituted from an angle of perception. There is a horizon of the past and one of the present, and these mirror one another, making each of them variable and subject to reformulation according to the viewpoints adopted. The dual horizons thus indicate an ongoing readjustment, which turns them into a frame for conceiving how understanding occurs. "In fact the horizon of the present is being continually formed in that we have continually to test all our prejudices. An important part of this testing is the encounter with the past and the understanding of the tradition from which we come. Hence the horizon of the present cannot be formed without the past. There is no more an isolated horizon of the present than there are historical horizons. Understanding, rather, is always the fusion of these horizons which we imagine to exist by themselves" (273).

"Fusion of horizons" is crucial to Gadamer's theory of understanding. It indicates that the encounter with the past is never an assimilation of what appears to be alien, but always "a critical appropriation of otherness."[7] Understanding, then, occurs as a constant negotiation between oneself and otherness, which means that both the horizon of tradition and that of self-understanding are continuously under adjustment. Any work of art that has come down to the present appears somewhat alien to the horizon which limits the present situation. However, one can only become aware of one's own situation when it is either reflected in the mirror of something different from oneself or when one is invaded by something from outside oneself. Thus fusion of horizons is marked by a duality: it interweaves past and present, and simultaneously upholds difference. It forms the umbrella for the ongoing conversation, and yet it is nothing but a metaphor for the experience of how self-understanding develops.

Just as with Ingarden, the capstone of Gadamer's hermeneutical theory is a metaphor. Irrespective of the fact that it might be an apt description for the never-ending process of self-understanding, the metaphor has to be taken apart in order to derive a method that will allow us to grasp what happens in a "fusion of horizons." Although Gadamer's book was called *Truth and Method*, he did not seem particularly concerned with "method," not least as he developed his argument in terms of history. But he did give a few hints as to how the dovetailing of horizons might be conceptualized.

Resuscitating the past for the purpose of self-understanding requires a methodologically organized approach, because otherwise individual arbitrariness would prevail.

Furthermore, understanding is not to be achieved for its own sake: therefore Gadamer quite rightly maintains: "It is the problem of application that exists in all understanding [ ... ] Interpretation is not an occasional act subsequent to understanding, but rather understanding is always an interpretation, and hence interpretation is the explicit form of understanding" (274). Thus method becomes crucial for the whole process, and Gadamer is fully aware of it, as evinced by a methodological proposal: "The voice that speaks to us from the past – be it text, work, trace – poses a question and places our meaning in openness. [ ... ] We must attempt to reconstruct the question to which the transmitted text is the answer [ ... ] For the text must be understood as an answer to a real question" (337). And he then makes explicit reference to Collingwood, who proposed a question-and-answer logic as the fundamental method of hermeneutics (338).

## Method Derived from Theory

If we are to break down the vague metaphor "fusion of horizons" into a methodological framework of interpretation, we shall have to give it a more concrete form. All the defining terms, from dovetailing to linking and interlocking, are just synonyms of fusion, and hence do not explain anything, let alone allow us to conceive of how such a fusion may work. R. G. Collingwood (1889–1943), in his attempt to outline how history can be reenacted in the present, proposed a question-and-answer logic. "I began by observing that you cannot find out what a man means by simply studying his spoken or written statements, even though he has spoken or written with perfect command of language and perfectly truthful intention. In order to find out his meaning you must also know what the question was (a question in his own mind, and presumed by him to be in yours) to which the thing he has said or written was meant as an answer. It must be understood that question and answer, as I conceive them, were strictly correlative."[8] Therefore Collingwood made it a point in all his teaching "never [to] think you understand any statement made by a philosopher until you have decided, with the utmost possible accuracy, what the question is to which he means it for an answer."[9]

The correlation of question and answer is an important tool for interpretation, as it permits us to reenact a past horizon in our present situation, and simultaneously to control the workings of such reenactments. Each work of art is to be conceived as an answer to a question or problem prevalent in the respective historical situation within which it was produced. The work as an answer is bound to contain the question in the form of an issue that had to be addressed. Through the logic of question and answer we are able to reconstruct the context of the work to which it has reacted, thereby making us present to a historical situation that has never been our own. Thus a truly historical interpretation of the work of art emerges, which allows us both to reenact the work on its own terms, and to begin to understand its otherness. Furthermore, the question-and-answer logic does not subject tradition to preconceived principles, as all the philosophies of history do; instead of downgrading tradition to a foil for umbrella concepts, it allows tradition to speak to the present in its own language.

## An Example

Let us consider Henry Fielding's *Tom Jones* in order to demonstrate how the question-and-answer logic may work as a method of interpretation. What is the answer that *Tom Jones* provides? Fielding is very direct in his *Bill of Fare to the Feast* when he says: "The Provision then which we have here made is no other than HUMAN NATURE."[10] Depicting the latter will be successful to the degree in which it can be marked off from those contextual realities which appear as questionable. For our present purpose, it will suffice to single out the characters and focus on the relationship between the hero and those whom he encounters. The minor characters appear to represent the questions to which the hero is the answer. The aim of depicting human nature is fulfilled through incorporating the prevailing norms of eighteenth-century thought systems and social systems that govern the conduct of those figures with whom the hero is in constant interaction.

What are these norms which lay claim to be representative of human nature? In general, they are arranged in more or less explicitly contrasting patterns: Allworthy (*benevolence*) is set against Squire Western (*ruling passion*); the same applies to the two pedagogues, Square (*the eternal fitness of things*) and Thwackum (*the human mind as a sink of iniquity*), who in turn are also contrasted with Allworthy. There are various other sets of opposites – the view of love, for instance, as shown in Sophia (the ideality of natural inclination), Molly Seagrim (seduction), and Lady Bellaston (depravity). All these serve as contrasts to the position of the hero, so that the relationship between his perspective and theirs is transformed into a tension, which is most strikingly represented by the Tom–Blifil contrast: Blifil follows the norms of his mentors and is corrupted; Tom acts against them and gains in human qualities.

Thus we find an extensive assembly of eighteenth-century views regarding human nature. Allworthy embodies the latitudinarian morality of benevolence, Squire Western the basic principle of eighteenth-century anthropology, Square the deistic norms of the orderliness of things, Thwackum the orthodox Anglican norm of the corruption of human nature, and Mrs. Western the upper-class social conventions concerning the natural superiority of nobility. The hero, though linked with all of them, cannot be subsumed under these norms; instead, he keeps violating them. Whenever this happens, the resultant situation may be judged in one of two different ways: either the norms appear as a drastic reduction of human nature, in which case we view them from the standpoint of the hero; or the violation shows the imperfections of human nature, in which case it is the norm that conditions the view. In both cases we have the same structure of interacting positions being transformed into a determinate meaning. For those characters who incorporate a norm – in particular Allworthy, Squire Western, Square, and Thwackum – human nature is defined in terms of one principle, so that all the possibilities which are not in harmony with the principle are given a negative slant. This applies even to Allworthy, whose allegorical name indicates his moral integrity which, however, frequently tends to cloud his judgment. In this way, the negation of other possibilities by the norm in question gives rise to a diversification of human nature, which takes on a definite form to the extent that the norm is revealed as a restriction on human nature.

The attention is now fixed not upon what the norms represent but upon what their representation excludes, and so human nature, as Fielding conceived of it, begins to arise out of what is adumbrated by the negated possibilities. In this way, the function of the norms themselves begins to change: they no longer represent the social regulators prevalent in the thought and social systems of the eighteenth century, but instead indicate the amount of human experience which they suppress, because as rigid principles they cannot tolerate modifications. Thus the norms embody the question to which Fielding's idea of human nature provides the answer.

Apart from their apparent one-sidedness in depicting human nature, the rigidity of the normative principles hinders the acquisition of experience through which human nature is actually formed, as is evinced by the development of the hero, whose spontaneous actions and impulsive nature threaten to leave him without any orientation in the course of his various adventures. Through experience he has to acquire *circumspection* and *prudence* to ensure self-preservation. It follows that the prevailing norms, which screen off experience, pose a real danger to this objective, since they suppress the contingent elements of life which lie beyond their range of efficacy. On the other hand, the hero makes us fully aware of the danger to self-preservation which arises when spontaneity (however well meant) and impulsiveness are indiscriminately indulged in during the flow of experience. Self-preservation is therefore ensured neither by prevailing norms nor by spontaneous reactions but by a mode of conduct arising from self-control in the midst of changing experiences. If such a mode of conduct is to be developed, it requires a sharpened sense of discernment with regard to the different alternatives inherent in each situation.

Now we are able to spotlight the question-and-answer relationship. The eighteenth-century norms regarding human nature pose a problem, as they identify human nature with a reified principle. Fielding provides a solution, as he shows that human nature is a process of learning from experience through self-control. The latter, however, will not only ensure self-preservation but will also launch human nature toward self-perfection. This contrast means no less than that all normative determinations of human nature fail to grasp what in actual fact it might be like, because it is a potential which unfolds through experience into a range of diversifications that herald its self-perfection. Obtaining knowledge of oneself through experience versus preconceived principles of selfhood is the insight the question-and-answer logic allows us to perceive. We are now able to reenact a past to which we become present, and such a presence may turn into a viewpoint from which we may look at ourselves.

## Notes

1  Friedrich Schleiermacher, *Hermeneutics: The Handwritten Manuscripts*, trans. James Duke and Jack Forstman, ed. Heinz Kimmerle, Missoula: Scholars, 1977, p. 110. The sources of all other quotations from this volume are given in the text with references to the appropriate pages.

2   Immanuel Kant, *Critique of Judgment*, trans. Werner Pluhar, Indianapolis: Hackett, 1987, p. 75.

3   Ibid., p. 217.

4   Hans-Georg Gadamer, *Truth and Method*, trans. and ed. Garret Barden and John Cumming, New York: Continuum, ²1988, p. 74. The sources of all other quotations from this volume are given in the text with references to the appropriate pages.

5   Gerald L. Bruns, *Hermeneutics Ancient and Modern*, New Haven: Yale University Press, 1992, pp. 201–2.

6   Hans-Georg Gadamer, *Truth and Method*, trans. Joel Weinsheimer and Donald G. Marshall, New York: Continuum, ²1989, p. 355.

7   Bruns, *Hermeneutics*, p. 237.

8   R. G. Collingwood, *An Autobiography*, Oxford: Oxford University Press, 1939, p. 31.

9   Ibid., p. 74.

10  Henry Fielding, *The History of Tom Jones A Foundling*, ed. Fredson Bowers, Middletown: Wesleyan University Press, 1975, p. 32.

# 4

# Gestalt Theory: Gombrich

The gestalt theory of art is an offshoot of gestalt psychology, which brought about a revolutionary change in our understanding of how perception works. Gestalt psychology was opposed to the time-honored stimulus-and-response theory advanced by John Locke (1632–1704) and elaborated on by the psychology of association. The latter held sway up to the end of the nineteenth century, until Christian von Ehrenfels (1890)[1] turned it upside down by pinpointing the mechanics of perception. This takes place not through data impinging on the human mind, as the stimulus-and-response theory had it, but by projecting the mind itself onto the world outside. The active agent is not the data received but the creative mind, and to accord activity to the former turns the latter into a passive repository. The older theory would render the data responsible for the kind of perceptions that can be made, whereas gestalt psychology now conceived perception as an active operation, which was the exact reversal of the Lockean model.

Gestalt theory argues that whatever is encompassed in an act of perception is constituted as a field, which basically consists of center and margin. A field requires structuring, which is achieved by balancing out the tension between the data, thus grouping them into a shape. It is the creative eye of the perceiver that does the grouping, and this marks a decisive switch between Locke's the active/passive poles, and provides a more plausible account of how perception works. A field arises out of the relationships between data – relationships that are neither given nor brought about by a stimulus but are the result of a grouping activity guided by the perceiver's underlying assumptions. This makes all perception into a projective act of seeing, which in turn produces a gestalt.

The gestalt is neither a property of the data nor an arbitrary product of the perceiver's imagination; instead, it designates our relationship to the world. This holds true in spite of various attempts that have been made to trace the roots of gestalt formation to certain areas in the human body, for instance by Wolfgang Köhler[2] – an important proponent of gestalt psychology – who suggested the location to be in the central nervous system. Irrespective of whether his assumption was correct or not, a percept either has a gestalt or is nonexistent, just as perception becomes an experience in proportion to the degree to which a gestalt is closed. We must now look at the basic operations that accomplish this closure.

As the tension between data has to be resolved by grouping them, gestalt-formation is guided by three principles: those of economy, similarity, and figure and ground. All of them are prerequisites for structuring the perceptual field and for providing closure. (1) The principle of economy has to bring about some kind of equilibrium within the perceptual field, and hence acts as a filter of data. Balance is achieved by selecting those data that appeal to the interest-governed eye of the perceiver, who would be overwhelmed if all data in the field were taken into account. Economy, therefore, means screening off all the data irrelevant to the purpose that informs perception. (2) The principle of similarity "refers to factors that cause some parts to be seen as belonging more closely together than others. [ ... ] This principle asserts that the degree to which parts of a pattern resemble each other in some perceptual quality will help determine the degree to which they are seen as belonging together."[3] (3) The principle of figure and ground is perhaps the most important one. During the process of perception we always select specific items from the mass of data available to our senses – a selection that is governed by our expectations. This assembly turns into a figure that is surrounded by the diffuse data which we have, so to speak, ignored. Within this figure-and-ground relationship certain distinctions must be drawn. "The most important of these is the fact that the perceived figure and the perceived ground are not formed in the same way, and in a certain sense the perceived ground has no form at all. A field which had previously been perceived as ground, and is then for the first time perceived as figure, can have a surprising effect, and this effect is due to the new form which the observer had not been conscious of before, and which he now perceives."[4] In giving contours to one another, figure and ground can interchange, and in so doing become a structural pattern for varying and even expanding perception, since the relationship involves a straightforward switch from "formed things" to

**Figure 1**   Duck/rabbit image

"unformed material."[5] The famous example is the duck/rabbit interchange, depending on what the common contour makes us select as a figure. But we cannot see the duck and the rabbit simultaneously.

Perception is governed by these three principles, through which a gestalt balances out the tensions between data and between data and observer by screening off those that are not relevant to the perceiver's expectations. It imposes a meaningful order upon contingency, and this gives rise to perception. Gestalts are neither standardized nor measurable, as they are bound to have different shapes and functions according to the perceptual preferences of the perceiver. Hence a gestalt cannot be qualified as objective or subjective; rather, it objectifies the way in which we process data.

It also defies categorization, as it is neither cognition, invention, analysis, nor intuition. It exceeds the fusion of thinking and observing, as it is a visual judgment; it is not an invention, but a guided projection for processing data; and it is not an analytic operation, but a synthetic unit that provides closure.

## Schema and Correction

Perception is a performative process, the outcome of which is a percept created by the perceiver. This basic conception of gestalt psychology provides the **heuristics** for Ernst H. Gombrich's (1909–2001) theory of the fine arts, as expounded in *Art and Illusion: A Study in the Psychology of Pictorial Representation*.[6] Representation, Gombrich contends, can no longer be conceived as mimesis in the Aristotelian sense of the term, i.e., as imitation of what is given, because representation is a form of production not to be derived from imitation. Gombrich illuminates the thrust of his argument by quoting a passage from Philostratus's life of the Pythagorean philosopher Appollonius of Tyana, "who probed much more deeply into the nature of mimesis than Plato or Aristotle." The following dialogue takes place between Appollonius and Damis, his disciple.

"Tell me Damis, is there such a thing as painting?" "Of course," says Damis. "And what does this art consist of?" "Well," says Damis, "in the mixing of colours." "And why do they do that?" "For the sake of imitation, to get a likeness of a dog or a horse, or a man, a ship, or anything else under the sun." "Then," Apollonius asks again, "painting is imitation, mimesis?" "Well, what else?" answers the stooge. "If it did not do that it would just be a ridiculous playing about with colours." "Yes," says his mentor, "but what about the things we see in the sky when the clouds are drifting, the centaurs and stag antelopes and wolves and horses? Is God a painter who uses his leisure hours to amuse himself in that way?" No, the two agree, these cloud shapes have no meaning in themselves, they arise by pure chance; it is we who by nature are prone to imitation and articulate these clouds. "But does this not mean," probes Apollonius, "that the art of imitation is twofold? One aspect of it is to use the hands and mind in producing imitations, another aspect the producing of likenesses with the mind alone?" The mind of the beholder also has its share in the imitation. Even a picture in monochrome, or a bronze relief, strikes us as a resemblance – we see it as form and expression. "Even if we drew one of these Indians with white chalk," Apollonius concludes, "he would seem black, for there would be his flat nose and stiff curly locks and prominent jaw [ . . . ] to make the picture black for all who can use their eyes. And for this reason I should say that those who look at works of painting and drawing must have the imitative faculty and that no one could understand the painted horse or bull unless he knew what such creatures are like." (154f.)

This lengthy quotation contains Gombrich's idea of representation in a nutshell. It is the accessibility of the imitated object that becomes the prime concern, because we do not know what the object is like when it is separated from our modes of seeing it. Hence it has to be made conformable to a repertoire of schemata and patterns that are shared by the artist and the beholder of the work. What is to be represented is not objects so much as conditions of perception, so that natural phenomena can be viewed in the manner intended by the artist. For even the simple act of perception teaches us that we can never see objects as a whole but only *as* something, and so imitation of an object can only take place through imitating the conditions of perception. Consequently the imitated object is present as an idea, even if one is under the illusion that the object itself is present.

This marks a monumental shift in representation from the qualities of the object, to perception. Thus the Appollonius example fits in perfectly with Gombrich's concept of imitation, which is to be thought of principally as a performative act, in accordance with the way in which gestalt psychology conceived of perception. Representation, then, is not a copy of what can be seen, because there is no pure seeing, but develops, according to Gombrich, as an interlocking of "schema and correction."

The schema is an indispensable component of representation. "Every artist has to know and construct a schema before he can adjust it to the needs of portrayal" (99). It precedes the external world, and in organizing given data it functions as a scaffolding for what is to be represented. Its basic structure is pretty similar to that of a gestalt, except that the latter concludes the process of perception, whereas the schema initiates representation. The nature of the schema is thus twofold: it is a scaffolding (1) in terms of form, functioning as a selective screen, and (2) in terms of content, encapsulating the modes of seeing handed down by tradition. "Without some starting point, some initial schema, we could never get hold of the flux of experience. Without categories, we could not sort our impressions. Paradoxically, it has turned out that it matters relatively little what these first categories are. We can always adjust them according to need. Indeed if the schema remains loose and flexible, such initial vagueness may prove not a hindrance but a help. An entirely fluid system would no longer serve the purpose; it could not register facts because it would lack pigeonholes. But how we arrange the first filing system is not very relevant" (76). The schema as an aid to perception is indispensable insofar as there is no pure seeing. Seeing only occurs when shaped by the selective screen of schemata, which finally reveal that the world is available only in terms of representation.

Basically, there are two sources from which schemata are drawn. On the one hand they are stored in the artist's perceptual experience, and on the other they are inherited from the tradition of painting. "The perfect painter is endowed with the gift of seeing the universal in the particular, of looking across the dross of matter at the 'essential form' which [ ... ] shaped the resisting clay from within. We need not doubt that painters experienced this very thrill. And yet one suspects that the pattern they found behind the visible world was not one laid out up in heaven but the remembered shapes they had learned in their youth. [ . . . ] Do we not tend to judge human bodies by their resemblance to those Greek statues that have become traditionally identified with the canon of beauty?" (134). The important thing here is the painter's relation to schemata which his predecessors had elaborated, and into which their forms of seeing had been inscribed, because the inherited schema serves to transmit a previous view of the world. It provides the necessary amount of redundancy against which the newly created vision can be portrayed by the artist and read by the beholder.

Simultaneously, such inscriptions into schemata that have come down from the past enable us to trace a particular history of the fine arts. "Seen in this light, that dry psychological formula of schema and correction can tell us a good deal, not only about the essential unit between medieval and postmedieval art, but also of their vital difference. To the Middle Ages, the schema is the image; to the postmedieval artist, it is the starting point for corrections, adaptations, the means to probe reality and to wrestle with the particular" (148). This becomes all the more obvious in the eighteenth century, which marks the rise of caricature in painting. Representing the particular – as does the caricature – becomes successful to the degree in which the schema is deliberately distorted. The schema, however, is still required if the disfigurement is to convey all the particulars of the "target," which holds true from Hogarth to Daumier. Thus distortion becomes the fountainhead of realistic representation. "What a painter inquires into is not the nature of the physical world but the manner of our reactions to it. He is not concerned with causes but with the mechanisms of certain effects. His is not a psychological problem – that of conjuring up a convincing image despite the fact that not one individual shade corresponds to what we call 'reality.' In order to understand this puzzle [ . . . ] science has to explore the capacity of our minds to register relationships rather than individual elements" (45). And gestalt psychology, from which Gombrich draws his basic arguments, has provided such an explanation.

As the schema precedes the external world, it is a construct, and even though it bears the inscription of a previous correction, it functions for the subsequent painter as an aid to perception. The correction to be inserted cannot therefore be deduced from the schema itself, but derives from the painter's observation of the world. To make the observation visible means recasting the schema in order to accommodate what the painter intends to represent. How does this work? "Our formula of schema and correction," Gombrich writes, "in fact, illustrates this very procedure. You must have a starting point, a standard of comparison, in order to begin that process of making and matching and remaking which finally becomes embodied in the finished image. The artist cannot start from scratch but he can criticize his forerunners" (272). Now the graduated process that gives rise to the painted image comes into full view. Correction is basically a "criticism" of the "forerunner," and it operates by a dovetailing of making and matching. Making comes before matching in Gombrich's classic formula. "Before the artist ever wanted to match the sights of the visible world he wanted to create things in their own right" (99). Making is a creative act, which manifests itself by subjecting the schema to manifold corrections until it matches the artist's vision.

There is a great variety of operations, by means of which the pairing of making and matching inscribes itself as correction into the schema inherited by the painter. The most radical one is to dispose with the schema altogether because, as Gombrich maintains, the "tendency of our minds to classify and register our experience in terms of the known must present a real problem to the artist in his encounter with the particular. Indeed, it may well be this difficulty which brought about the downfall of the formula in art" (144). This happened in Impressionism, when the evocation of light became the object to be made. A different handling of the basic pattern occurs in Turner, who was Constable's great rival. Whereas for Constable "[m]aking still comes before matching" (271), in Turner "the structure of objects is often quite swallowed up by the modifications of the moment – mist, light, and dazzle. Matching wins over making" (250). Another variant is to be ascertained in Cubism, which exposes everything presented through central perspective as an illusion. "If illusion is due to the interaction of clues and the absence of contradictory evidence, the only way to fight its transforming influence is to make the clues contradict each other and to prevent a coherent image of reality from destroying the pattern in the plane" (238). It may also happen that instead of the schema being dropped, a great many schemata will be assembled on the canvas, encroaching upon one another, and increase the ambivalences to such an extent "that even coherent forms are made to play hide-and-seek in the elusive tangle of unresolved ambiguities" (242). Dispensing with the schema leaves the eye without anchorage; accumulating schemata overtaxes perception; and making overwhelmed by matching tries to restore an innocent eye. These variations mark an historical articulation of art, but they also indicate the role of the beholder, whose perception is worked upon, and who is made to interpret what is to be seen.

The "beholder's share" is one of the cornerstones of Gombrich's theory. Representation is shown to be a performative process, articulated by the correction of the schema. Since the painted "object" which thus emerges is not the copy of something given, it is bound to engage the beholder, who feels compelled to figure out what is on the canvas. There are several reasons for getting the beholder involved. First of all, representation gives presence to something for a potential addressee, since it is never done for its own sake. Furthermore, correction – the result of making and matching – remains a blank that can only be dealt with by spelling out the clues to be discerned in the correction of the schema. This draws the beholder into the process; "it is the guess of the beholder that tests the medley of forms and colours for coherent meaning, crystallizing it into shape when a consistent interpretation has to be found" (204). And this is all the more necessary as in "the reading of images [ . . . ] it is always hard to distinguish what is given to us from what we supplement in the process of projection which is triggered off by recognition" (204). Consequently, the beholder will never arrive at a definitive interpretation by means of which correction as a blank can be filled. Ambiguities will remain, and they are due not only to the impossibility of probing into the artist's mind but also to rep-resentation itself. "There is a limit to what pictures can represent without differentiating between what belongs to the picture and what belongs to the intended reality" (201). Ambiguities can never be seen simultaneously, and always force a decision in favor of one or the other aspect, because "[r]epresentation is always a two-way affair. It creates a link by teaching us how to switch from one reading to another" (203). However, such an activity makes the beholder do something similar to what the artist practices all the time. What "we call 'reading' an image may perhaps be better described as testing it for its potentialities, trying out what fits" (190f.). Such an engagement allows the beholder to experience the thrill of making. These are the moments when beholder and artist are in close communion.

The beholder's share turns out to be a vital component of Gombrich's theory, because representation is no longer conceived as depicting a given object but stands for performance, and this process becomes tangible only through the beholder's realization. Gaps and omissions have to be bridged or supplemented, prodding the beholder's imagination into action, and as they can never be definitively resolved the inexhaustibility of the work of art moves into focus. This cannot be spelt out by the work itself but requires the participation of the beholder.

"All communication consists 'in making concessions' to the recipient's knowledge" (196), but it cannot be equated with the latter, as it would no longer convey information. It is the gray area between new information and existing knowledge that gives rise to ambiguity. "Ambiguity [ . . . ] can never be seen as such. We notice it only by learning to switch from one reading to another and by realizing that both interpretations fit the image equally well" (211). Thus the picture is made to unfold into its multifaceted aspects. "The image, it might be said, has no firm anchorage left on the canvas – it is only 'conjured up' in our minds. The willing beholder responds to the artist's suggestion because he enjoys the transformation that occurs in front of his eyes. It was in this enjoyment that a new function of art emerged gradually and all but unnoticed during the period we have discussed. The artist gives the beholder increasingly more to do, he draws him into the magic circle of creation and allows him to experience something of the thrill of 'making' which had once been the privilege of the artist. It is the turning point which leads to those visual conundrums of twentieth-century art that challenge our ingenuity and make us search our own minds for the unexpressed and inarticulate" (169). Through such introspection, Gombrich's theory comes full circle.

The beholder's share is an integral part of this theory, as the fundamental pairing of schema and correction is not self-explanatory. The schema refers to something, whereas its correction does not. Thus we have a scaffolding and a blank, because there is no reference for "making" that inscribes itself as correction into the schema. Making cannot be conceptualized, since creation eludes cognition. It is the beholder's share that is supposed to fill this blank, and a blank is different from a metaphor, which otherwise serves as the capstone of theories when explanation reaches its limit. The beholder's share assumes a twofold function. (1) The sequence of schema and correction cannot be viewed from a transcendental vantage point that would determine the process, and so representation as a performative process requires an active agent to make it tangible. (2) Through the beholder's engagement the painting translates itself into an experience. This may range from enhancing our capabilities of perception through seeing the world differently, to a penetration of one's own mind. The basis of all this is provided by gestalt psychology, the framework of which encompasses a gestalt theory of art that heightens our awareness of how our perceptual apparatus works. The gestalt theory conceives of the painting in terms of an event that arises out of the correction inscribed into the schema. This event has no reference, which accounts for a shift in theory-building from a semantic to an operational model. The focus is not on cognition and understanding but on how artistic "making and matching" translates into experience.

## An Example

Creativity looms large in Gombrich's theory, but creativity eludes cognition. The beholder's share, therefore, serves as a mode of illuminating what making entails, and the concept is supported by a range of examples from the history of fine arts that reveal many of the secrets of making. Whenever indeterminacies have to be minimized, theories become operational and function as a method of interpretation, because they have to prove their efficacy by opening up the work of art. The beholder's share and the history of fine arts enable us to focus on what happens when schemata are corrected, which we will now illustrate briefly by looking at Pablo Picasso's *Guernica* in Gombrich's terms.

It is a painting of disaster, which becomes all the more telling as the cause of the disaster is not apparent. The evil suggested is both absent and present, as is indicated by the missing reference of the multiple – though seemingly dispersed – schemata, a dispersal that may well be taken for a large-scale correction. What we are given to see are primarily human beings and animals who, however, are deformed and incoherently displayed on the canvas, thus defying a perspectival reading. The apparent incoherence and fragmentation of the schemata adumbrate something that either cannot be perceived or is beyond the scope of perception. The schemata are marked by a duality, which resists resolution. Despite their incoherence, they are cast in a shape that invokes a nonvisual dimension, which is not depicted but whose impact they are designed to formulate. The schemata still carry their ordinary signification in their wake, but they move beyond it.

This duplicitous character triggers various forms of reading, each of which can be conceived as a correction. The woman with the dead child suggests biblical allusions – to Herod, or perhaps to Pietà. Such biblical and artistic allusions are made to converge with an historical actuality, i.e., the bombing. Thus a diversified referentiality occurs and fuses what is otherwise different, without confirming any of these suggestions. The schema evaporates into a grim atmosphere through the corrections inserted.

**Figure 2** Pablo Picasso, *Guernica*, 1937, oil on canvas. Museo Nacional Centro de Arte, Reina Sofia, Madrid. Photo Bridgeman Art Library, London © Succession Picasso/DACS 2005.

The schemata of animals are, in contradistinction to the fleeing and burning women, metaphorical by nature. Picasso once said of the horse that it was the Spanish people. But even if it were not so clearly stated, the horse and the bull metaphorically represent features of Spanish life. The schema as metaphor establishes the overall background, which the correction marks as mutilated. Another level of reference is spotlighted by the destroyed monument, which inverts what is to be commemorated. Out of the broken sword of the warrior blooms a flower, which turns the corrected schema into a metonymy for peace. Finally, the lamp above sheds light over everything, yet it also forms an eye – a correction that might suggest that the eye sees what cannot be seen.

Here we are confronted with a set of scattered and fragmented schemata indicative of far-reaching corrections, each of which assumes a specific pattern of the intention that governs the making. To a certain degree, then, making becomes tangible by means of allusion, mutilated metaphor, metonymy, and the perception of the invisible. These diversified modes of correction point in different directions, making the painting explode semantically and yet guiding this explosion toward an emerging totality of the visibly disfigured schemata, which can only be realized by the beholder.

For this to happen we have to take another set of schemata into consideration. The basic scaffolding of the painting resembles an altar with one wing on each side. The crowded middle part suggests a triptych flanked by terror and anxiety on the right-hand side and by death and mourning on the left. The lamp at the top corresponds diagonally to the flower at the bottom. While these schemata stand for a scene, the picture itself figures a "metascenic event,"[7] brought about by the insertion of the corrected schemata into the overarching schema of the triptych and the correspondence of lamp and flower. Such a correction makes the altar into a location of horror and the correspondence into a tangential relationship. In each case the superimposition of the individually corrected schemata on the overall schema reverses established expectations, and simultaneously guides the beholder toward perceiving something that exceeds perception.

Finally, *Guernica* is based on an historic event: the bombing of a town. Yet the welter of schemata turns the incident into something which transcends perception. We see women, animals, a monument, and a warrior; all of them simultaneously mean, and do not mean, what they denote, because owing to the corrections they figure something else, without ever abandoning what they have meant in the first instance. Thus double meaning emerges and develops into a tilting game between perceiving and conceiving.

Perception itself is able only to grasp the fragmented schemata. Conception in turn is dependent on what is to be perceived if we are to visualize the unseeable. There is an incoherence on the perceptual level, which functions as a pointer toward coherence on the conceptual level. The one cannot work without the other. What arises out of the interpenetration of incoherence and coherence is something that has no reference outside itself, and thus requires a performative act by the beholder. It is this cohering of the mutually exclusive which now functions as an overall correction of ordinary expectations in order to drive home what has happened. Now the beholder becomes engaged, because the corrections observed trigger a creative impulse that leads us to "make" what the painting is meant to depict. Such making gains salience by being matched with the individual ideas of the beholder. For instance, if incoherence goes together with coherence, it might be conceived as a message that the senselessness of historical events can be overcome. But this is by no means the only version that the beholder might "make."

Gombrich's basic concept as outlined is a tool that may also be employed for interpreting literary texts. To illustrate this process and its consequences, we might refer to an example already discussed in another context. In Fielding's *Tom Jones*, Allworthy is introduced as the *homo perfectus*; he lives in Paradise Hall "and [ . . . ] might well be called the Favourite of both Nature and Fortune."[8] In a new chapter, Dr. Blifil enters the Allworthy family circle, and of him we learn: "the Doctor had one positive Recommendation. This was his great Appearance of Religion. Whether his Religion was real, or consisted only in Appearance, I shall not presume to say, as I am not possessed of any Touch-stone which can distinguish the true from the false."[9] However, it is said that the doctor seems like a saint. We are given certain signs which provide a basic schema of the characters concerned: Blifil gives an appearance of deep piety and Allworthy that of a perfect man. Simultaneously, however, the narrator lets out a warning signal that one must differentiate between true and false appearances, which is a hint that the schemata may need correction.

Next Blifil meets Allworthy and, owing to the narrator's signals, two different segments of the characters' basic dispositions are made to confront each other with reciprocal effect. The correction of the schemata gets under way. We are induced to anticipate Blifil's hypocrisy and Allworthy's naiveté. Blifil's appearance of piety is put on in order that he may impress Allworthy, with a view to worming his way into the family and perhaps gaining control of their estate. Allworthy trusts him because perfection is simply incapable of conceiving a mere pretense of ideality. The realization that the one is hypocritical and the other naive involves building a gestalt out of no fewer than three different segments – two of character and one of narrative perspective. But this gestalt is not explicit in the text – it is "made" by the reader, and is guided insofar as it arises out of the corrections of schemata.

Now if the naive Allworthy/hypocritical Blifil gestalt is regarded as self-sufficient, the conclusion must be simply that Allworthy is taken in by a con artist. But generally readers will not confine themselves to this conclusion, and questions arise such as "how" and "why" the perfect man is being duped. The corrections, as markers of "making," stimulate the reader into imagining the answers. These are, of course, individual, and emerge from the reader's "making," and all bear the inscription of what the making has been matched against. But as there are multiple and historically different results, the artist's "making" reveals itself as finally unfathomable, and this in turn generates ever new experiences in readers, as they are spurred into an incessant process of making.

## Notes

1  Christian von Ehrenfels, "Über Gestaltqualitäten," in Ferdinand Weinhandel, ed., *Gestalthaftes Sehen*, Darmstadt: Wissenschaftliche Buchgemeinschaft, 1960, pp. 11–43.

2  Wolfgang Köhler, *Gestalt Psychology: An Introduction to New Concepts in Modern Psychology*, Winnipeg: Mentor Books, 1965, pp. 94, 107, 118.

3  Rudolf Arnheim, *Art and Visual Perception: A Psychology of the Creative Eye*, Berkeley and Los Angeles: California University Press, 1966, p. 67.

4  Edgar Rubin, *Visuell wahrgenommene Figuren*, Copenhagen: Glydendal, 1921, pp. 36f. (The translation is mine.)

5  Ibid., p. 48.

6  E. H. Gombrich, *Art and Illusion: A Study in the Psychology of Pictorial Representation*, London: Phaidon Press, [2]1962. The sources of all other quotations from this volume are given in the text references to the appropriate pages.

7  See Max Imdahl, *Zur Kunst der Moderne* (Gesammelte Schriften I), ed. Angeli Jahnsen-Vukićević, Frankfurt/Main: Suhrkamp, 1996, p. 435, to whom I am indebted for some of his suggestions, although he interprets the painting in terms of Cubism and not gestalt theory.

8  Henry Fielding, *The History of Tom Jones A Foundling*, ed. Fredson Bowers, Middletown: Wesleyan University Press, 1975, p. 34.

9  Ibid., p. 64.

# 5

# Reception Theory: Iser

What has come to be called reception theory is by no means as uniform as it may seem. Its various ramifications are marked by a basic duality, incorporating both the reception of the literary text and its effects on its potential reader. These are two different sides of a related problem. An aesthetics of reception explores reactions to the literary text by readers in different historical situations. It is largely dependent on available evidence, as it tries to grasp prevailing attitudes that have shaped the understanding of a literary work in a given period of time. Such an attempt aims, according to Hans Robert Jauß (1921–97), at a "renewal of literary history,"[1] and in so doing it seeks to reconstruct the "horizon of expectation"[2] entertained by the reading public which, in determining what it considered artistic, revealed its own standards. In this respect reception functions as a divining rod for tracing the recipients' taste at a particular historical moment. Simultaneously, "the horizon of expectation" allows us "to conceive the meaning and form of a literary work in the historical unfolding of its understanding."[3] "It brings to view," Jauß writes, "the hermeneutic difference between the former and the current understanding of a work; it raises to consciousness the history of its reception, which mediates both positions."[4] By delineating the historical conditionality of readers' reactions, an aesthetics of reception turns literature into a tool for reconstituting the past.

While an aesthetics of reception deals with real readers, whose reactions testify to certain historically conditioned experiences of literature, my own theory of aesthetic response[5] focuses on how a piece of literature impacts on its implied readers and elicits a response. A theory of aesthetic response has its roots in the text; an aesthetics of reception arises from a history of readers' judgments. Thus the former is systematic in nature, and the latter historical, and these two related strands together constitute reception theory.

If the study of literature arises out of our concern with texts, then there is no doubting the importance of what happens to us as readers of those texts, and of what a text makes readers do. A literary work is not a documentary record of something that exists or has existed, but it brings into the world something that hitherto did not exist, and at best can be qualified as a virtual reality. Consequently, a theory of aesthetic response finds itself confronted with the problem of how such emerging virtual realities, which have no equivalent in our empirical world, can be processed and indeed understood.

## Reaction to a State of Criticism

Reception theory did not derive its parameters from a philosophy, as phenomenological and hermeneutical theories did, nor from a discipline such as psychology as in the case of gestalt theory. Instead, it was engendered by the dilemma in which the study of literature found itself in the late 1950s and 1960s: namely, the conflict of interpretation. The cultural heritage no longer served as an unquestioned means of promoting what used to be called *Bildung*; it became a problem because there were no longer uniform guidelines for such education, as had been the case in the past. Until the advent of modern art it was taken for granted that texts had a content, which was considered as a carrier of meaning. Interpretation had to uncover the text's meaning, which legitimized the whole process because meanings were considered to represent values that could be employed for the purpose of education. Thus the excavation of meaning became a prime concern which, however, began to raise the question as to why the meaning had been concealed within the text, and why authors should indulge in such a game of hide-and-seek with their interpreters. What turned out to be even more puzzling was why the meaning – once found – should change again, even though the letters, the words, and the sentences of the text remained the same. Eventually, this situation created an awareness of the fact that the presuppositions governing interpretation were to a large extent responsible for what the text was supposed to mean. Therefore the claim to have found *the* meaning implied justification of one's own assumptions and presuppositions, and this triggered what since has become known as the conflict of interpretation.[6]

This conflict unfolds as a competition, with each approach trying to assert itself at the expense of others in order to demonstrate its own importance, as well as the depth and breadth of its insights and its range. However, what the conflict of interpretation reveals, and what makes it interesting, is the inherent limitation of all presuppositions, and hence their restricted applicability to the task they are meant to perform. What critical attitudes were still dominant at the time when the nature of presuppositions became the subject of scrutiny?

The main approaches searched for the author's meaning or intention, for the message the work was supposed to convey, or for the aesthetic value that was to be considered as a final reconciliation of the text's ambiguities, its diversity of tropes and figures, and the harmonizing of its various layers. Intention had always been held in high esteem, because it embodied one last vestige of the Romantic view of the artist as creator. The message remained essential because, in the nineteenth century, art and literature were promoted to the status of a secular religion. This "Religion of Art" became the dominant orientation in seeking answers to basic questions of human life. As for the classical concept of harmony, it derived its dignity from the fact that the reconciliation of opposites in a work of art was believed to make it into what Hegel called "the vessel for the appearance of truth."[7]

When access to modern literature was blocked by such norms, i.e., intention, message, and value, the questions that in the past had seemed to be natural began to reveal themselves as offshoots of an historically conditioned approach to literature and the arts. It is, however, a basic feature of the history of interpretation that questions once asked are not without influence when new ones are framed: they do not simply disappear from view, but turn into signs of a now blocked path of interpretation. The problems produced by old questions give rise to new ones, so that the old questions serve as pointers to new directions. Thus the classical preoccupation with the author's intention has led to our concern with the reader's response to a text. The old semantic search for the message led to an analysis of those operations through which the imaginary object of the text is assembled. The resolution of opposites, bound up with the aesthetic value of the work, has led to the question of how human faculties are stimulated and acted upon by the literary text during the reading process.

These questions could not have arisen had it not been for the old answers that they replaced. The latter, then, are not dead and buried but live on as a negative fountainhead for new questions. Thus the author's intention, the work's message, the value manifested in the harmonious reconciliation –

all of them constitute a background to the theory of aesthetic response. The old answers take on an unanticipated function when expectations regarding the traditional norms of interpretation are frustrated, notably by modern literature and art. Thus the author's intention was replaced by the impact a piece of literature has on its potential recipient. The message, no longer to be ascertained, triggered interest in what has since come to be called text processing, i.e., what happens to the text in the act of reading. And finally, attention turned to the triadic relationship between author, text, and reader. Basically the focus switched from what the text means to what it does, and thus at a stroke relieved literary criticism of a perennial bugbear: namely, the attempt to identify the author's actual intention.

## Interface between Text/Context and Text/Reader

If we assume that the literary text does something to its reader, three initial problems have to be addressed. First, whatever happens to the reader is due to the fact that the literary text is in the nature of an event, i.e., an occurrence without reference,[8] and hence has to be coped with and responded to through text processing. The second point is: to what extent do the structures of the literary text prefigure the processing to be done by the reader, and how much latitude does the reader have? The third point concerns the relationship of a piece of literature both to its sociohistorical context and to selected dispositions of its reader. Inspecting the reaction of literature to its environment is all the more important, as literature makes inroads into social and cultural systems. It disrupts their structure and semantics by transplanting dislocated social and cultural fragments into the text.

Thus reception theory focuses primarily on two points of intersection: the interface between text and context, and that between text and reader. Every literary text normally contains selections from a variety of social, historical, cultural, and literary systems that exist as referential fields outside the text. This selection is itself an overstepping of boundaries in that the elements selected are lifted out of the systems in which they fulfill their specific function. This applies both to cultural norms and literary allusions, which are incorporated into every new literary text in such a way that the structure and semantics of the systems concerned are decomposed. We have to bear in mind that literary texts do not relate to contingent reality as such, but to systems through which the contingencies and complexities of reality are reduced to meaningful structures. The structures, however, are broken up and rearranged when selected features reappear in the text. These rearrangements move the systems themselves into focus, so that they can be discerned as the referential field of the text. So long as they are organizational units of the given world, in which they fulfill their regulatory function, they are taken for reality itself and thus remain unobserved. The selection, however, breaks their given order, thereby turning them into objects for observation.

The observability of referential fields is given its perspectival slant by each of the fields being split up into elements that are either actualized by the text or remain dormant within it. The elements chosen initially spotlight a field of reference, thus opening it up for perception, but they also permit perception of those elements that have been excluded. These, then, form the background against which the observation is to take place. It is as if what is present in the text must be judged in the light of what is absent. Therefore the literary text does not copy the referential fields to which it relates, but instead represents a reaction to those extratextual systems whose elements have been incorporated in the text.

This reaction is basically triggered by the system's limited ability to cope with what it was set up to organize, thereby drawing attention to the deficiencies of the system. This can best be illustrated by an example. The Lockean system of empiricism was the predominant thought system in eighteenth-century England. The system is based on a number of selective decisions regarding the acquisition of human knowledge, which was of increasing concern at the time in view of the general preoccupation with self-preservation. The dominance of this system can be gauged from the fact that existing systems endeavored to adapt themselves and so were relegated to subsystems. This was especially so with regard to theology, which accepted empirical premises concerning the acquisition of knowledge through experience, and so continually searched for natural explanations of supernatural phenomena.[9] By thus subjugating theological systems, empiricism extended the validity of its own assumptions. However, it is in the nature of a system that it gains its stability by excluding other possibilities. In this case the possibility of an a priori knowledge was negated, and this meant that knowledge could only be acquired subjectively. The advantage of such a doctrine was that knowledge could be gained from the individual's own experience; the disadvantage was that all traditional postulates governing human conduct and relationships had to be called into question. "Hence it comes to pass," Locke maintained, "that men's names of very compound *ideas*, such as for the most part are moral words, have seldom in two different men the same precise signification, since one man's complex *idea* seldom agrees with another's, and often differs from his own, from that which he had yesterday or will have tomorrow."[10] Here lie the boundaries of the empirical system, which can only stabilize itself by excluding what its general assumptions are unable to embrace. Locke solved the problem of how humans acquire knowledge from their experience, but in doing so he created the new problem of finding a possible basis for human conduct and relation. All systems are bound to exclude certain possibilities, and so they automatically give rise to deficiencies. It is to these deficiencies that literature latches on. This accounts for the intense preoccupation of the eighteenth-century novel and drama with questions of morality, for they attempted to balance out the deficiencies of the dominant thought system of the time. Since the whole sphere of human relations was absent from this system, literature brought it into focus.

Such an interrelationship applies equally to the inroads made by the literary text into the systems of its environment, and for illustration we may again turn to Locke. For him, the association of ideas represented a fundamental prerequisite for obtaining knowledge, as it was the combination of contingent sense data that brought about the extension and consolidation of knowledge in the human mind. The association of ideas was, then, one of the dominant features of the empirical system. In *Tristram Shandy*, this basic norm is selected, and held up for inspection. The association of ideas becomes an *idée fixe*, thus demanding a recodification of the whole basis of the empirical system. Sterne brings to the fore the human dimension that had been glossed over in Locke's system. Man's habitual propensity for combining ideas was for Locke a natural guarantee for the stabilization of knowledge, but Sterne now seizes on this same propensity to show the arbitrariness of such associations – as proved by the meanderings of Walter Shandy and Uncle Toby. Individual explanations of world and life shrink to the level of personal whim. This arbitrariness not only casts doubt on the dominant norm of the Lockean system, but also reveals the unpredictability and impenetrability of each subjective character. The result is not merely a negation of the Lockean norm but a disclosure of what remained eclipsed in Locke, namely, subjectivity as the selecting and motivating agency behind the association of ideas.[11]

This, however, is only one result of Sterne's recodification of the empirical norm when transplanted into the literary text for observation. Once the reliability of human knowledge is undermined by the revelation of its dependence on personal fixations, the norm under attack itself becomes the background for a new insight: the problematic nature of human relations. This revelation, in turn, leads Sterne to uncover the inherent social disposition of the human being, which now promises reliability in human affairs.

Literature endeavors to counter the problems produced by systems through focusing on their deficiencies, thus enabling us to construct whatever was concealed or ignored by the dominant systems of the day. At the same time, the text must implicitly contain the basic framework of the systems concerned, as this is what causes the problems that literature reacts to.

If the literary work arises out of the reader's own social and cultural background, it will serve to detach prevailing norms from their functional context, enabling the reader to observe how such social regulators function, and what effect they may have on people subject to them. Readers are thus placed in a position from which they can take a fresh look at the forces which guide and orient them, and which may have hitherto been accepted without question. If, however, these norms have faded into history, and readers are no longer entangled in the systems concerned, their recodification will allow readers not only to reconstruct the historical framework to which the text has reacted, but also to experience for themselves the deficiencies brought about by these norms, and to recognize the answers implicit in the text. The literary recodification of social and cultural norms thus has a dual function: it enables contemporary readers to perceive what they normally cannot see in the ordinary process of day-to-day living, and it enables subsequent generations of readers to grasp a reality that was never their own.

Focusing on the interface between text and context moves into view the text's responses to the situation within which it was produced. The text, however, interacts not only with its sociocultural environment but also, and in equal measure, with its readers. Highlighting what happens in text processing, therefore, is a central objective of a theory of reception. Analysis of the act of reading suggests that the literary text is a "structured prefigurement," which implies that what is given on the page has to be worked out. Sterne already wrote in *Tristram Shandy*: "no author, who understands the just boundaries of decorum and good-breeding would presume to think all: The truest respect which you can pay to the reader's understanding, is to halve this matter amicably, and leave him something to imagine, in his turn, as well as yourself. For my own part, I am eternally paying him compliments of this kind, and do all that lies within my power to keep his imagination as busy as my own."[12] However, such a relationship is marked by a fundamental asymmetry between text and reader. There is no common code between transmitter and receiver governing the way in which the text is to be processed; at best such a code is to be established in the reading process itself. The imbalance between text and reader is undefined, but it is this very indeterminacy that increases the reader's involvement, although this is not without control. The control is exercised by the text, but it is not exactly in the text. This is well illustrated by a comment Virginia Woolf made on the novels of Jane Austen: "Jane Austen is thus the mistress of deeper emotion than appears at the surface. She stimulates us to supply what is not there. What she offers is, apparently, a trifle, yet is composed of something that expands in the reader's mind and endows with the most enduring form of life scenes which are outwardly trivial. Always the stress is laid upon character [ . . . ] The turns and twists of the dialogue keep us on the tenterhooks of suspense. Our attention is half upon the present moment, and half upon the future [ . . . ] Here, indeed, in this unfinished and in the main inferior story, are all the elements of Jane Austen's greatness."[13] What is said appears to take on significance as a reference to what is not said, and so it is the implications and not the statements that give shape and weight to the meaning. The "enduring form of life" Virginia Woolf speaks of is not manifested on the printed page; it is a product arising out of the interaction between text and reader. This interaction is a process set in motion and regulated not by a given code but by a mutually restrictive and magnifying interplay between the explicit and the implicit, between revelation and concealment. Since the structure of the text consists of segments that are determinate, and of links between them that are indeterminate, the basic pattern of the text is formed by an interaction between the expressed and the unexpressed. The expressed itself evolves to the degree in which the reader actualizes the unexpressed, and so the reading process transforms the text into a correlate in the reader's mind.

As no story can ever be told in its entirety, the text itself is punctured by blanks and gaps that have to be negotiated in the act of reading. Whenever the reader bridges a gap, communication begins. The gaps or structured blanks – which in their most elementary form occur, for instance, when a new character appears in a novel – function as a kind of pivot on which the whole text–reader relationship revolves, because they stimulate the process of ideation to be performed by the reader on terms set by the text. There is, however, another place in the textual system where text and reader converge, and that is marked by various types of negation. Blanks and negations both control the process of meaning assembly in their own different ways. The blanks leave open the connection between textual perspectives which, in a narrative for instance, outline the author's view through the perspective of the narrator, the characters, the plot, and the fictitious reader inscribed in the text. They spur the reader into coordinating these patterned perspectives – in other words, they induce the recipient to perform basic operations *within* the text. The various types of negation invoke familiar and determinate elements of knowledge only to cancel them out. What is canceled, however, remains in view, and thus brings about modifications in the reader's attitudes to what is familiar or determinate – that is, the reader is guided to adopt a position *in relation to* the text.

Blanks indicate that the different segments and patterns of the text are to be connected even though the text itself does not say so. They are the unseen joints of the text, as they mark off patterns and textual perspectives from one another, and simultaneously prompt acts of ideation on the reader's part. Consequently, when the patterns and perspectives have been linked together, the blanks "disappear." As the reader's wandering viewpoint in the act of reading travels between all these segments, its constant switching during the time flow of reading intertwines them, thus bringing forth a network within which each perspective opens a view not only on other perspectives but also of the intended imaginary object. The latter itself is a product of interconnection, the structuring of which is to a great extent controlled by blanks.

Sterne's *Tristram Shandy* is a good example. Here the reader's traveling viewpoint has to switch between an increasing number of textual perspectives, and hence begins to oscillate between those of the characters, the narrator, and the fictitious reader, as well as the fragmented segments of the story, and the meanderings of the plot line, subjecting all of them to a reciprocal transformation. The segment on which the viewpoint focuses in each particular reading moment becomes the theme, and the theme of one moment becomes the horizon against which the next segment takes on its actuality and so on. As the perspective of the fictitious reader serves mainly to outline *attitudes* toward the events in the text, it follows that the transformation must apply to the contents of such attitudes – in other words, the attitude of the fictitious reader is transformed by the real reader. The narrator's perspective, which denotes *evaluation* of the events, may undergo a similar transformation when it comes into conflict with other perspectives during the theme-and-horizon process; instead of directing the proceedings he appears to be continually surprised. The story suspends "good continuation," thus inverting both subjective and measured time, and the expected causality of the plot line breaks up into unforeseeable ramifications. Everything appears to go against the grain, leading to a multiplicity of blanks – even relating to what is generally expected in a novel – which the reader is meant to negotiate. And yet while these invisible joints of the text are being negotiated, an overall pattern tends to emerge: the unfathomableness of individuality.

The emergence of such an idea is supported by the fact that readers must react not only to the instruction given by the blanks in the text but also to the products of their own ideating activity whenever revisions are needed. The discontinuities of textual segments trigger synthesizing operations in the reader's mind, because the blanks lead to collisions between the individual ideas formed, thus preventing "good continuation," which is a prerequisite for understanding. These colliding ideas condition each other in the time flow of reading. Even if an idea has to be discarded in order to accommodate new information, it will nevertheless condition its successor, and thereby affect the latter's composition. The chain of ideas which thus emerges in the reader's mind is the means by which the text is translated into the imagination. This process, which is mapped out by the structured blanks of the text, can be designated the **syntagmatic axis of reading**.

The **paradigmatic axis of reading** is prestructured by the negations in the text. Blanks indicate connections to be established; negations indicate a motivation for what has been nullified. Negations mark dominant positions that are questioned; they require a degree of introspection in order to elicit a positive counterpart to what has been nullified, because the negated items isolated from their respective social and cultural contexts need to be reshuffled.

Let us turn now to an example of how negations operate in the reading process. In Fielding's *Joseph Andrews* Abraham Adams, the real hero of the novel, is introduced through a catalogue of virtues, which embrace practically every norm that was regarded as belonging to the ideal eighteenth-century man; and yet these very virtues make Adams totally unsuited to the demands of everyday life. As far as adaptability and practicality are concerned, they reduce him to the level of a newborn child – as Fielding himself declares at the end of his introductory characterization. Rejecting the norms *en bloc*, however, would result in total disorientation, and in any case Fielding could scarcely dismiss virtue as stupidity. And so the negation does not indicate any radical alternative, but rather suggests a different view of these virtues. They themselves are not questioned, but the expectations associated with them are thwarted because, as a result of the negation, they are no longer seen from their Christian or Platonic basis; the standpoint now is the everyday world. The resultant dislocation suggests that what matters now is not the nature of the norms but how they function and how they are to be applied in practice. This dislocation of the norms from their traditional basis obviously means that they must be reassessed in the everyday world, and this reassessment becomes the imaginary object for the reader – "imaginary" because in the text it appears only as a "defined deficiency." "Thus the negative act is constitutive for the image."[14] There is no doubt that the negative slant given to the knowledge offered induces the reader to ideate the as yet hidden cause governing the negation – and in doing so the reader formulates what has been left unformulated.

Without going into further details of how negation operates in the example, we can see that it has an important bearing on communication. This activity would not be necessary if what is communicated were not to some extent unfamiliar. Literature brings something into the world that is not there. This something must reveal itself if it is to be comprehended. However, as the unfamiliar elements cannot be manifested under the conditions that pertain to familiar or existing conceptions, what literature brings into the world can only reveal itself by means of questioning what it reproduces from the world. This comes about by dislocating extratextual norms, meanings, and structures, and draining them of their empirical reality, as once described by Adorno: "everything that works of art contain, as regards form and materials, spirit and matter, has emigrated from reality into the works, and in them has been deprived of its reality."[15] Negation is the structure underlying the invalidation of the reality manifested. It is the unformulated constituent of the text.

Thus negation cannot be deduced from the given referential realities which it questions nor can it be conceived as serving whatever essentialist idea it heralds. It is the nonformulation of the not-yet-comprehended, and as such it marks a relationship to what it disputes, but it also provides a basic link between the reader and the text. If the reader is to conceive the cause underlying the questioning of the world, he/she must transcend this world in order to observe what he or she is otherwise so inextricably entangled in. Through this repositioning the communicatory function of literature realizes itself.

Negation and blanks as basic constituents of communication are thus enabling structures that demand a process of determining which only the reader can implement. This gives rise to the subjective hue of the text's meaning. However, as the text does not have one specific meaning, what appears to be a deficiency is, in fact, the productive matrix, which enables the text to be meaningful in a variety of historically changing contexts.

Reception theory has helped to elucidate why and how the same literary text can mean different things to different people at different times, because it has taken into consideration the two-sidedness of the literary work with its two poles: the artistic and the aesthetic. The artistic refers to the text created by an author, and the aesthetic to the realization accomplished by the reader, the interaction of which unfolds the work's potential. Reception theory is an operational model par excellence, and simultaneously a theory of the literary text.

## Notes

1   Hans Robert Jauß, *Toward an Aesthetics of Reception*, trans. Timothy Bahti, Minneapolis: Minnesota University Press, 1982, p. 20.
2   Ibid., p. 25.
3   Ibid., p. 32.
4   Ibid., p. 28.
5   Wolfgang Iser, *The Act of Reading: A Theory of Aesthetic Response*, Baltimore: Johns Hopkins University Press, 1979, [5]1991, and Wolfgang Iser, *The Implied Reader: Patterns of Communication from Bunyan to Beckett*, Baltimore: Johns Hopkins University Press, 1974, [5]1990.
6   For details see Paul Ricœur, *The Conflict of Interpretation*, ed. Don Ihde, Evanston: Northwestern University Press, 1974.
7   Georg Friedrich Wilhelm Hegel, *Ästhetik*, ed. Friedrich Bassenge, Berlin: Aufbau Verlag, 1970, pp. 96–108, and 1105.
8   See Alfred North Whitehead, *Science and the Modern World*, Cambridge: Cambridge University Press, 1953, pp. 116f. and 130.
9   See for instance John Toland, *Christianity not Mysterious* (1696), and Matthew Tindal, *Christianity as Old as the Creation* (1730).
10  John Locke, *An Essay Concerning Human Understanding*, book III, chapter 9, London: Dent 1961, p. 78.
11  For further details see Wolfgang Iser, *Laurence Sterne, "Tristram Shandy"* (Landmarks of World Literature), Cambridge: Cambridge University Press, 1988.
12  Laurence Sterne, *Tristram Shandy*, book II, chapter 11, London: Dent, 1956, p. 78.

13  Virginia Woolf, *The Common Reader (First Series)*, London: Hogarth Press, 1957, p. 174.

14  Jean Paul Sartre, *Das Imaginäre: Phänomenologische Psychologie der Einbildungskraft*, trans. Hans Schöneberg, Reinbek: Rowohlt, 1971, pp. 207 and 284f., my translation.

15  Theodor W. Adorno, *Ästhetische Theorie* (Gesammelte Schriften 7), Frankfurt/ Main: Suhrkamp, 1970, p. 158, my translation.

# 6

# Semiotic Theory: Eco

Semiotics as a theory of signs dates back to the philosophy of John Locke (1634–1702) and has been given a systematic exposition by Charles S. Sanders Peirce (1839–1914). It is basically concerned with the properties of signs and their functions, i.e., the way in which signs operate in designating an object for an *interpretant*. "A sign, or *representamen*," Peirce writes, "is something which stands to somebody for something in some respect or capacity. It addresses somebody, that is, it creates in the mind of that person an equivalent sign, or perhaps a more developed sign. The sign which it creates I call the *interpretant* of the first sign. [ . . . ] A *Sign* or *Representamen*, is First which stands in such a genuine triadic relation to a Second, called *its Object*, as to be capable of determining a Third, called its *Interpretant* [ . . . ] The triadic relation is *genuine*, that is its three members are bound together by it in a way that does not consist in any complexus of dyadic relations."[1] This triadic interrelation is schematically represented by the diagram below, which maps out the structure of signification.

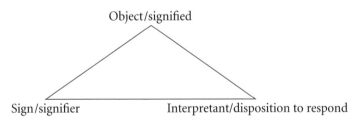

Object/signified

Sign/signifier          Interpretant/disposition to respond

The process of signification requires a distinction between types of signs, whose different properties allow them to operate in a specific manner. Thus Peirce came up with another of his "**trichotomies**," as he called them, by defining signs as iconic, indexical, and symbolic. An iconic sign is similar to what it represents: it "is an image of its object and, more strictly speaking, can only be an *idea*."[2] An indexical sign represents an object not immediately present, such as smoke being an index of fire. "Anything which focusses attention is an index."[3] The symbolic sign designates an object; "it must *denote* an individual, and must *signify* a character. A *genuine* symbol is a symbol that has a general meaning."[4] Although we shall be concerned in what follows with the iconic sign, we should be aware that the latter is only one of a set of signs, all of which have different denotative functions.

Peirce laid the foundation of modern semiotics, which had a considerable impact on human and natural sciences in the twentieth century and spawned ever new concepts of sign usage in order to illuminate what the processes of signification were able to communicate. Eventually, semiotics laid claim to being a "unified science," as it considered itself to be universal in character. The claim is based on the fact that in both the humanities and the sciences the production, function, and operation of signs play an important part, for which semiotics provides the parameters. Hence, although semiotics is not primarily concerned with the work of art, the latter is regarded as a special case not only of sign-function but also – and more importantly, as we shall see – of the production of codes, because the signifier requires a code if the interpretant is to grasp exactly what the signifier has designated as the signified. In the context both of art and code production, the iconic sign is of crucial importance, but has also created problems of definition.

## The Iconic Sign

What makes the work of art into an interesting paradigm for semiotics is the fact that its assembly of signs does not refer to a given object, in the sense in which the diagram above charts the triadic relationship. Charles Morris (1901–79) – a leading semiotician of the twentieth century – argues that the work of art consists of "iconic signs" or is an iconic sign itself. "A sign is *iconic* to the *extent to which* [my italics] it itself has the properties of its denotata [*see* **denotatum**]; otherwise it is *non-iconic*."[5] However, Morris begins to modify this straightforward definition, when he writes: "A portrait of a person is to a considerable extent iconic, but it is not completely so since the painted canvas does not have the texture of the skin, or the capacities for speech and motion, which the person portrayed has. The motion picture is more iconic, but again not completely so. A completely iconic sign would always denote itself, since itself would be a denotatum."[6] What exactly does this mean? Is the iconic sign self-referential or, by being identical to what it denotes, does it actually bring forth the thing it designates?

In view of these mounting difficulties, Morris tones down his initial definition: "An iconic sign, it will be recalled, is any sign which is similar in some respect to what it denotes. Iconicity is thus a matter *of degree* [my italics]."[7] And what the degree might be he now details in the following manner: "An icon can designate, but it can also appraise and prescribe. A portrait of a person, together with the name of the person, is, as Peirce held, no less a statement than the verbal description of a person. And by the same token something can be appraised by icons (can for instance be caricatured or idealized in paint or sound), so that the arts may signify in the appraisive mode. They may also signify prescriptively since a command can be given visual form or signified musically by the use of sounds similar to the speech melodies of spoken imperatives."[8]

This is a rather substantial modification of what Morris initially said about the painting as an iconic sign, in spite of the fact that he admitted that paint, canvas, texture, and a few other characteristics are not iconic, since they are the material through which the iconic sign manifests itself. When he takes "appraisive" and "prescriptive" features to be properties of the iconic sign, he is clearly adding something to the latter, especially if the painting issues "visual commands" or enforces a prescriptive "reading." Is the reading, then, part of the self-designating denotatum, or are appraisal and prescription meant to induce attitudes in the interpretant, which for Morris is "a disposition to respond?"[9] As long as the iconic sign remains confined to being similar to what it denotes, "the definition is more or less tautological and in any case rather naïve,"[10] as Eco has maintained. Therefore, it gains its value not so much from similarity but rather from what its self-designating denotatum elicits. "The icon naturally has an important place in the fine arts because the valuative aim is more surely reached if an object can be presented for inspection which itself is prized and which iconically embodies the very characteristics of a **goal-object** concerning which the aim is to induce valuation."[11] If the iconic sign begins to function by stimulating evaluation, the latter is not engendered by likeness or similarity but by the code that governs the iconic sign. Behavior, then, regulates signification, because, as Morris put it, "signs are identified within goal-seeking behavior."[12]

What is the upshot of this discussion? As the iconic sign does not denote a given object, it becomes self-designating, and thus, as Peirce had already said, is just an "idea" that begins to function only when governed by a code, which according to Morris is behavioristic. The code, however, is not a property of the iconic sign but is something posited that regulates the way in which the sign is meant to operate. Peirce did not run into this kind of trouble, because for him semiotics was "a formal doctrine of signs," and thus only another name for logic, as epitomized by the properties of signs. Considering the work of art, however, as an iconic sign raised two interconnected problems: what exactly is likeness, and what is the code according to which it is made to function?

It is scarcely surprising that Morris's position came under scrutiny, in a manner exemplified by both Benbow Ritchie and Isabel Creed-Hungerland, who advocate different concepts of the iconic sign and its mode of operation. At first glance Ritchie seems to latch on to Morris's behavioristic attitude when he writes: "Formal signs [ . . . ] are iconic of value."[13] What does this mean, if it is not identical to what Morris had in mind? Ritchie asserts: "Anything is a value when it is believed to be relevant to the fulfilment of an impulse,"[14] and he illustrates this statement with an example. A painter like Matisse, he writes, being very much concerned with "the structural uses of color," tries to make yellow, blue, and red patches play into one another on canvas. "Suppose, for example, that we have a patch of [ . . . ] yellow between a red and a blue patch. When the yellow is perceived in relation to the red patch it seems to share the 'aggressive' character of the red. On the other hand when it is perceived in relation to the blue patch, it seems to share the latter's 'cool reticence.'"[15] Thus the red patch becomes a sign of a newly formed value, "since it is perceived and used as a link between the aroused expectations and further values," as signified by "the blue line which has the restraint demanded by the red patch," and so the interplay unfolds in ever new variations "until the experience ends with the creation of a total complex value which fulfils the impulse."[16] Hence it is not the red patch in itself that Ritchie considers a value, but rather what it sparks off by developing an "impulse," which realizes itself in a concatenation of relationships that shade into one another.

There may still be a behavioristic touch to Ritchie's argument in the emphasis on value, which, however, as the fulfillment of impulses is different from Morris's "valuative aim." Moreover, iconic signs are supposed to denote the relationship between the formalistically conceived values in an aesthetic object. Hence an "aesthetic syntactics" is advocated, which "would be a study of the syntactical relations between the formal icons of value [and thus] we could describe any particular work of art as a certain kind of syntactical system."[17]

Such a syntax need not necessarily be confined to value as the fulfillment of an impulse, but would easily be applicable to the way in which rhetorical tropes and figures are organized in a work of art. The "aesthetic syntax" as the iconic sign would still retain its likeness to what it denotes, although the similarity is substantially different from what Morris considered it to be. But just as Morris needed a code for the iconic sign to function as evaluation, so Ritchie also posits a code by his conception of value as fulfillment of an impulse which operates the syntactical system.

Isabel Creed-Hungerland advocates a different approach by giving a twist to Ritchie's example: "As Mr. Ritchie's account of the red–blue combination makes clear, the two colors are perceived not only as contrasting (and I would add, as creating tensions) in terms of their distance, in a color scheme, from one another, but also in terms of the exciting quality of the particular red and the soothing quality of the particular blue, i.e. in terms of the contrasting expressive qualities." The iconic sign as aesthetic syntax is replaced by the iconic sign as expressiveness.

Creed-Hungerland makes a similar point in criticizing Morris. Likeness, she contends, is not enough, and has to be "modified or transformed by differences [ . . . ] *in* the work of art if the associations evoked are molded by the perceptual structure and become part of its expressiveness, an expressiveness which can reinforce or work together with the expressiveness of line, shape, or color."[18]

But what is expressiveness, and how is it to be identified? The answer is contained in her brief description of Ernst Barlach's sculpture *The Avenger*. The "outlines and volume seen as abstract [ . . . ] would be perceived as moving strongly in one direction. There would still be a quality of harshness, severity, and strength in the three-dimensional design. But the recognition of the iconic character of the form reinforces the movement and the emotions appropriate to a fiercely moving avenger are felt as the characteristics of the perceptual form." The latter denotes expressiveness, conveyed by certain contortions of the bodily movement, of which Rodin's *L'Homme qui marche* would also be a telling example. However, is the perceptual form an iconic sign denoting expressiveness, or is the latter a code that endows the contortions of the perceptual structure with expressiveness? Owing to the countervailing structures of the perceptual form, Creed-Hungerland seems to take it as an iconic sign denoting expressiveness.

If the iconic sign has the properties of what it denotes (Morris), one might conclude that whatever is iconic must be a work of art. In this respect Ritchie and Creed-Hungerland have reservations, defining the iconic sign as either denoting syntactical relationships in or expressiveness of the work of art. However, all of them agree that the iconic sign is similar to what it denotes, although both Ritchie and Creed-Hungerland confine their definitions of it to certain features within the work of art. One could well imagine that there might be further specifications, such as the interplay of super-signs (character, narrator, plot line, and story in a narrative), which would eventually unfurl a taxonomy of iconic signs. Such a taxonomic listing of what the iconic sign denotes in each of the instances would make a semiotic theory of the arts somewhat peripheral, as the iconic sign would then only spotlight different features in every case.

More important, however, than the changing definitions of the iconic sign are the different codes that are brought to bear in order to make the icon function in particular ways. As these codes are not part of the art work, and are postulated from an outside stance, they reflect trends that are or have been dominant at certain times – for instance, behaviorism, formalism, expressionism. As long as the iconic sign is defined in terms of similarity to its denotatum, a code is required to make it function, and this, in view of changing definitions for both sign and code, poses a problem for a semiotic theory of art.

## The Aesthetic Idiolect

Umberto Eco (b. 1930) caused a turnabout in the semiotic approach to art by breaking away from the discussion of iconicity altogether, maintaining: "if the iconic sign is similar to the thing denoted *in some respects*, then we arrive at a definition which satisfies common sense, but not semiotics."[19] For him, "the aesthetic text represents a sort of summary and laboratory model of all the aspects of sign-function" (261), which means no less than that "the aesthetic text" is paradigmatic for the whole process of semiosis. Eco starts out by asserting "that art, above and beyond its own 'linguistic' form, also conveys a *'je ne sais pas quoi.'* In this way aesthetics becomes the philosophy of the unspeakable" (265). Unspeakability arises from the specific sign-function in the aesthetic text, because the sign is both *"ambiguous* and *self-focusing"* (262).

Ambiguities, on the one hand, harbor double meanings, succinctly expressed by Shakespeare's Richard III when he says, "I moralize two meanings in one word" (III.i.83), and arise out of code violation, when for instance in Spenser's *Shepheardes Calender* – as we shall see in our example – Colin Clout means a whole string of different persons that contrast substantially in their character.

Self-focusing, on the other hand, foregrounds the pattern according to which the message is formed. If the pattern places itself side by side with the message, what is to be communicated is how the message is formed and meant to be received. Thus the self-focusing sign designates instructions for perception and conception of the message. Such an aesthetic sign-function exceeds the norms operative in the language system, as "it focuses my attention and urges me to an interpretive effort (while at the same time suggesting how to set about decoding) it incites me toward the discovery of an unexpected flexibility in the language with which I am dealing" (263). If that happens, "the text becomes self-focusing: it directs the attention of the addressee primarily *to its own shape*" (264). Self-focusing is an overcoding in two respects, which means that the sign is to be read according to two different codes: (1) the message to be conveyed is overcoded by simultaneously presenting the pattern according to which it has been formed; (2) the sign-sequence is overcoded, as the prevalent norms of the language system have been outstripped, thus revealing the "unspeakable" within the language system.

"Looking at a work of art, the addressee is in fact forced to question the text under the pressure of a twofold impression: on the one hand he 'guesses' that there is a *surplus of expression* that he cannot completely analyze [ ... ] On the other hand he vaguely senses a *surplus of content*. The second feeling is clearly aroused by the surplus of expression but it occurs even when this surplus of expression is not consciously grasped" (269f.). Obviously, neither the ambiguous nor the self-focusing sign infringes codes randomly, but each follows a precise design which, however, cannot be identified with any existing codes. Thus a "deviational matrix" (271) emerges, which is dual in character as it spotlights the codes that have been violated, and simultaneously points to the hidden motivation that caused the violation. Such a duality tends to generate several messages within the same work. But as the work of art does not rearrange codes in order to produce multiple and conflicting messages for its own sake, "the deviational matrix [ ... ] entails a rearrangement of the codes themselves. It thus presents the proposal of a *new coding possibility*" (272). In other words, the infringed codes caused by ambiguous and self-focusing signs trigger the search for a code that will allow us to read the ongoing rearrangements and the apparently conflicting messages of the text. "The rule governing all deviations at work at every level of a work of art, the unique diagram which makes all deviations mutually functional, is the **aesthetic idiolect**" (272). The term is self-explanatory up to a point: in reading all the deviations caused by the ambiguous and self-focusing signs, one has to trace the underlying motivations. But as the guideline for such an activity has been produced by the work itself, the rule governing the reading has to be discovered, since it makes all the deviations function. Thus each reading of the aesthetic idiolect is an actualization of something that by its very nature is a potential, which can never be totally actualized. "A responsible collaboration is demanded of the addressee. He must intervene to fill up semantic gaps, to reduce or to further complicate the multiple readings proposed, to choose his own preferred paths of interpretation, to consider several of them at once (even if they are mutually incompatible), to re-read the same text many times, each time testing out different and contradictory presuppositions. Thus the aesthetic text becomes a multiple source of unpredictable '*speech acts*'" (276) because the latter are realizations of how the addressee feels engaged by "being spoken to." The offshoot of such an activity generated by the idiolect consists in "(a) a combinatorial knowledge about the entire range of possibilities available within the given codes; (b) a historical knowledge about the circumstances and the codes (indeed all the norms) of a given artistic period" (276). Hence the variability of historical reception and understanding of the work of art, because tracing the idiolect is guided by the sociocultural setting that conditions its readability.

This is one of the consequences arising from the aesthetic idiolect of the work. The other one appears to be of equal importance. Generated by the deviational matrix, the idiolect calls for new coding possibilities, which makes the work of art into a paradigm of code changing and code production. And as the relationship between the signifier and the signified is always governed by a code, which is not simply behavioristic by nature, as semioticians like Morris claimed, the work of art provides a fundamental insight into how codes are produced by violating codes. This means no less than "*to change the way in which 'culture' sees the world* [ . . . ] If aesthetic texts can modify our concrete approach to states of the world then they are of great importance to that branch of sign production that is concerned with the labor of connecting signs with the states of the world"

(274f.). While the ambiguous and self-focusing signs operative on the expression level point up the unspeakable in the language system, the idiolect spells it out, and in doing so integrates unspeakability into our social world, the outcome of which is twofold: it epitomizes code changing and code production, and it turns into a "metacommunication" for the process of signification, i.e., in communicating, it simultaneously communicates what happens in such a process of communication.

## An Example

To illustrate the sign-function as outlined by Eco we may select a Renaissance text for the following reason: throughout the Middle Ages the sign relationship was ternary by nature; it emerged in late antiquity and persisted until it became problematical in the Renaissance. "Ever since the Stoics," Foucault writes, "the system of signs in the Western world had been a ternary one, for it was recognized as containing the significant, the signified and the 'conjuncture.' "[20] The latter functioned as an unquestioned code and was identical with the medieval world picture, so that the "conjuncture" represented the all-encompassing world order, which functioned as the regulating code for the sign relationship. When the arrangement of signs became binary, owing to the abandonment of the preestablished "conjuncture," the connection between the signifier and signified turned into a problem.

In Spenser's *Shepheardes Calender* (Appendix B) traditional sign relationships came under stress. This is already discernible in the external organization of the eclogues. Each one is headed by a woodcut exhibiting the appropriate image of the zodiac for the twelve-month calendar. Then comes the *Argument*, followed by the eclogue itself, which concludes with an *Emblem*. Eclogue and *Emblem* lead to a *Glosse* that to a degree opens up the territory hidden in the eclogue. Such a sequence testifies to the fact that the medieval "conjuncture" has ceased to function as a code, and that new regulations of sign relationships have become pertinent.

The eclogues are virtually teeming with ambiguous signs. Colin Clout, the central figure, is sometimes a poet, sometimes Spenser himself, sometimes just a shepherd, and sometimes the English people as a whole. The same is true of the shepherdess Eliza, who at different times embodies the beloved, Queen Elizabeth, and the grieving Dido. The figure of Pan takes on curious ambiguities: god of the shepherds, Jesus, Henry VIII, and even Satan. While the allegorical mode imposed a predetermined relationship on what the personification was meant to signify, these ad hoc similitudes actually release a welter of potential correlations. The shepherds take on multiple meanings, which may be literary, moral, religious, or political. Often the meanings are so interwoven that, despite the temporary dominance of one of them, the others shade into the one actually present. If Colin Clout is shepherd, poet, Spenser, and the English people, and if Eliza is shepherdess, Dido, and Queen Elizabeth, the preordained interdependence of the two levels, otherwise fixed by the allegorical mode, begins to fade, and we obtain a host of semantic adumbrations that impinge on every meaning of every situation in each eclogue. Consequently, when the shepherds foreshadow certain political figures, the resemblance becomes increasingly complex, and ambiguities begin to proliferate.

Of course, it is through the *Glosse* at the end of each eclogue that shepherd and shepherdess are made ambiguous, as they keep signifying something different from what they appear to be. Generating ambiguous signs through explanations reverses the function of the "conjuncture"; instead of stabilizing the relation between signifier and signified, the *Glosse* makes the connection multivalent. Salient features of the idiolect thus begin to emerge on the expression level.

This is equally true of self-focusing signs, which become particularly telling in the *February Eclogue*. Various literary genres are telescoped together. We have a song-contest, a medieval *altercatio*, a fable, a forensic plea, which is a traditional rhetorical genre, and an emblem. However, none of these genres fulfills its generic function. The eclogue begins with a typical song-contest between two shepherds. This, however, is reduced to a mere outline, because instead of trying to outdo each other in praise of the adored shepherdess, the two shepherds switch to an altercation between youth and old age. In this way the generic feature of the pastoral is replaced by another genre, the "debate." The confrontation between youth and age demands a decision, but instead of a judgment as a basic component to be expected in the genre we get a fable, and this, instead of ending with a moral, leads finally to a forensic plea. In the fable, the oak and the brier quarrel over the importance they have for each other and over the trouble they cause each other. They take their case to man – representing humankind – who, called upon to pass judgment, makes a wrong decision that destroys both oak and brier. A moral conclusion would now be pertinent, but here as elsewhere the expectation aroused by the genre is not fulfilled.

79

There is no victor in the song-contest, no decision in the debate, no moral to the fable, and no endorsement of an expected outcome owing to the two differing emblems, while the *Glosse* adds that the attitudes depicted may be seen from different standpoints and hence will give rise to different conclusions. The constitutive components of the genres are eliminated and replaced by another, though different, genre. Now the genres are representative only to the degree in which they invoke and run counter to established expectations. Their nesting divests them of their inherited representational function and transforms them into self-focusing signs that stand side by side with the message to be conveyed. Such signs arise out of a code violation of what is normally expected of the genres, and the nesting creates a "deviational matrix," which generates new coding possibilities guided by the self-focusing signs. As we know from Eco's exposition, the sign becomes self-focusing when, instead of designating the message, it foregrounds the pattern according to which the message has been formed and is to be received. It signals a rearrangement of codes, as evinced by decomposing the genres, which are robbed of their representational quality and thus simultaneously point to something unspeakable.

Self-focusing and ambiguous signs give salience to the idiolect, which is self-produced by the work of art and has a code of its own arising out of the code changes it has wrought. The idiolect comes to life through multiple readings depending on interconnected pathways that are mapped by the ambiguous and self-focusing signs. One reading might be as follows: we discern in the eclogues a definite undermining of representation, which the ambiguous sign causes to explode into multiplicity, and which the self-focusing sign strips of its reference. Obviously, the world can no longer be encompassed by representation, which shrinks and becomes partial, thus pointing to something beyond itself, toward which the idiolect gestures. If there are two worlds, one of which can be perceived by representation while the other appears to elude our grasp, then the problem of orientation looms large. The idiolect highlights the fact that an expanding world cannot be captured through inherited codes, because a featureless future is now dawning on the Renaissance horizon. Making this open-endedness palpable requires both code changing and code production in order to chart what is as yet beyond grasp. Any change in the semantic system entails changing the way in which a culture conceives of the world. However, the self-produced code of the work of art gains salience by multiple readings of the idiolect, each of which will depend on the path one takes within the maze of signs.

# Notes

1 Charles S. Sanders Peirce, *The Philosophy of Peirce: Selected Writings*, ed. Justus Buchler, London: Routledge and Kegan Paul, ³1956, pp. 99f.
2 Ibid., p. 105.
3 Ibid., p. 108.
4 Ibid., p. 112.
5 Charles Morris, *Signs, Language and Behavior*, New York: Braziller, 1955, p. 18.
6 Ibid., p. 23.
7 Ibid., p. 191.
8 Ibid., p. 194.
9 Ibid., p. 18.
10 Umberto Eco, *A Theory of Semiotics*, Bloomington: Indiana University Press, 1976, p. 192.
11 Morris, *Signs, Language and Behavior*, p. 195.
12 Ibid., p. 7.
13 Benbow Ritchie, "The Formal Structure of the Aesthetic Object," in Eliseo Vivas and Murray Krieger, *The Problem of Aesthetics*, New York: Holt, Rinehart, 1975, p. 232.
14 Ibid., p. 227.
15 Ibid., p. 228.
16 Ibid., p. 230.
17 Ibid., pp. 232f.
18 Ibid., p. 238.
19 Eco, *Theory of Semiotics*, p. 193. The sources of all other quotations from this volume are given in the text with references to the appropriate pages.
20 Michel Foucault, *The Order of Things*, New York: Vintage, 1973, p. 42.

# 7

# Psychoanalytical Theory: Ehrenzweig

Sigmund Freud, the great "revolutionary theorist"[1] of the twentieth century, who launched an archeological excavation into the innermost recesses of the human psyche, "was widely read in classical literature, from Sophocles, Shakespeare, and Goethe to contemporary poetry."[2] Works of art served more than one purpose for him, not least as "a defense and an illustration of psychoanalysis to the general and nonscientific public," especially in his period of isolation prior to the Great War.[3] And yet Freud never advanced a theory of art on the basis of his findings; instead, he produced case studies, the most famous of which is his Leonardo essay, and all of them have a story-like character. "We might consider Freud's writing an exploration and elaboration of the late-nineteenth-century genre, the clinical narrative. [ ... ] Freud never made extended and consistent use of his theory in the analysis of art, and much of his theory which would have been most helpful in developing a philosophy of art was never put to that use."[4] Works of art were more often than not taken as a testing ground for psychoanalytical discoveries – a practice still evident in literary criticism today. Endorsing the findings of psychoanalysis, however, is not a psychoanalytical theory of art. Moreover, Freud frequently probed into the artist's life – Leonardo's and Michelangelo's, for instance – in order to explain features of their work. Thus "[p]sychoanalytic studies of art," Kuhns writes, "frequently make the mistake of jumping outside the work to the life of the artist, yet when the purpose of the inquiry is to give a psychoanalytical interpretation *of art*, the object itself and its own establishment of reality must be the focus of attention."[5] Hence art for Freud is, according to Ricœur, "the nonobsessional, nonerotic form of substitutive satisfaction. The 'charm' of aesthetic creation does not indeed arise from the return of the repressed. But where, then, is its place between the pleasure principle and the reality principle? This is the great question which remains in suspense behind the short essays on 'applied psychoanalysis.'"[6] Ricœur himself, however, shies away from "posing the immense question of creativity" in his presentation of "Art and Freudian Systematics."[7] A psychoanalytical theory of art, therefore, has to address artistic creativity on Freudian grounds, which Freud himself actually evaded.

## The Creative Process

Anton Ehrenzweig (1908–66) tried to meet this challenge by advancing basic principles of artistic creativity in his book *The Hidden Order of Art: A Study in the Psychology of Artistic Imagination*. Like all art critics of a Freudian persuasion, he also focused on the interrelationship between the "primary" and the "secondary" process in order to spotlight features of the creative process. Freud had explained this duality of "thinking" as follows: "We have found that processes in the unconscious or in the id obey different laws from those in the preconscious ego. We name these laws in their totality the *primary process*, in contrast to the *secondary process* which governs the course of events in the preconscious, in the ego."[8] This duality provides guidance as to how the human psyche functions, with the primary process representing the pleasure principle, and the secondary process the reality principle. Together they "exhaust the processes of thought and they together must account for products such as art. It is in this part of the theory that some of the most interesting possibilities for a psychoanalytic theory of art still rest [ . . . ] Great art will somehow grapple with primary process thinking, both to use it and to refer to it in its manifest content."[9]

An elucidation of this interplay is Ehrenzweig's point of departure, and he sets out to provide "an aesthetic analysis of art's deep substructure,"[10] which means two things at the same time: art arises out of primary process "thinking," but the apparent chaos of this seems nevertheless to have a structure.

Although we have now become used to psychoanalytical terminology, it sometimes strikes us as strange, and this is because it charts a territory that to a large extent eludes the grasp of language, and yet has to be explored. For this reason psychoanalysis from Freud onward has borrowed a great many terms from mechanics, physics, mathematics, biology, mythology, folklore, archaic language, and recently even from computer language as heuristic tools for exploring what we might call the territory of the unconscious. Ehrenzweig's theory of creativity teems with such jumbled terminology, because the creative process resists being subsumed under any kind of familiar referentiality.

"The hidden structure of art," Ehrenzweig contends, "is created on lower levels of awareness that are nearer to the undifferentiated techniques of the primary process" (78). Hence the inner fabric of the latter has to come under scrutiny. This is all the more pertinent as "neglect of the undifferentiated structure of primary process phantasy has been responsible for the deadlock which has held up the progress of psycho-analytic aesthetics for over half a century. What Freud called primary process structures are merely distortions of articulate surface imagery caused by the underlying undifferentiation of truly unconscious phantasy" (263). "Undifferentiated structure of primary process phantasy" sounds like an oxymoron, and we may be inclined to accept it, because outlining the creative process cannot start out from what is familiar. Whatever an undifferentiated structure may indicate, Ehrenzweig meant it as a replacement for Freud's pleasure principle, without denying that the latter may well be a representation of the primary process. The pleasure principle, however, cannot be, as we shall see, the fountainhead of art, because it excludes such vital elements as "ego decomposition."

How is art engendered in the primary process, and to what extent does it help to illuminate its "undifferentiated structure"?

> In the first (schizoid) phase of creativity the artist's unconscious projections are still felt as fragmented, accidental, alien and persecuting. In the second phase the work acts as a receiving "womb." It contains and – through the artist's unconscious scanning of the work – integrates the fragments into a coherent whole (the unconscious substructure or matrix of the work of art). In the third phase the artist can re-introject his work on a higher near-conscious level of awareness. He so enriches and strengthens his surface ego. At the same time secondary processes of revision articulate previously unconscious components of the work. They thus become part of art's conscious superstructure. In this manner a full exchange occurs between conscious and unconscious components of the work as well as between the artist's conscious and unconscious levels of perception. His own unconscious also serves as a "womb" to receive split-off and repressed parts of his conscious self. The external and internal processes of integration are different aspects of the same indivisible process of creativity. (104f.)

This in a nutshell is Ehrenzweig's description of how the creative process works. The "phases" thus described do not develop as a sequence, although for analytical charting of the primary and secondary processes they have to be displayed sequentially. There is a constant interaction between these phases, the very modes of which keep changing from telescoping to interference and superimposition. The phases are just constituents of the creative process, the outcome of which is generated by their acting upon one another, and these multiple interactions imbue each work of art with its individuality. Although such operations elude the grasp of theory, the phases themselves are nevertheless clearly discernible through their flow and contraflow. In the unconscious[11] first phase there is an "undifferentiated structure of primary process phantasy" which, of course, is not departmentalized and is therefore undifferentiated, but has structural inscriptions marked as schizoid fragmentation and unconscious **scanning**. What do these "phases" indicate?

Ehrenzweig alludes to schizoid painting to exemplify how the initial phase of creation is arrested by **splintering** the projections, and freezing them into fragmented shapes. "True schizophrenic art only offers the surface experience of fragmentation and death without being redeemed by low-level coherence. Cubist painting resembles schizophrenic art almost too closely. There are some glassy all too rigid splinters that refuse to join into bigger entities, the same proximity of fear and sweetness, of laughter and tragedy. But there the similarity ends. In schizophrenic art no oceanic envelopment heals the surface fragmentation. Oceanic dedifferentiation is felt and feared as death itself" (122).

The schizoid splintering is by no means an aberration; instead, it marks the initial phase of the creative process, which goes awry only when the scattered fragmentations congeal into bizarre shapes. But why is such splintering considered the actual beginning of the creative process at all? Because "creating a work of art means externalizing the inner workings of the ego; its submission to the superego's fragmenting and scattering action" (249). The conscious ego becomes alienated from itself when abandoning itself to its unconscious phantasies. It is no longer in command of itself and, submitting to the dominance of the superego, it disperses into fragments.

But this makes the second phase of the creative process all the more expedient, which Ehrenzweig has described in computer-like language as "unconscious scanning." This means that the splinters have now to be enveloped by a syncretistic vision, which reassembles them in an unconscious "womb." Thus "unconscious scanning, which can hold mutually exclusive serial structure in a single focus, can contemplate all designs in a single act of comprehension" (106). This can be best illustrated by what Ehrenzweig has called "the empty stare," when the painter gazes at the canvas, trying to figure out how the details could fit together. "More than ever an undifferentiated empty stare is needed to transcend [ ... ] sharp divisions and forge the total work into a single and indivisible whole" (31). The stare signals a shift in ego functioning from its initial dispersal to unconscious scanning. "Creativity can almost be defined as the capacity for transforming the chaotic aspect of undifferentiation into a hidden order that can be encompassed by a comprehensive (syncretistic) vision" (127).

The third phase of the creative process occurs on a "higher near-conscious level of awareness" (104), when the latency of unconscious scanning is given a manifest gestalt. This is the mainspring for double meaning in art, because the manifest surface is shot through by the latent syncretistic vision, which more often than not makes itself felt through disfigurements of the surface structure. According to Ehrenzweig, "[a] truly fertile 'motif' – in music or drama as well as the visual arts – often has something incomplete and vague about its structure. It bears the imprint of the undifferentiated vision which created it in the first place and which guides its use" (48). Double meaning, then, is the offshoot of the interface between the conscious and the unconscious levels, which reveals in what is said or perceived, the hidden and absent. "[S]ignifying one thing at the same time signifies *another* thing without ceasing to signify the first,"[12] and such an operational mode generates "the complex diffuse substructure of all art" (77). The interplay between the manifest and the latent meaning generates a multiplicity of interpretations and responses, which in the end are nothing but efforts to integrate the latent and manifest content into a coherent account.

What this may entail Ehrenzweig exemplifies by the actions a Cubist painting makes the beholder perform.

> Cubism went out of its way to deny the eye stable focusing points round which the rest of the composition could be organized. Instead, the eye was sent on a fool's errand. When it fastened on one feature the cubistic fragments fell into a new pattern, which was shattered again as soon as the eye wandered on and was caught by another feature. The picture kept heaving in and out as the eye tried to infuse some measure of stability into the pattern. (67)

One might even be inclined to say that such a painting effects a transfer of the creative process into the beholder, who has to undo any coherence arrived at, thus being transposed into the phase of unconscious scanning. This brings the interplay between the manifest and the latent content of double meaning to fruition.

This delineation of the creative process, however, does not yet explain why it comes about in the first place. "The creative mind," Ehrenzweig contends, "must identify itself with the fate of the 'dying god' in order to surrender control to the powers of the deep" (63). Hence it is "ego decomposition" (284) that sets the creative process in motion. A surface fragmentation of the ego is needed in order to bring low-level sensibilities into action. The evidence Ehrenzweig provides for this basic concept is to be found in the many myths of the dying and self-creating god that run as a perennial theme through human civilization. The analogy is illuminating, but not explanatory, and it exposes a structural problem inherent in most soft theories. Closure is the hallmark of theory, but psychoanalytical theory cannot explain why "ego decomposition" is the fountainhead of creation. Whenever theoretical explications leave off, examples take over, and Ehrenzweig parades an impressive collection of them, which make up almost half of his book. We have seen to what extent phenomenological and hermeneutical theories achieve closure through metaphors as their capstones. Operational theories are by contrast more or less open-ended, which poses a problem insofar as they claim to explain what they have scrutinized, but can only do so through examples, each of which is limited in its range of generalization.

Ehrenzweig appears to be aware of this, as is evidenced from his attempt to spotlight the principle that all his examples yield – namely, an illumination of the minimal content of art. The latter arises out of the ego rhythm through which the "phases" of the creative process – projection, fragmentation, dedifferentiation, integration, and reintrojection – become operative. Ehrenzweig endorses the findings of his fellow "London psycho-analysts, D. W. Winnicott and Marion Milner," who

> have stressed the importance for a creative ego to be able to suspend the boundaries between self and not-self in order to become more at home in the world of reality where the objects and self are clearly held apart. The ego rhythm of differentiation and dedifferentiation constantly swings between these two poles and between the inside and the outside world [ . . . ] Temporary dedifferentiation if it is extreme, as in oceanic states, implies

paralysis of surface functions and so can act very disruptively. But the ego could not function at all without its rhythm oscillating between its different levels. [ . . . ] Seen in this way, the oceanic experience of fusion, of a "return to the womb," represents the minimum content of all art. (121, 177, 121)

Thus the interface between **oceanic dedifferentiation** and **structured focusing** through which the self is decomposed and reintegrated marks the wellspring of artistic creativity. It does not explain the work of art, but it does account for its engendering.

## An Example

Ehrenzweig maintains: "The minimum content of art, then, may be the representation of the creative process in the ego" (174), whose phases of fragmentation, dedifferentiation, unconscious scanning and reintrojection are clearly to be observed in the "Circe" chapter of James Joyce's *Ulysses*. Bloom functions as a paradigm of ego decomposition. Right from the start he keeps splintering into a welter of fragments, which in their dynamic dissipation convey the impression that the ego has exploded.

No thoroughfare. Close shave that but cured the stitch. Must take up Sandow's exerciser again. On the hands down. Insure against street accident too. The Providential. *(He feels his trouser pocket.)* Poor mamma's panacea. Heel easily catch in tracks or bootlace in a cog. Day the wheel of the black Maria peeled off my shoe at Leonard's corner. Third time is the charm. Shoe trick. [ . . . ] Keep to the right, right, right. If there is a fingerpost planted by the Touring Club at Stepaside who procured that public boon? I who lost my way and contributed to the columns of the *Irish Cyclist* the letter headed, *In darkest Stepaside*. Keep, keep, keep to the right. Rags and bones, at midnight. A fence more likely. First place murderer makes for. Wash off his sins of the world.[13]

The chapter teems with instances of such "schizoid fragmentations," in which memories, relationships, actual events, and interchanges with other characters are in continual dispersion. What makes this scattering even more striking is the permanent conversation Bloom is engaged in. But instead of a give and take, the utterances slide away in unforeseeable directions.

The fragmentation of Bloom is enhanced by authorial interventions into the disconnected interchange between the characters, continually giving Bloom new shapes by showing him from astonishing angles. There is a passage in which the author even exhibits Bloom's "schizoid splintering" of himself.

> *(The crossexamination proceeds re Bloom and the bucket. A large bucket. Bloom himself. Bowel trouble. In Beever street. Gripe, yes. Quite bad. A plasterer's bucket. By walking stifflegged. Suffered untold misery. Deadly agony. About noon. Love or burgundy. Yes, some spinach. Crucial moment. He did not look in the bucket. Nobody. Rather a mess. Not completely. A* Titbits *back number.) (Uproar and catcalls. Bloom, in a torn frockcoat stained with whitewash, dinged silk hat sideways on his head, a strip of sticking-plaster across his nose, talks inaudibly.)* (441)

This authorial intervention can be read in two ways: it either represents Bloom's dedifferentiation, thus endorsing the depiction of the initial phase of ego decomposition, or the author himself is splintering into fragments, thus revealing how the ego's dissipation sets the creative process in motion. At any rate, what we are given to witness is a scattering ego as a basic feature of creativity. There is an interesting remark by Ehrenzweig concerning Joyce's language, which ties in with the observations just made. The "schizoid splintering of the language function does not prevent a creative use of language if unconscious linkages are preserved. James Joyce's splinter language is of this kind. His phantastic word conglomerates are not just violent compressions of language splinters, but establish counterpoints of dreamlike phantasies that run on below the surface and link the word clusters into an unending hypnotic stream" (118).

The fragmentation, however, is not confined to language and to Bloom only; it disrupts the coherence of the chapter itself, in which scenes of Dublin are presented in a series of dialogues, reminiscent of dramatic form. The very use of this form automatically precludes narration. If one regards the lining up of events as a basic element of narrative, it would seem as though the novel was trying to free itself from this basic condition. Even where there is some narration, it is only in the form of stage directions, and this divests it of its real narrative character. However, despite its layout, the chapter can scarcely be called a play at all. The monologues, dialogues, stage directions, exits, and entrances have almost completely lost their dramatic function. The conflicts between the characters end as abruptly as they began, and the cast grows bigger and bigger, for it is not only the characters of the novel that take part in this conversation – we are also suddenly confronted with Lord Tennyson, Edward VII, and Shakespeare, with the intervention of a whistling gasjet, a jarring doorhandle, a barking retriever, a ringing out of voices of the damned and those of the blessed, even a personified end of the world, and a two-headed octopus spouting forth in a Scottish accent. There is almost no end to the line of such unexpected, bizarre figures. And yet the dialogue hardly ever reaches the level of a conversation; instead, it continuously goes off in unforeseeable directions, making the endless interchange peter out into incommunication. From the diffraction of the "dialogue" to the suddenly emerging strange and monstrous figures there is dispersion all over, the outcome of which is a litter of frozen scraps.

Bloom's splintering ego tends to lead to oceanic states, which mark the beginning of his "unconscious scanning" when substructures of a reassembling ego are formed. Such a change is to be witnessed early on in the chapter. "What do ye lack? Soon got, soon gone. Might have lost my life too with that mangongwheeltracktrolleyglarejuggernaut only for presence of mind. Can't always save you, though. If I had passed Truelock's window that day two minutes later would have been shot. Absence of body" (431).

After this groping attempt at gathering fragments into an unconscious "womb," Bloom assumes a multiplicity of shapes. First, he finds himself in court accused of lewd behavior toward the ladies of Dublin society, and trying to clear himself by gasping for words. "O cold! O shivery! It was your ambrosial beauty. Forget, forgive. Kismet. Let me off this once. *(He offers the other cheek.)*" (446).

Soon after, Bloom enjoys being hailed as Lord Mayor of Dublin, decreeing in stately language: "My subjects! We hereby nominate our faithful charger Copula Felix hereditary Grand Vizier and announce that we have this day repudiated our former spouse and have bestowed our royal hand upon the princess Selene, the splendour of the night" (459). And he continues: "My beloved subjects, a new era is about to dawn. I, Bloom, tell you verily it is even now at hand. Yea, on the word of a Bloom, ye shall ere long enter into the golden city which is to be, the new Bloomusalem in the Nova Hibernia of the future" (461). Now the beautiful women of Dublin's upper crust go into ecstasies over him and, in the passion of their hero-worship, many commit suicide, and Bloom is the illustrious hero of the whole nation.

There is a turnabout in Bloom's unconscious scanning in the brothel scene. Seeing himself confronted with Bella Cohen, the whore-mistress, he changes into a woman and creeps timidly under the sofa in order to play a subservient role opposite Bella, who meanwhile has swollen up into a masculine monster. In his despair Bloom cries out "Justice! All Ireland versus one! Has nobody . . . ? *(He bites his thumb.)*" (515).

Unconscious scanning is a collection of schizoid fragments forming fluid shapes, and this happens to Bloom all the time. These shapes lack stability, as evinced by their continual melting into one another and also by their being abandoned again when they tend to congeal into a definitive outline. But even the shapes themselves are marked by this fluidity, since Bloom assumes the very features into which other characters cast him, as is most evident in his encounter with Bella Cohen. The rapid changes of Bloom's rather contradictory appearances are indicative of unconscious scanning as a manic stage, which has not as yet reached the order of a secondary process. Thus Bloom turns into a paradigm of the ego rhythm by highlighting the intersection between oceanic dedifferentiation and structured focusing which, as we have seen, represents the minimum content of art.

Something similar happens later in the novel, when quite a few passages of authorial intervention make the now familiar characters and events melt into oceanic states, while simultaneously unforeseeable shapes begin to arise (see for instance 547). Just as in Bloom's case, the authorial interventions combine dissolution and reassembly. This basic structure of the creative process reminds one of what Coleridge described as the operations of secondary imagination: "It dissolves, diffuses, dissipates, in order to recreate; or where this process is rendered impossible, yet still at all events it struggles to idealize and to unify."[14]

The "Circe" chapter as a whole allows us to perceive the reintrojection which, as a secondary process ordering, brings the creative process to fruition. Whatever we have been given to observe is framed by Dublin at midnight. However, instead of an urban nightscape, the unfolding spectacle makes the topography of Dublin explode into the frenzy of a Walpurgis night. But for all its confusion, it is an orchestrated phantasmagoria, which the creative ego rhythm produces as it pulsates between oceanic dedifferentiation and structured focusing. Composing phantasmagoria is an extremely powerful challenge to artistic creation because of the manner in which at one and the same time it encompasses and lifts the boundaries of characters and events. The Walpurgis night is a vivid illustration of Ehrenzweig's concept of interacting phases which, as we have seen, work simultaneously to create the individual work of art.

## An Afterthought – Specular Imaging: Lacan

Jacques Lacan (1901–81) did not develop a theory of the arts, and stated explicitly that he would refrain from entering "into the shifting, historical game of criticism, which tries to grasp what is the function of painting at a particular moment, for a particular author at a particular time." Yet he goes on to say that "it is at the radical principle of the function of this fine art that I am trying to place myself."[15] What does this mean in the light of his declared abstention from practicing art criticism? The answer to this question will guide, but also limit, our account. Lacan incorporates a few works of painting and literature without actually theorizing them; instead they appear to serve a specific function, and it is to this that the following remarks will be confined, because it reveals a different relationship between art and psychoanalysis from that which has hitherto been observed. This is all the more pertinent as Lacan is invoked by diverse intellectual fields, ranging from academia through film to popular culture. In the course of these various invocations, his concepts and tools are used in order to explore and elucidate their special concerns, but we shall restrict our focus to pinpointing why certain works of art matter to his brand of psychoanalysis.

In asking what "the radical principle of the function" of art might be, at which Lacan intends to place himself, we shall deliberately ignore his assessments of those paintings and pieces of literature that he subjects to an "applied psychoanalysis." Since the thrust of the latter consists "in tracing poetry to a clinical reality, to reduce the poetic to a 'cause' outside itself, the crucial limitation of this process of reduction is that the cause, while it may be necessary, is by no means a sufficient one."[16] Thus what Lacan has to say about Shakespeare's *Hamlet*, Sophocles's *Antigone*, or Duras's *Le Ravissement* can be set aside, as we are looking for the "function" to be discerned in his so frequently glossed interpretation of Edgar Allan Poe's *Purloined Letter*, and Hans Holbein's painting of *The Ambassadors*.

The importance of Poe can be gauged from the fact that Lacan devoted a seminar to this crime story, and opened his *Écrits* with an essay on Poe. In order to provide a frame for our inquiry, we must resort to Lacan's basic idea of the mirror-stage because of its relevance to the function accorded to the work of art. The mirror-stage plays a decisive role in "the formation of the I as we experience it in psychoanalysis."[17] A child, by looking into the mirror and making all kinds of gestures, "experiences in play the relation between the movements assumed in the image and the reflected environment, and between this virtual complex and the reality it dupli-cates."[18] In the mirror image the child perceives itself as its own other, but the "moment in which the mirror-stage comes to an end inaugurates, by the identification with the *imago* of the counterpart [ . . . ] the dialectic that will henceforth link the I to socially elaborated situations."[19] What dis-tinguishes the child's displaying itself before the mirror, even if its "most perfect likeness is in the image [ . . . ] would still be the *jouissance* of the other."[20] This *jouissance*, however, also prefigures the alienating trend that occurs when the relation "between the *Innenwelt* and the *Umwelt* [the inner world and the outer world]"[21] is established.

This relationship guides Lacan's elaboration of the function that art has for psychoanalysis. Mirroring the other is no longer confined to the formation of the I and its destiny in the social world, but is employed as a schema to develop the imbrication of art and psychoanalysis.

I

What was it in Poe's story that intrigued Lacan enough to devote one of his seminars to it? Barbara Johnson gave this answer: "A literary text that both analyzes itself and shows that it actually has neither a self nor any neutral metalanguage with which to do the analyzing, calls out irresistibly for analysis."[22] Since there appears to be no tangible subject matter, or it remains hidden, we have to turn to Lacan's analysis first, before address-ing the question of how literature makes this into more than just another case history.

Lacan starts out from the following premise: "As is known, it is in the realm of experience inaugurated by psychoanalysis that we may grasp along what imaginary lines the human organism, in the most intimate recesses of its being, manifests its capture in a *symbolic* dimension" (39). So we might assume that the "imaginary" is dually coded; it has a psychoanalytical and a literary reference, both of which have to be translated into symbolic lan-guage if the "imaginary" is to be fathomed. Such a translation means the entrance of otherness into what is identical with itself.

Lacan conceives the layout of Poe's tale as follows:

> There are two scenes, the first of which we shall straightway designate the primal scene, and by no means inadvertently, since the second may be con-sidered its repetition [ . . . ] The primal scene is thus performed, we are told,

in the royal *boudoir*, so that we suspect that the person of the highest rank, called the "exalted personage," who is alone there when she receives a letter, is the Queen. This feeling is confirmed by the embarrassment into which she is plunged by the entry of the other exalted personage, of whom we have been told prior to this account that the knowledge he might have of the letter in question would jeopardize for the lady nothing less than her honor and safety. Any doubt that he is in fact the King is promptly dissipated in the course of the scene which begins with the entry of the Minister D [ ... ] At the moment, in fact, the Queen can do no better than to play on the King's inattentiveness by leaving the letter on the table "face down, address upper-most." It does not, however, escape the Minister's lynx eye, nor does he fail to notice the Queen's distress and thus to fathom her secret. [ ... ] After dealing in his customary manner with the business of the day, the Minister draws from his pocket a letter similar in appearance to the one in view, and having pretended to read it, he places it next to the other. A bit more conversation to amuse the royal company, whereupon, without flinching once, he seizes the embarrassing letter, making off with it, as the Queen, on whom none of his maneuver has been lost, remains unable to intervene for fear of attracting the attention of her royal spouse, close at her side at that very moment. [ ... ] Second scene: [ ... ] Dupin [the detective] calls on the Minister. The latter receives him with studied nonchalance affecting in his conversation romantic *ennui*. Meanwhile Dupin, whom this pretense does not deceive, his eyes protected by green glasses, proceeds to inspect the premises. When his glance catches a rather crumpled piece of paper – apparently thrust carelessly in a division of an ugly pasteboard card-rack, hanging gaudily from the middle of the mantelpiece – he already knows that he's found what he's looking for. (41–2)

Under the pretense of recovering his snuffbox, which he had deliberately left at the Minister's office, Dupin returns the next day and does the very same thing the Minister had done, filching the letter and replacing it with a counterfeit one.

The two scenes mirror one another insofar as each of them is similarly structured, which also applies to the unfolding drama of seeing and not seeing. In the first instance the King does not see the letter; the Queen sees that the King does not see it, whereas the Minister sees it. This is duplicated in the second scene. The Minister sees that the detective does not see the letter during their conversation, whereas Dupin sees that the Minister does not see what he sees. There is a further level of mutual mirroring: the Queen appears to be embarrassed by the fact that the letter may catch the King's attention, which is doubled by the Minister's "studied nonchalance," meant to lure Dupin away from seeing the letter, which is openly displayed. There is still one more level of mutual mirroring, which appears to be decisive for the analysis of the two scenes: the Queen hides something which should not be exposed, lest it might jeopardize her conjugal relationship; the Minister hides his intentions as to how he will avail himself of what he has stolen. Hence the drama which develops has a threefold dimension: one of blindness and sight, one of deceiving and exposure, and one of hiding and displacing.

The repetition of the primal scene thus engenders an intersubjective chain, tying together the multiple mirrorings through which the participating subjects enter into one another. This is effected by the letter, which passes through all the subjects concerned. There is, however, no mention of the content of the letter, and nobody appears to make use of it. At this juncture Lacan begins to exploit the semantic duality of the letter, which could be both an epistle and a typographical character. The latter is just a "unit of signification without any meaning in itself."[23] Consequently, nobody says anything in Poe's tale about what the signifier points at, let alone what it signifies. Only the Prefect, who sends the police to track down the letter, takes it for an epistle which testifies, according to Lacan, to "the realist's imbecility" (55), because what we are given to observe is "the itinerary of the signifier" (40), which travels through the intersubjective chain and unites the participants in a drama of hiding and exposing. If the letter lacks content, it is no longer to be taken as an epistle but as a signifier, which produces certain effects within the intersubjective chain. These effects are variable according to what each subject has displaced. The "displacement is determined by the place which a pure signifier – the purloined letter – comes to occupy in their trio" (45). The Queen displaces her fear of discovery, and the Minister that of the potential use of the letter, whereas Dupin disentangles himself by taking the money for delivering the letter to the Prefect, although he "rectifies" the robbery by another theft.

Thus each of the subjects is inhabited by the signifier, which means being occupied by otherness, because, according to Lacan's basic idea, "*the unconscious is the discourse of the Other,*" highlighted in the instance under discussion by "the manner in which the subjects relay each other in their displacement during their intersubjective repetition" (45). If the letter as signifier is the presence of the other in the person's unconscious, then it mirrors the latter in its dispositions and individuality. The mutual mirroring of the two scenes can now be considered as the macro-level being doubled by the micro-level. Under these auspices the final sentence of Lacan's analysis need not raise so many eyebrows as it has frequently done. It reads: "Thus it is that what the 'purloined letter,' nay, the 'letter in sufferance' means is that a letter always arrives at its destination" (72). If the letter as signifier is otherness in the person's unconscious, then it will always reach its destination, because in Barbara Johnson's words, " 'Otherness' becomes in a way the letter's sender."[24] "Writings scatter to the winds blank checks in an insane charge," Lacan contends, and "were they not such flying leaves, there would be no purloined letters" (56).

Of course, one could fine-tune this rough sketch of Lacan's reading of *The Purloined Letter*, but our concern is with the function Lacan attributes to literature, although we might be able to spot a parallel between the detective and the analyst; this, however, is not very revealing, not least as Dupin is just one of the cast, and is certainly not Poe himself. Furthermore, there is no rivalry between Lacan the analyst and Poe the poet. Instead, Lacan's sophisticated description of the floating letter is permeated by remarks on what literature is able to achieve. First of all, he contends, it is the itinerary of the signifier "which makes the very existence of fiction possible" (40), because the traveling signifier leaves no signified in its wake, and the lack of a signified points to what the fiction keeps hidden. Hence what appears to elude us provokes interpretation, which is nothing but a translation of the blank into the symbolic order. Simultaneously, it seems that "a fictive tale even has the advantage of manifesting symbolic necessity to the extent that we believe its conception arbitrary" (40). As the latter could not be the case, because the fictional tale is composed, a gap opens up between a surmised arbitrariness and the compulsion to translate this into the symbolic order.

This gap is focused upon by Lacan's comment on a passage in Poe's tale in which Dupin maintains "the remote source of his [i.e., the Prefect's] defeat lies in the supposition that the Minister is a fool, because he has acquired the renown as a poet. All fools are poets."[25] Lacan objects to the Prefect's conclusion, because of "a false distribution of a middle term, since it is far from following from the fact that all madmen are poets" (52). Obviously, there is something that qualifies a poet other than being mad, and hence a fool, namely, "the poet's superiority in the art of concealment." This is the art that Lacan admires, not least as "we ourselves are left in the dark" (52) in relation to the poet's sophisticated contrivance, whose distinction lies in offering the hidden for rediscovery. The construal of enigmas remained Lacan's lifelong interest in literature, once again stressed in his reading of Joyce's *Finnegans Wake* toward the end of his career. "It is because the signifiers collapse into each other, are recomposed and mixed up – read *Finnegans Wake* – that something is produced that, as signified, may seem enigmatic, but is clearly what is closest to what we analysts, thanks to analytic discourse, have to read."[26]

Thus literature becomes a mirror that reflects the strategies of the psychoanalyst. Bringing oneself before the mirror means "even if he achieved his most perfect likeness in that image, it would still be the *jouissance* of the other that he would cause to be recognized in it."[27] Being mirrored by the other reveals the intimate connection between psychoanalysis and literature, which allows for both monitoring and fine-tuning of the armory of analysis. Literature as the "*jouissance* of the other" is an erotically tinged enjoyment of the other, and the function of art is to allow psychoanalysis to find itself in the mirror of its own other.

## II

The mirror reflects whatever is in front of it, whereas the picture exceeds perception. This is one of the reasons why paintings play a role for Lacan in elucidating another of his basic concepts: that of the gaze, which the specular image, even if it still allows "seeing myself seeing myself," is unable to capture. "I see only from one point, but in my existence I am looked at from all sides"[28] marks Lacan's starting-point for describing the split between the eye and the gaze. "The spectacle of the world, in this sense, appears to us as all-seeing. This is the phantasy to be found in the Platonic perspective of an absolute being to whom is transferred the quality of being all-seeing [ . . . ] The world is all-seeing, but it is not exhibitionistic – it does not provoke our gaze. When it begins to provoke it, the feeling of strangeness begins too" (75).

Lacan approaches the dialectic between eye and gaze by juxtaposing two Greek painters:

> In the classical tale of Zeuxis and Parrhasios, Zeuxis has the advantage of having made grapes that attracted the birds. The stress is placed not on the fact that these grapes were in any way perfect grapes, but on the fact that even the eye of birds was taken in by them. This is proved by the fact that his friend Parrhasios triumphs over him for having painted on the wall a veil, a veil so lifelike that Zeuxis, turning towards him said, *Well, and now show us what you have painted behind it*. By this he showed that what was

at issue was certainly deceiving the eye (*tromper l'œil*). A triumph of the gaze over the eye. (103)

The eye is trapped by the visible, which might indicate that there is something in the paintings that eludes perception. This absence is the location of the gaze, screened off, according to Lacan, by the dominance of the geometrically organized vision. Since the eye is deluded, the *trompe-l'œil* painting revolves around a trapped vision and an absent gaze. If the painting of the veil provokes a spectator "to ask what is behind it," then "the *trompe-l'œil* of painting pretends to be something other than what it is" (112). However, this "something other" cannot be seen, because it is not there, so that this type of painting is nothing but an "appearance that says it is that which gives the appearance." Hence it does not represent anything, not even the deception of the eye (103), and *trompe-l'œil* marks the gaze as a blank, because there is nothing beyond the deceived eye.

As long as the gaze is qualified by the fact that in my existence I am looked at from all sides, or that the world around me is "all-seeing," it remains fairly unspecific, not least as I am unaware of being looked at. But the split between the eye and the gaze – a major premise of Lacan's theory – can only be fathomed through their relationship, which Lacan maps out as follows: "In our relation to things, in so far as this relation is constituted by the way of vision, and ordered in the figures of representation, something slips, passes, is transmitted, from stage to stage, and is always to some degree eluded in it – that is what we call the gaze" (73). The latter runs counter to vision, irritates it, makes it slide into other foci, resulting in a destabilized vision, which is not caused by seeing. Thus the gaze inscribes itself into what the eye focuses upon, and simultaneously appears to need the eye in order to become tangible. The gaze is not perception, though it requires a medium to manifest itself. "For Lacan," Slavoj Žižek writes, the "gaze marks the point in the object (picture) from which the subject viewing it is already *gazed at*, i.e., it is the object that is gazing at me."[29] Hence the gaze is no longer a mirror image.

The split between the eye and the gaze brings about their interdependence, the nature of which has the structure of *anamorphosis*. "In my seminar," Lacan emphasizes, "I have made great use of the function of *anamorphosis*, in so far as it is an exemplary structure" (85). What this exemplarity is, and how it works, is mapped out by Lacan's choice of Hans Holbein's *The Ambassadors* (1533).

Vision is ordered according to a mode that may generally be called the function of images. This function is defined by a point-to-point correspondence
of two unities in space. Whatever optical intermediaries may be used to establish their relation, whether their image is virtual, or real, the point-to-point
correspondence is essential. That which is of the mode of the image in the
field of vision is therefore reducible to the simple schema that enables us to
establish anamorphosis, that is to say, to the relation of the image, in so far
as it is linked to a surface, with a certain point that we shall call "geometral"
point. Anything that is determined by this method, in which the straight
line plays its role of being the path of light, can be called an image. (86)

The image thus indicates the "normal" perspective of seeing, which Lacan
dubs "geometral," stressed by "the point-to-point correspondence" of
markers that organize the visual space. It is this schema according to which
the subject perceives, and this is in line with what Lacan has said about
the mirror image. However, the "geometral dimension of vision does not
exhaust [ ... ] what the field of vision as such offers us as the original
subjectifying relation. This is why it is so important to acknowledge the
inverted use of perspective in the structure of anamorphosis" (87). The extent
to which the geometrically organized vision is limited can be gauged by
the simple empirical fact that "*You never look at me from the place from
which I see you*" (103). The limitation of the scopic field is undone by
*anamorphosis*, which works as a distortion of the subject-centered geometrical
perspective. "Distortion may lend itself [ ... ] to all the paranoiac ambiguities, and every possible use has been made of it, from Arcimboldi
to Salvador Dali. I will go so far as to say that this fascination comple-
ments what geometral researches into perspective allow to escape from
vision" (87).

What eludes being seen needs perception to register it, and this structures Lacan's interpretation of Holbein's *The Ambassadors*. What is to be
seen on the visual surface of the painting are "two figures frozen in their
showy adornments. Between them is a series of objects that represent in
the painting of the period the symbols [ ... ] of the sciences and arts as
they were grouped at the time in the *trivium* and *quadrivium*" (88). The
portrayal of these two stately figures appears to represent achievement,
the perception of which is, however, disturbed by an object in front of the
painting "which from some angles appears to be flying through the air,
at others to be tilted [ ... ] You cannot know – for you turn away, thus
escaping the fascination of the picture," because it seems to suggest "a
cuttlebone," a "loaf of two books" (88), or what have you. "One thinks it

**Figure 3**   Hans Holbein the Younger, *The Ambassadors*, 1533, oil on panel. National Gallery, London. Photo Bridgeman Art Library, London.

is a question of the geometral eye-point, whereas it is a question of a quite different eye – that which flies in the foreground of *The Ambassadors*" (89).

As we try to figure out what the object at the bottom of the painting might be, and how it relates to what the ambassadors appear to represent, *anamorphosis* begins to work. According to the dictionary, *anamorphosis* is an "image distorted so that it can be viewed without distortion only from a special angle," an operation that causes a transformation of the picture by implying, according to the Greek root of the word, "a forming it anew." Thus we are forced to change the angle of our vision, switching from a frontal glance to a lateral one in order to spell out the signification of the "flying cuttlebone," as it appears to a frontal view. "Begin by walking out of the room," Lacan suggests to the members of his seminar, "in which no doubt it [Holbein's painting] has long held your attention. It is then, turning around as you leave [ ... ] you apprehend in this form ... What? A skull" (88). The lateral glance resolves the distortion and in doing so forms the picture anew. The achievements the two ambassadors represent are now undercut by the skull, for the strange object that puzzled the eye becomes integrated into the picture by the lateral glance, which simultaneously suspends the dominance of the frontal view. The geometrically organized central perspective dwindles to insignificance, just as the represented achievements do, when the observer looks sideways on the picture. However, forming the picture anew inevitably changes the position of the spectator. The floating object in the foreground, Lacan writes,

> is there to be looked at, in order to catch, I would almost say, *to catch in its trap*, the observer, that is to say, us. It is, in short, an obvious way, no doubt an exceptional one, and one due to some moment of reflection on the part of the painter, of showing us that, as subjects, we are literally called into the picture, and represented here as caught [ ... ] the secret of this picture is given at the moment when, moving slightly away, little by little, to the left, then turning around, we see what the magical floating object signifies. It reflects our own nothingness, in the figure of the death's head. (92)

Being drawn into the picture makes the ground slide from under the observer's feet, but this happens by our being forced to switch from frontal to lateral viewing. "The anamorph undoes more than the conventions of realistic geometrical perspective; it undoes temporarily the effect of the mirror-stage by giving us the experience of being looked at and controlled rather than being the viewer who occupies the position of control. That experience is one version of what Lacan calls the gaze. Instead of controlling the vanishing point, we experience vanishing and dissolution in the conceptual space projected by the representation's seeming incoherence."[30] The gaze through which the picture looks at the spectator is not manifested by perceptible details but emerges in the dramatic turnabout, when the signification of the seemingly ungraspable object is integrated into the picture.

Canceling the validity of what perception is able to see – the splendidly dressed figures and the emblematic presence of arts and science – allows the gaze to radiate from the picture. The eye is "made desperate," because of "the envy that makes the subject pale before the image of a completeness closed upon itself" (116). The completeness of the painting reveals itself through the workings of *anamorphosis* in the course of which the spectator's perception is looked at by what the lateral glance has brought about. This is a way of experiencing the totality of the painting.

However, if Lacan intends to place himself "at the radical principle of the function of this fine art" (110), "completeness" stands in need of qualification. The aura that envelops it is not enough, although it certainly exercises an attraction. The gaze cannot be confined to being looked at by the picture, because this is only the mode in which it works. "What we see here, then, is that the gaze operates in a certain descent, a descent of desire, no doubt. But how can we express this? The subject is not completely aware of it – he operates by remote control. Modifying the formula I have of desire as unconscious – *man's desire is the desire of the Other*" (115). The other as an awakening of the subject's desire is a fundamental concept of Lacan's brand of psychoanalysis, and if artistic achievement culminates in "completeness," it becomes the other that is desired.

## Notes

1  Richard Kuhns, *Psychoanalytic Theory of Art: A Philosophy of Art on Developmental Principles*, New York: Columbia University Press, 1983, p. 2.
2  Paul Ricœur, *The Conflict of Interpretation*, ed. Don Ihde, Evanston: Northwestern University Press, 1974, p. 197.
3  Ibid.
4  Kuhns, *Psychoanalytic Theory of Art*, pp. 3f.
5  Ibid., p. 115.
6  Ricœur, *Conflict of Interpretation*, p. 197.
7  Ibid., pp. 196–208.
8  Sigmund Freud, "An Outline of Psychoanalysis," in *The Standard Edition of the Complete Psychoanalytical Works of Sigmund Freud*, 23, ed. James Strachey, Anna Freud, Alix Strachey, and Alan Tyson, London: Hogarth Press, 1964, p. 164.
9  Kuhns, *Psychoanalytic Theory of Art*, p. 34.
10 Anton Ehrenzweig, *The Hidden Order of Art: A Study in the Psychology of Artistic Imagination*, Berkeley and Los Angeles: California University Press, 1967, p. xiv. The sources of all other quotations from this volume are given in the text with references to the appropriate pages.
11 "Ordinarily," Ehrenzweig writes, "drives and phantasies are repressed and made unconscious because of their unacceptable content. Here it is maintained that images

and phantasies can become unconscious because of their (undifferentiated) structure alone. This implies an expansion of the term 'unconscious'" (291).

12   Ricœur, *Conflict of Interpretation*, p. 63.

13   James Joyce, *Ulysses*, London: Bodley Head, 1958, pp. 416f. The sources of all other quotations from this volume are given in the text with references to the appropriate pages.

14   Samuel Taylor Coleridge, *Biographia Literaria* I (Collected Works 7), ed. James Engell and W. Jackson Bate, Princeton: Princeton University Press, 1983, p. 304.

15   Jacques Lacan, *The Four Fundamental Concepts of Psycho-Analysis*, ed. Jacques-Alain Miller, trans. Alan Sheridan, New York and London: Norton, 1981, p. 110.

16   Shoshana Felman, *Jacques Lacan and the Adventure of Insight: Psychoanalysis in Contemporary Culture*, Cambridge, Mass.: Harvard University Press, 1987, p. 38.

17   Jacques Lacan, *Écrits: A Selection*, trans. Alan Sheridan, London: Routledge, 2001, p. 1. The English translation does not contain the Poe essay, which opens the first volume of the original French *Écrits*.

18   Ibid., p. 2.

19   Ibid., p. 6.

20   Ibid., p. 46.

21   Ibid., p. 4.

22   Barbara Johnson, *The Critical Difference: Essays in the Contemporary Rhetoric of Reading*, Baltimore: Johns Hopkins University Press, 1980, p. 145.

23   Jeffrey Mehlman, "Introductory Note: Jacques Lacan Seminar on 'The Purloined Letter,'" *Yale French Studies* 48 (1972), p. 38.

24   Barbara Johnson, *Critical Difference*, p. 145.

25   Edgar Allan Poe, *Selected Prose, Poetry, and Eureka*, ed. W. H. Auden, New York: Rinehart, 1950, p. 107.

26   Quoted in Jean-Michel Rabaté, *Jacques Lacan: Psychoanalysis and the Subject of Literature*, Houndmills: Palgrave, 2001, p. 175. It is a modified translation from Jacques Lacan, *Seminar XX. On Feminine Sexuality: The Limits of Love and Knowledge 1972–73*, trans. B. Fink, New York: Norton, 1998, p. 37.

27   Lacan, *Écrits: A Selection*, p. 46.

28   Lacan, *Four Fundamental Concepts of Psycho-Analysis*, p. 72. The sources of all other quotations from this volume are given in the text with references to the appropriate pages.

29   Slavoj Žižek, *Looking Awry: An Introduction to Jacques Lacan through Popular Culture*, Cambridge, Mass.: MIT Press, 1991, p. 125.

30   John Paul Riquelme, "Joyce's 'The Dead': The Dissolution of the Self and the Police," in Rosa M. Bollettieri Bosinelli and Harold F. Mosher, Jr., eds., *ReJoycing: New Readings of Dubliners*, Lexington: University Press of Kentucky, 1998, pp. 135f. Riquelme uses Lacan's interpretation of the Holbein painting in order to elucidate Joyce's short story.

# 8

# Marxist Theory: Williams

In his Preface to *A Contribution to the Critique of Political Economy* (1859) Karl Marx stated a basic principle that became a guideline for Marxism:

> In the social production of their existence, men inevitably enter into definite relations, which are independent of their will, namely relations of production appropriate to a given stage in the development of their material forces of production. The totality of these relations of production constitutes the economic structure of society, the real foundation, on which arises a legal and political superstructure and to which correspond definite forms of social consciousness. The mode of production of material life conditions the general process of social, political and intellectual life. It is not the consciousness of men that determines their existence, but their social existence determines their consciousness.[1]

The formula of base and superstructure – the very heart of Marxism – makes all art dependent on the base from which it arises. The fact that art is conditioned, perhaps even determined, by "the material forces of production" poses the question: Why is there such a peripheral phenomenon as art at all, and what is its function?

Marx himself focused primarily on the complex relations between base and superstructure: "It is known in the case of art that determinate times of artistic flowering by no means stand in a proportional relation to the general development of society, therefore [they do not stand in a proportional relation] to the general development of the material basis, to the general development, as it were, of the bone-structure of its organization."[2] Obviously, material and artistic production are not always in sync in the course of history, and if art appears to be ahead at times, what does this indicate? As Marx and Engels did not address this question, Terry Eagleton gives this answer on their behalf: "The materialist theory of history denies that art can *in itself* change the course of history; but it insists that art can be an active element in such change."[3] At best art helps to accelerate processes that are under way at the base, but both art and these processes are still conditioned by the development of society. Clearly, the formula of base and superstructure requires a more detailed definition when it comes to assessing "artistic production."

Furthermore, there is a hotly debated remark that Marx made regarding historical forms of art, which – though tied to the material conditions of a bygone society – can still provide pleasure. "However, the difficulty does not lie in understanding that Greek art and epic are tied up with a certain social form of development. The difficulty is that they still give us artistic enjoyment and serve in a certain relationship as the norm and unreachable standard."[4] If the base vanished long ago, how can a superstructural phenomenon turn into an "unattainable model"? Does Marx's connoisseurship win over his ideological stand? Despite the many explanations Marxists have come up with for such an obvious infringement of the "law" of base/superstructure, it is clear that the arts cannot easily be subsumed under this law. Georg Lukács, a prominent proponent of a Marxist theory of art, complained in a programmatic essay "Art and Objective Reality" as late as 1934 that Marxist aesthetics was lagging far behind the general development of Marxist theory.[5] He regretted that Marx had broken off his manuscript without tackling the thorny problem of why he still enjoyed the Greek epic. There are, then, loose ends in Marx's conception of the arts and these may account for the proliferation of art theories of a Marxist persuasion.

## Reflectionist Theory

Art is part of the superstructure, and that makes its relationship to the base a vital concern, not least as its function is not as obvious as those of legal and political institutions. Marx never gave a systematic exposition of the function of art, but as all superstructural phenomena are conditioned by the base, art too must have a function. Georg Lukács was one of the first to tackle this issue by advancing a reflectionist theory, maintaining that art is a mirror of society. Plausible as this may seem according to the Marxist premise, it nevertheless poses problems. Since it is the reality of society that is to be reflected, art tends to be identified with realism – an idea Lukács entertained throughout his career, as highlighted in one of his later essays of 1956, "Critical Realism and Socialist Realism."[6] Whatever deviates from socialist realism is not considered to be art at all. Hence Lukács contends that "modernism means not the enrichment, but the negation of art" (46). For him Joyce features "the reduction of reality to a nightmare," and Beckett's *Molloy* "presents us with an image of the utmost human degradation – an idiot's vegetative existence. Then, as help is imminent from a mysterious unspecified source, the rescuer himself sinks into idiocy" (31f.).

We may ask ourselves whether Joyce and Beckett are reflections of bourgeois society, and if they are, the depravity of the latter must be such that it can only be mirrored by the self-liquidation of art. Lukács, however, did not seem to have this in mind; instead, he used examples of the kind referred to as a "negative foil" in order to give salience to social realism as "a truthful reflection of reality" (23). But when it comes to delineating artistic procedures, we are confronted with a host of abstractions, such as "that the fusion of the particular and the general [ . . . ] is the essence of realistic art" (45). Or, "realism is the interpenetration of contingency and necessity."[7] Or, "socialist perspective, correctly understood and applied, should enable the writer to depict life more comprehensively than any preceding perspective" (98). Or, pinning down the essence of realism, "Concreteness, then, in my sense involves an awareness of the development, structure and goal of society as a whole" (96). All these concepts reflect Lukács's Hegelian heritage, which he combines with the Marxist formula. The Hegelian concepts serve as parameters for basic structures of socialist society, because a reflection of the latter cannot confine itself to appearances but has to incorporate the categories that underlie them.[8]

These lofty conceptualizations of realism gain a certain vividness through what Lukács considers "a correct aesthetic (i.e. the creation of a typology)" (97). A type appears to be an adequate "form" for casting general ideas in individual trappings. It provides a certain tangibility to the mirroring of the base and its transmission to a potential recipient. "A character is typical," Lukács writes, "when his innermost being is determined by objective forces at work in society" (122). This duality is necessary in order to give salience to the class structure of society, which is conveyed by focusing on the type from either inside or outside:

By the "outside" method a writer obtains a typology based on the individual and his personal conflicts; and from this base he works towards wider social significance. The "inside" method seeks to discover an Archimedian point in the midst of social contradiction, and then bases his typology on an analysis of these contradictions. Many realist writers use both methods; and both methods may coexist in the same work of art. Dickens is a case in point: his plebeian characters are explored from the inside, his upper- and middle-class characters from the outside. [ ... ] It is evident that writers will tend to present an inside picture of the class on which their own experience of society is based. All other social classes will tend to be seen from the outside. (91)

Up to this point the reflectionist theory still holds, albeit with the claim that "the alliance of socialism with realism may be said to have its roots in the revolutionary movement of the proletariat" (101). However, as Lukács maintains that socialist realism is superior to what he calls "bourgeois critical realism," he appears to imply that socialist realism – the pinnacle of art – is either an ideal or something not yet fully realized. In this respect art must be a model for what society is meant to achieve, thus being ahead of its material base. This does not mean that art has emancipated itself from its function of reflecting the material conditions of society, but since mirroring too must have a function – if art is not to be considered superfluous – this consists in signposting ideals for social development.

At this juncture, we can clearly see a duality in the reflectionist theory. Although art is still related to the social base, its reflection is no longer the sole concern; instead art acts upon and shapes the very base itself through patterns that have not been derived from what it is supposed to mirror. Thus the reflectionist theory had to be modified, if not drastically revised. It was the Czech philosopher Karel Kosík who pointed the Marxist theory of art in a different direction. "Every work of art has a unified and double character: it is an expression of reality, but it also forms the reality that exists, not next to or before the work but actually in the work itself [ ... ] the work of art is not an illustration of *concepts* of reality. As work and as art, it represents reality and so indivisibly and simultaneously *forms* reality."[9] Dispensing with the straitjacket of the reflectionist theory, art is now conceived as a social force that molds the very society of which it is an integral part. This opens the way for the Marxist theory to be restructured by moving the formative power of art into focus.

## Production

Kosík's position is a halfway house between the reflectionist theory and that of production proposed by Raymond Williams (1921–88) in his *Marxism and Literature* (1977). Art for Kosík does not mirror the base but represents it, and in doing so slants what is depicted, thus shaping reality. It is the formative process that Williams takes to be the hallmark of Marxism, based on Marx's idea that human beings create both the world and themselves. "At the very centre of Marxism," Williams writes,

> is an extraordinary emphasis on human creativity and self-creation. Extraordinary because most of the systems with which it contends stress the derivation of most human activity from an external cause: from God, from an abstracted Nature or human nature, from permanent instinctual systems, or from an animal inheritance. The notion of self-creation, extended to civil society and to language by pre-Marxist thinkers, was radically extended by Marxism to the basic work processes and thence to a deeply (creatively) altered physical world and a self-created humanity.[10]

But Williams is aware that this "notion of creativity," although promulgated by Marx himself, was "throughout the development of Marxism [ . . . ] a radically difficult area," because "some important variants of Marxism have moved in opposite directions, reducing creative practice to representation, reflection, or ideology" (206).

For this reason Williams questions certain central concepts that have dominated Marxist tradition, since they have impeded, if not inhibited, the development of a theoretical framework that would allow for the productivity of creative art. The latter is notably absent from the reflectionist theory, and without explicitly mentioning Lukács Williams states, with tongue in cheek,

> Art reflected reality; if it did not it was false or unimportant. And what was reality? The "production and reproduction of real life," now commonly described as "the base," with art part of its "superstructure." The ambiguity is then obvious. A doctrine about the real world expressed in the materialism of objects leads to one kind of theory of art: showing the objects (including human actions as objects) "as they really are." But this can be maintained, in its simplest form, only by knowing "the base" as an object. [ . . . ] To know "the base" as a process at once complicates the object-reflection model which had appeared so powerful. (96)

Taking the base as an "object," which art is supposed to mirror, amounts to a reification of the social reality, whereas the base developing as a dynamic process in actual fact produces itself. Therefore, it cannot be reduced to a hazy notion of material life. "In all our activities in the world we produce not only the satisfaction of our needs but new needs and new definitions of needs. Fundamentally, in this human historical process, we produce ourselves and our societies, and it is within these developing and variable forms that 'material production,' then itself variable, both in mode and scope, is itself carried on" (91). If the formative process of the base is to be reflected by any superstructural phenomenon, the latter must itself be formative. However, reflection is prone to freeze the productive forces into an object. In any case, reflection of the base even in terms of the dynamics of production leaves the question unanswered why it should be done at all. This predicament may well have been the reason why Lukács considered the Marxist approach to art as less developed than the materialist theory.

The relationship between base and superstructure has always been a vexing question for a Marxist theory of art, not least as the nature of the connection between the two poses a problem that appears to elude analysis. Hence the gap between base and superstructure has been bridged according to Williams by metaphors of which reflection has become the most prominent.

Obviously, the latter did not provide the expected solution, and thus was replaced by mediation. It is "easy to see the attraction of 'mediation,'" Williams writes,

> as a term to describe the process of relationship between "society" and "art," or between "the base" and "the superstructure." We should not expect to find [ ... ] directly "reflected" social realities in art, since these [ ... ] pass through a process of "mediation" in which their original content is changed. [ ... ] The change involved in mediation can be simply a matter of indirect expression: the social realities are "projected" or "disguised," and to recover them is a process of working back through the mediation of their original forms. Relying mainly on the concept of "ideology" as (class-based) distortion, this kind of reductive analysis, and of "stripping," "laying bare" or "unmasking," has been common in Marxist work. (98)

In this respect "mediation" is a more effective metaphor for bolstering up the function of art than reflection, which only doubles up what exists.

Both reflection and mediation are fine-tuned by their more "sophisticated variants" of homology and correspondence (105). "Both 'correspondence' and 'homology,' in certain senses, can be modes of exploration and analysis of a social process which is grasped from the beginning as a complex of specific but related activities. Selection is evidently involved, but as a matter of principle there is no *a priori* distinction between the necessary and the contingent, the 'social' and the 'cultural,' the 'base' and the 'superstructure'" (105).

These basic metaphors of Marxist theory, developed over time, intended to repair the deficiencies of previous explanations. It was the idea of reflection which to a large extent spawned the other metaphors, because it raised the question why the base should be reflected, and what such a reflection was able to achieve. Mediation provides an answer insofar as art has to strip away all the disguises to be observed in material life and exposes what the masks are meant to hide. In doing so, mediation is guided by a virtual and as yet not realized ideality, thus turning art into a tool for change. Homology and correspondence single out different structures and levels of the base in order to create an awareness of social complexity, the untangling of which is made into an experiential reality. All these metaphors reveal a different conception of art, ranging from the reflection of "the ideal whole" through exposure of the hidden to an exhibition of the multifariousness of material life. Why are Marxist theories of art so diverse? The straightforward answer would be: because the gap between base and superstructure has to be bridged. In other words, it is this gap that generates the various metaphors, with each of them advancing a different idea of the function of art. The very diversity of the functions proposed points to the fact that the gap, in the final analysis, is unbridgeable.

What all these variants of a Marxist theory fail to address is the "creative practice" to be observed in all human activities, and awareness of this shortcoming marks Williams's point of departure. "Orthodox analysts," Williams writes, "began to think of 'the base' and 'the superstructure' as if they were separable concrete entities. In doing so they lost sight of the very processes – not abstract relations but constitutive processes – which it should have been the special function of historical materialism to emphasize" (81). Dogmatizing the framework means sustaining the duality between what is taken for different entities. Consequently, the diverse metaphors discussed above are basically nothing but a repetition of this dualism, owing to which the variants of a Marxist theory of art have proved unsatisfactory. Therefore, Williams calls for a "theoretical revision of the formula of base and superstructure and of the definition of productive forces" (136). And he contends: "Cultural work and activity are not now, in any ordinary sense, a superstructure: not only because of the depth and thoroughness at which any cultural hegemony is lived, but because cultural tradition and practice are seen as much more than superstructural expressions – reflections, mediations, or typifications – of a formed social and economic structure. On the contrary, they are among the basic processes of the formation itself and, further, related to a much wider area of reality than the abstractions of 'social' and 'economic' experience" (111).

While base and superstructure pale into abstractions, their concrete replacement is a triadic relationship between the "Dominant, Residual, and Emergent" (122–7), which sets the productive process in motion. Out of this dynamic interrelationship arises the complexity of material reality in all its social, cultural, and artistic diversity. But even this triad is not hierarchically structured. What is dominant or hegemonic "is always a more or less adequate organization and interconnection of otherwise separated and even disparate meanings, values and practices, which it specifically incorporates in a significant culture and an effective social order" (115). The residual "has been effectively formed in the past, but it is still active in the cultural process, not only and often not at all as an element of the past, but as an effective element of the present" (122). Distant as the residual element may seem in relation to what is dominant, it functions as guidance for social and cultural formation. "The case of the emergent is radically different [ . . . ] the formation of a new class, the coming to consciousness of a new class, and within this, in the actual process, the (often uneven) emergence of elements of a new cultural formation. Thus the emergence of the working class as a class was immediately evident (for example, in nineteenth-century England) in the cultural process. [ . . . ] A new class is always a source of emergent cultural practice." This practice, especially if it is oppositional rather than alternative, will be incorporated into the social process. "This can be seen in the same period in England, in the emergence of the then effective incorporation of a radical popular press" (124).

The triangular interrelation is the blueprint for the production of material reality, which is not created by any agency outside itself but generates itself through the multifarious combinations of its constituents. The latter can even exchange places. The residual may become dominant, resulting in an orthodox social formation, as happened to socialism. Then what was previously dominant will change into a more or less aggressive opposition, thus turning itself into a residual element that is still effective in the present. If the "emergent" becomes dominant, the formative process will tend to become revolutionary. Although the range of possible combinations remains unforeseeable, the bottom line of Williams's argument conceives of material life as a continually emerging reality. Hence it is "understanding emergent culture, as distinct from both the dominant and the residual" (126) that matters most for him.

This makes art into an interesting case of cultural practice, because "what is now in question, theoretically, is the hypothesis of a mode of social formation, explicit and recognizable in specific kinds of art, which is distinguishable from other social and semantic formations by its articulation of *presence*" (135). But what does "presence" mean? It is a key concept of Williams's theory, and designates changes in the "structures of feeling," which are taken as propellants that trigger new turns in the process of social formation. If "structures of feeling" – admittedly a difficult term, intended to replace static concepts like ideology or worldview – are defined as going "beyond formally held and systematic beliefs" (132), then art becomes a showcase revealing how these changes occur and what is thus brought into presence. The latter is always in the nature of an emergent phenomenon, the engendering of which is made tangible by art. How is presence, in the sense defined, achieved by the work of art? Williams singles out various levels to demonstrate how the emergent presence comes about – namely, "Signs and Notations," "Conventions," "Genres," "Forms," and "Authorship." The all-pervading feature of these levels is that they combine various factors, out of which arises something that cannot be identified with, let alone reduced to, any one of these interacting factors.

Language is the first case in point: "For it is at once a material practice and a process in which many complex activities of a less manifestly material kind – from information to interaction, from representation to imagination, and from abstract thought to immediate emotion – are specifically realized" (165). The interfusion of the linguistic material of sound and letters with attitudes makes the interconnections issue into meaning that "is always produced [and] never simply expressed" (166). The written words are signs, and thus material in character, and yet they are not just signs but "notations of actual productive relationships" (170), which keep differentiating themselves. "Notations of order, arrangement, and the mutual relationship of parts; notations of pause, of break, of transition; notations of emphasis: all these can be said to control, but are better described as ways of realizing, the process of the specific productive relationship that is at once, in its character as notation, a way of writing and a way of reading" (171). Since notations have to be grasped, reading also becomes a mode of production which, more often than not, progresses through trial and error, thus engendering further relationships that are different from those of writing, but are nevertheless stimulated by the latter.

If "notations are relationships, expressed, offered, tested, and amended in a whole social process, in which device, expression, and the substance of expression are in the end inseparable" (171f.), then it becomes all the more obvious why Williams is so strongly opposed to all kinds of dualism. Dualities are "crippling categorizations" (146) and this is particularly true of literature. Dichotomies such as fact/fiction, discursive/imaginative, referential/emotive solidify categorical divisions, thus failing to grasp the mechanics of emergence.

Notations are governed by conventions, which function both negatively and positively. On the one hand, they "can uncover the characteristic belief of certain classes, institutions and formations," and on the other they "can show the real grounds of the inclusions and exclusions, the styles and ways of seeing, that specific conventions embody and ratify" (173). In any event, the choices made are not aesthetic in character but are guided by "radical social assumptions of causation and consequence" (176). Hence "the reality of conventions as a mode of junction of social position and literary practice remains central" (179). Conventions can spotlight both what has been eclipsed and what is to be asserted, thus revealing hidden motifs or intentions.

Genres consist of interrelationships between "(i) *stance*; (ii) *mode of formal composition*; (iii) *appropriate subject-matter*" (183) which open up wide-ranging combinations, each one of which keeps yielding ever new possibilities. This productive interaction is certainly a break away from what Williams might call a bourgeois theory of genres, which neatly categorizes generic forms, thus conceiving them as basically static. By contrast, Williams lays stress on the operations of the genres by foregrounding their internal mobility that energizes what is to be produced. Recognition and investigation "of the complex relations between processes at each of these levels in different arts and in forms of work, are necessarily part of any Marxist theory. Genre, in this view, is neither an ideal type nor a traditional order nor a set of technical rules. It is in the practical and variable combination and even fusion of what are [ ... ] different levels of the social material process that what we have known as genre becomes a new kind of constitutive evidence" (185). Stances, modes of composition, and subject matter are the material base of genres whose interfusion turns them structurally into an exhibition of and a response to the social process.

Finally, form and authorship are conceived along the same lines. "For a social theory of literature, the problem of form is a problem of the relations between social (collective) modes and individual projects. [ . . . ] But it is clear that the collective mode which can sustain and contain all individual projects is only one of the number of possible relationships. Individual variations on such basically collective forms as heroic stories, 'romances,' and 'myths' are almost always possible" (187f.). Again the "collective" and the "individual" are the material components the interface of which potentially generates an unforeseeable range of forms, each of them articulating a social situation that they have produced.

Something similar applies to Williams's idea of authorship. Apart from social conditions in which authors' dependence ranges from patronage to the bookselling market, there is a more theoretical concept of authorship in Marxist terms. It defines itself "as a reciprocal discovery of the truly social in the individual, and the truly individual in the social. In the significant case of authorship it leads to dynamic senses of social formation, of individual development, and of cultural creation, which have to be seen as in radical relationship without any categorical or procedural assumption of priorities. Taken together, these senses allow a fully constitutive definition of authorship, and its specification is then an open question: that is to say, a set of specific historical questions, which will give different kinds of answer in different actual situations" (197). Just as with form, the individual and the social are the material constituents of authorship, and it is out of the combination of the two that the production of authors emerges.

Given the various levels of his theory of literature, the impression prevails that Williams subjects the basic constituents of literature to a reconceptualization. In doing so he breaks away from a common understanding that literature is a form of representation by advancing the idea of literature as a process of production. In this respect literature is just one of the many formative processes through which humans create themselves and their realities.

Williams is, however, somewhat reticent about what distinguishes literary production from all the other processes in which it is embedded. At best we can say that literature, in being related to and by articulating "presence," gains its importance through what Williams has called "the structure of feeling," thus heralding a change of belief in the overall patterning of social life. If this were correct, then Williams's basic theoretical moves become plausible. (1) He has to dispense with the base/superstructure model, because literature was accorded a minor function under these auspices, and social reality was frozen into a duality. (2) He has to replace the notion of literature as representation, because nothing precedes what such representation refers to, and so literature has to produce what might become an object for representation. (3) He has to take literature as a paradigm of emergence, since it gives presence to changing beliefs. Stressing the emergent character of literature makes Williams into a progressive neo-Marxist. What, however, remains an open question is how to conceive of the workings of these combinations and interconnections of factors that make emergence happen. This may not have been Williams's question, because he wanted to show production as the be-all and end-all of social life by navigating through all the rocks and shallows of Marxist orthodoxy.

## Examples

The realistic novel is a good illustration of Williams's ideas, because it not only reflected social situations but also produced them. Charles Dickens's *Oliver Twist* is a case in point. Shortly before Oliver asks for a second plate of gruel, the narrator portrays the board members of the workhouse as "very sage, deep, philosophical men"; when turning their attention "to the workhouse, they found out at once, what ordinary folks would never have discovered – the poor people liked it! It was a regular place of public entertainment for the poorer classes; a tavern where there was nothing to pay; a public breakfast, dinner, tea, and supper all the year round; a brick and mortar elysium, where it was all play and no work." Hence the board members decided to change it, and so "they established the rule, that all poor people had the alternative (for they would compel nobody, not they), of being starved by a gradual process in the house, or by a quick one out of it."[11] Small wonder, then, that when Oliver asks for more, they are outraged: " 'That boy will be hung,' said the gentleman in the white waistcoat. 'I know that boy will be hung.' Nobody controverted the prophetic gentleman's opinion."[12]

This is a "notation" of multiple relationships. It exposes the class structure of bourgeois society in a drastic manner, since those who have power not only oppress those who live in misery but appear to be determined to eliminate them. Thus the depiction of class structure becomes emotionally charged, and tends to produce sympathy for the socially oppressed. The almost factual presentation of the scene by the narrator makes it appear as if it were natural, thus provoking the reader to react against the prevailing inhumanity. This in turn produces an impetus for change.

The scene also reveals the productive force of "conventions." The economically oriented belief of the dominant class is uncovered by implicitly foregrounding the lack of any fellow feeling. Compassion is thus aroused in the reader, who wants to come to Oliver's rescue, and this involvement foreshadows another kind of convention developed later in the novel and represented by Mrs. Maylie and Brownlow, whose warm-hearted humanity provides a "real ground," as Williams says, for inclusions and exclusions of conventions. What the dominant convention excludes now emerges through the eclipse of the economic interest. Conventions are always limited, because they set standards for action and behavior, and what this reversal of basic standards produces is a social consciousness pertinent to a class-structured society. This makes it all the more obvious that literature is a formative process and not a reflection of the base.

In order to illustrate Williams's ideas of "genre" and "authorship" we shall consider William Makepeace Thackeray's *Vanity Fair*. When Becky Sharp writes a letter to her friend Amelia telling her what she is hoping to gain from her new position at the Crawley's country seat, the author's "stance" is revealed insofar as he calls this chapter "Arcadian Simplicity,"[13] which also manifests a specific "formal composition." This pointer ensures that the reader will not lose sight of the author's views on the social ambition and, especially, the flexibility with which the "famous little Becky Puppet"[14] performs her social high-wire act. This evocation of the author's "stance" throws Becky's intention into sharp relief, through which the "appropriate subject-matter" is moved into focus. Becky's naive desire to do all she can to please her new masters no longer seems to express the amiability she intended, but instead denotes her habitual opportunism. Simultaneously, the author's general metaphor for Becky – a puppet on a tightrope – begins to take on the specific form of opportunism characteristic in nineteenth-century society: the opportunist could only succeed through moral conduct, though this was not motivated by the selflessness normally inherent in morality. At this particular moment in the novel, the ability to manipulate reality – and with it the central code of conduct for the nineteenth-century middle class – emerges as the developing individualization of the author's "stance" as against the characters' perspective. This situation provides an impression of the internal mobility operative in the genre. "Stance," "formal composition," and "appropriate subject-matter" are the material components, whose interfusion produces a response to the social process.

The example also reveals the hallmark of authorship consisting in the reciprocal discovery of the social in the individual, and vice versa. As "Manager of the Performance"[15] the author is individualized, while the stances adopted by him disclose his social commitment. This reciprocity shapes the social formation that emerges; and so the author's individualization transmits his social consciousness to the reader, who is thus made to experience the social reality that the author had in mind.

According to Williams, literature as a social process of production is distinguished from all other processes out of which the material realities emerge by its relation to presence. A medieval example might serve to illustrate what that means, not least as medieval literature has always been a favorite testing-ground for Marxist premises. The courtly romance of Chrétien de Troyes is intimately related to what Williams has called "the structure of feeling" as the overall pattern of society. When courtly society came under stress from problems arising out of the feudal system, Chrétien responded to the threat by reaffirming the courtly values; he made the knights of his Arthurian romances embark on various quests, in the course of which these values were tested and proven, then the knights returned home, thus stabilizing the courtly society they had left. Isolation and reintegration form the pattern of all the adventures, in which Chrétien presents both the departure of the knights from Arthur's court and their adherence to the values of that court. The adventures embody situations that are no longer covered by the social system, but the pattern of isolation and reintegration fortifies this system against the threat of disintegration. Thus Chrétien takes up a presence, and in emphasizing the integrity of courtly society, epitomized by the epic nature of the Arthurian romances, he shores up an endangered structure.

In a Marxist framework, however, the question poses itself as to whether Chrétien's relation to presence is conservative or progressive; it could be the former if courtly society was considered to be doomed, and it could be the latter if the problems of this society called for solutions to be produced by formative processes.

## Notes

1 Karl Marx, *A Contribution to the Critique of Political Economy*, trans. S. W. Ryazenskaya, ed. Maurice Dobbs, New York: International Publishers, 1970, pp. 20f.
2 Karl Marx, *Introduction to the Grundrisse*, trans. Terrell Carver, Oxford: Blackwell, 1975, p. 84.
3 Terry Eagleton, *Marxism and Literary Criticism*, London: Methuen, 1976, p. 10.
4 Marx, *Introduction to the Grundrisse*, p. 86.
5 Georg Lukács, *Probleme des Realismus*, Berlin: Aufbau Verlag, 1955, p. 34.
6 Georg Lukács, *The Meaning of Contemporary Realism*, trans. John and Necke Mander, London: Merlin Press, [3]1972, pp. 93–135. The sources of all other quotations from this volume are given in the text with references to the appropriate pages.
7 Lukács, *Probleme des Realismus*, pp. 21f., my translation.
8 See also Eagleton, *Marxism and Literary Criticism*, p. 50.
9 Karel Kosík, *Die Dialektik des Konkreten*, Frankfurt/Main: Suhrkamp, 1967, pp. 123f., my translation.
10 Raymond Williams, *Marxism and Literature*, Oxford: Oxford University Press, 1977, p. 206. The sources of all other quotations from this volume are given in the text with references to the appropriate pages.
11 Charles Dickens, *The Adventures of Oliver Twist* (The New Oxford Illustrated Dickens), London and Oxford: Oxford University Press, 1959, p. 11.
12 Ibid., p. 13.
13 William Makepeace Thackeray, *Vanity Fair: A Novel without a Hero* I (Centenary Biographical Edition), London: Smith, Elder, 1910, pp. 112–28.
14 Ibid., p. lv.
15 Ibid., p. liii.

# 9

# Deconstruction: Miller

Is deconstruction a theory, a philosophy, or just an occurrence? From a deconstructionist angle all theories are "monsters," as Jacques Derrida (1930–2004) has called them, because the current "state of theory" reflects their mutual cannibalization. The "incorporation of some Marxist philosophemes into French structuralism, of structuralism into poststructuralism, of psychoanalytic theories into all the above" is a prominent case in point. "And you can imagine to what kinds of monsters these combinatory operations must give birth, considering the fact that theories incorporate opposing theorems, which have themselves incorporated other ones."[1] This state of affairs appears to be beyond remedy, because "these monstrosities are normal" and the only distinction to be made is "between normal monstrosities and monstrous monstrosities which never present themselves *as such*."[2] The latter hide what they are, whereas the former seem to be unaware of their character. The "monstrosity" is thus twofold. On the one hand the mutual amalgamation of theories reveals them as patchwork, though they claim nevertheless to provide totalizing explanations. On the other, this cobbling together of foreign imports is meant to bear out an assumption that has been posited. This "state of theory" marks the point of departure for deconstruction.

Deconstruction cannot regard itself as theory, particularly as the latter has one fundamental requirement: that of closure. Derrida writes: "Deconstruction resists theory then because it demonstrates the impossibility of closure, of the closure of an ensemble or totality on an organized network of theorems, laws, rules, methods."[3] Closure arises out of a basic decision which, in its determinacy, is bound to be limited, although the claim to all-encompassing explanations prevails. When this difference is pointed out, the claim to comprehensiveness turns into what Derrida calls a **supplement** which, as an addition, has to compensate for the deficiency arising from the limitations of the basic decision.

If deconstruction is not a theory, what is it? Derrida answers as follows: "[O]ne assertion, one statement, a true one, would be, and I would subscribe to it: Deconstruction is neither a theory nor a philosophy. It is neither a school nor a method. It is not even a discourse, nor an act, nor a practice. It is what happens, what is happening today in what they call society, politics, diplomacy, economics, historical reality, and so on and so forth."[4] What happens does not do so of its own accord, and so if deconstruction happens on all these different levels, what is the trigger that sets it in motion? The short answer to this question is: the reading process.

Deconstruction is a mode of reading, not confined to texts in the restricted sense of the term but applied in terms of textuality to almost everything there is. As a mode of reading it is bound to develop a reading strategy, which is organized by what Derrida calls a "jetty," whose operation is twofold: (1) It means "the force of the movement which throws something or throws itself [ . . . ] forwards and backwards at the same time [ . . . ] I will call the first jetty the *destabilizing* jetty or [ . . . ] the *devastating* jetty." (2) But it is also an "institutional and protective consolidation, which can be compared to the jetty, the pier in a harbor meant to break the waves and maintain low tides for boats at anchor and for swimmers [which is called] the stabilizing, establishing or simply *stating* jetty. [ . . . ] Of course, these two functions of the *jetty* are ideally distinct, but in fact they are difficult to dissociate, if not indissociable."[5] Reading, then, is throwing a "jetty" into the text, whose hierarchical order is destabilized by stating what the hierarchy has suppressed. "In a traditional philosophical opposition," Derrida writes, "we have not a peaceful coexistence of facing terms but a violent hierarchy. One of the terms dominates the other (axiologically, logically, etc.), occupies the commanding position. To deconstruct the opposition is above all, at a particular moment, to reverse the hierarchy."[6] Undoing hierarchical structures, which is the devastating operation of the "jetty," spotlights what the dominant features have relegated to absence, the articulation of which makes the hierarchy fall apart. The conflicts within the text, which the hierarchical order was supposed to tackle, thus come to the fore again. What deconstruction does is, in Barbara Johnson's pithy phrase, "the careful teasing out of warring forces of signification within the text."[7]

The jetty elucidates differences in the texts, thus showing that dominant positions have no foundation in themselves but are sustained by what they differ from: i.e., their otherness. This applies to everything. Whatever is present is not self-sustaining but lives on what it excludes, and by marking this difference deconstruction makes the excluded bounce back on the excluder. Thus all claims to origins other than what is different from the dominant positions are dismantled, and origin loses its metaphysical dignity. Difference, exposed by the jetty, becomes the hallmark of the deconstructionist mode of reading, which does two things at the same time: (1) It opens up a "play of difference" within whatever is identified as speech and writing, meaning and context, presence and absence, thus revealing that each of them is inhabited by what it is not. (2) If these phenomena are not grounded in themselves, the question of origin becomes unanswerable and is thus forever deferred.

Such a mode of reading may not be a theory in the received sense of the term, but it is not without theoretical constituents. The reading strategy of deconstruction is very elaborate and theoretically oriented, because it is structured by key concepts such as jetty, difference/**différance**, and supplement. However, it is distinguished from the structures of the theories discussed so far because it has freed itself from certain constraints of theory-building. This mode of reading is focused, but has no closure, no claim to comprehensive explanation, no panoramic view of the human condition; instead, it explores the open-ended dependence of every phenomenon on its otherness. It is an unbounded, free-ranging activity, which is in sync with the contemporary world, as evidenced by the impact deconstruction has made.

## Deconstruction at Work

There are a great many examples to choose from in order to illustrate the operation of a deconstructionist reading. A recent one is *Speech Acts in Literature* (2001), by J. Hillis Miller (b. 1928), which takes apart J. L. Austin's *How to Do Things with Words*. Focusing on **speech act theory** is particularly pertinent, because doing things with words is a basic concern of deconstruction, and one cannot confine the activity, as speech act theorists have done, to observing certain preordained procedures.

Speech act theory is derived from ordinary language philosophy and has conceptualized basic conditions that have to be fulfilled for a linguistic utterance to become successful. The speech act, as a unit of communication,

121

must not only organize the signs but must also condition the way in which these signs are received. For this reason John L. Austin (1911–60) introduced the distinction between constative and performative utterances, defining them as follows: "With the constative utterance [ ... ] we use an oversimplified notion of correspondence with facts. [ ... ] We aim at the ideal of what would be right to say in all circumstances, for any purpose, to any audience."[8] The performative utterance by contrast entails "*doing* something [ ... ] rather than *reporting* something" (13). It brings about a change within a situational context, and indeed it is only through their situational usage that performative utterances can take on their meaning. They are called performative because they produce an action: "The name is derived, of course, from 'perform,' the usual verb with the noun 'action': it indicates that the issuing of the utterance is the performing of an action – it is not normally thought of as just saying something" (6f.). Hence saying " 'I do (sc. take this woman to be my lawful wedded wife)' – as uttered in a marriage ceremony" (5) is a performative speech act. It is this very distinction between constative and performative utterances at which J. Hillis Miller aims his destabilizing jetty, which enables him to lay bare what has been covered up by the seemingly neat formula.

The first word of Austin's title, Miller writes, already arouses suspicion, because "in some uses of 'how,' the attempt to decide whether it is constative or performative leaves the other possibility hovering uneasily as a shadow in the background."[9] The very fact of writing a book entitled "how to do things with words" must make Austin's locutions conceived as constative utterances (being "right in all circumstances") regarding the nature of speech acts into "one vast somewhat dishevelled performative utterance of a specific kind" (23), because "how" insinuates the way in which something is brought about. Thus Austin's book tends to resemble a work of literature, since "the literary work as a whole" (1) is a performative speech act that makes something happen. However, it is literature that Austin explicitly excludes from his definitions, or rather considers to be the direct opposite of his concept of performatives which, when uttered, "the words must be spoken 'seriously' and so as to be taken 'seriously.' " Therefore, "I must not be joking, for example, nor writing a poem" (Austin 9). If Austin needs literature – basically performative in character – to contrast with his definition of performative utterances, then he inadvertently reveals that the latter elude cognition since there is no objective means of establishing "seriousness." Hence he can only back up the sincerity of the performative by saying that in each of these utterances "*our word is our bond*" (10).

However, such a moral commitment does not ensure "'how' a given utterance is to be taken, by different people for different uses in different circumstances, or just what its force will be" (Miller 54). For instance, "if I say 'I promise,' evidently I can know whether I really mean it or am just pretending to promise, whereas if the other says 'I promise,' this does not tell me anything about his or her intention to keep the promise" (173). Miller's destabilizing jetty makes Austin's categorical distinctions collapse, which results in the impossibility of knowing whether a speech act in a given case is either constative or performative. The Declaration of Independence is a case in point. It is "impossible to decide whether the text does no more than describe an act that has already occurred or whether the text itself as duly signed brings about the independence from England it names" (126).

Moreover, such equivocation discloses that there is no cognition of the action triggered by the performative utterance, and no knowledge of why the constative utterance is "right in all circumstances." Hence whatever Austin posits as a frame of reference is just a "supplement," added on for the sake of completing the incomplete. This applies particularly to the importance accorded to the first person singular, which is an unquestioned presupposition for all speech acts. Miller writes, "The standard theory of performative utterances depends [ . . . ] on the unitary 'I' or ego in full possession of its senses and intention" (72). This is a prerequisite for Austin if the performative is to be "felicitous," i.e., to bring about what is intended. "In order for a performative to be felicitous, I must mean what I say, and must know what I mean and that I mean what I say, with no *arrière pensée*, no unconscious motives or reservations. A Freudian notion of the unconscious would pretty well blow Austin's theory out of the water" (29). In other words, the ego presupposed by Austin for making the performative work is an ideal construct which, however, is supposed to be the origin of real and even controlled actions.

Its character as a supplement becomes all the more obvious when Austin illustrates the conditions which make the performative "infelicitous." These examples are ludicrous and sometimes even grotesque – for instance, when the christening of penguins is meant to exemplify a misfired speech act. "No examples are innocent. Of philosophers and theorists in general it can be said, 'By their examples ye shall know them'" (43).

Women come out especially badly in Austin's examples. A vein of misogyny runs all through *How to Do Things with Words*. It is the misogyny characteristic of Austin's gender, class, and national culture. Marriage, in the first mention of it, is said to be something in which you "indulge." It is the woman, not the man, who throws a monkey wrench into the marriage ceremony by saying "I will not." Women are also unable to keep the marriage bond, as in the example of the woman accused of adultery. If the worst comes to the worst you can try saying "shoot her!" or "I promise to send you to a nunnery," or "I wish you at the bottom of the sea," or "I divorce you." (50f.)

Thus Austin's ideal construct of the first person singular is stabilized by an array of examples, all of which highlight a deviation from what he considers proper conduct. Austin was after all "a professor of moral philosophy and had a professional obligation to raise moral issues. Austin wants among other things [ ... ] to guarantee that bigamists, welshers, and other such 'low types' can be both morally deplored [ ... ] and legally, juridically, punished" (132).

Thus the duality of Miller's "jetty" becomes transparent. It exposes Austin's first person singular as a construct that is needed in order to "supplement" the condition for the performative utterance to be felicitous. But simultaneously it shows that the multiplicity of misfired examples is guided by a law-and-order concept, implicitly meant to make the posited construct persuasive.

There is yet another basic presupposition for the performative utterance to become successful, namely, convention. The utterance must invoke a convention that is as valid for the recipient as for the speaker. The application of the convention must tie in with the situation – in other words it must be governed by accepted procedures. And, finally, the willingness of the participants to engage in a linguistic action must be proportionate to the degree in which the context of the action is defined. If these conditions are not fulfilled, or if definitions are too vague or inaccurate, the utterance will run the risk of remaining empty and so failing to achieve its ultimate goal which, in Austin's words, is "to effect the transaction" (Austin 7). For this to happen, Austin explicitly states: "There must exist an accepted conventional procedure having a certain conventional effect, that procedure to include the uttering of certain words by certain persons in certain circumstances" (14). As the context can never be fully determined, Miller writes, Austin's "conditions for a demonstrable felicitous performative can never be met" (Miller 99). Referring to Derrida, Miller argues "that the performative utterance creates the conventions it needs in order to be efficacious, rather than depending on their prior existence for its felicity.

It thereby transforms the context it enters rather than presupposing it and being based on it" (112). If the performative is liberated from the constraints that Austin has imposed on it, its utterance interferes with a context instead of being conditioned by it. Furthermore, a context can never be defined a priori, not least because "it is uncontrollably diverse in itself. It stretches out to vaguer and more distant fringes that are neither quite part of the context nor able to be put firmly beyond its borders as something we need to 'trench upon,' to borrow Austin's somewhat peculiar topographical figure" (100).

If the performative transforms the context into which it enters, and even sets certain limits, within which it intends to function, the context in turn will have repercussions on the utterance, whose intervention is not in the nature of one-way traffic. No intention is fully conscious of itself nor able to control what it means to achieve, and so the context disseminates the meaning of the performative. "Words [ . . . ] scatter like seeds or break open [ . . . ] and in doing so are inaugurally productive" (67). The performative may then be taken for something not intended, which can diminish or enhance its semantic potential, from which Miller concludes, "insofar as an utterance is performative, it is outside the realm of the knowable. This means that all acts of *Setzung*, far from being the region of a possible mastery, are a region of radical ignorance and intellectual weakness [ . . . ] The referential function of performative language presumably means the ability to do something with words and at the same time to know what that doing is. It turns out that this is impossible" (143). What Austin has initially proclaimed as "a revolution in philosophy" (Austin 3) "which seemed to promise so much clarity and so much beneficent understanding, turns out to be the very thing that transports 'us,' irresistibly, by logical stages, down the slippery slope into the bog. This brings us back around to 'bogging, by logical stages, down' as the best name for the splendid comic fiasco of *How to Do Things with Words*" (Miller 21).

Miller's reading of Austin has destabilized the framework that was meant to account for what speech acts are and how they operate. The very definition of the latter presupposes the dominance of logic, and whatever is dominant is bound to be exclusionary. Literature was the most prominent casualty of this exclusion, and yet Austin returns "so often and anxiously to this topic" (28). Obviously, he is aware that literature has to be displaced for the proposed definition to be true, and when he dubs literature as parasitic, he inadvertently acknowledges the similarity between the performative character of literature and that of speech acts.

125

Exorcising literature and vitiating logic make Austin "bog down" on the edges of his enterprise, which is both a good and a bad thing. "It is bad because it forbids further movement, good because it means that you are protected from reaching the center of the swamp, a kind of deadly black hole that Austin's work approached and at the same time vigorously resisted" (170). What is the "black hole" that appears to repel and attract Austin? Miller continues,

> It can, I think, be named. It has two facets. The first is the fear that the language for emotions may be predominantly performative, not constative. It really is the case that we fall in love only when we say "Je t'aime." Preexisting emotions have nothing to do with it. The other facet is the fear that it may be impossible ever to be sure whether the other is angry or loves me. The two fears are aspects of the same fear. [ . . . ] This is the aporia between the need to invoke conscious intention as a prerequisite to a felicitous performative utterance and the recognition that unless we say "My word is my bond" and disconnect the performative's efficacy from intention, the performative (promise, act of proffering, love, etc.) is moved back into an inaccessible, unverifiable, and wavering realm. How can we ever know for sure whether someone is "sincere" or not? (172f.)

Thus the black hole that marks the spot where explanation ends makes Austin's edifice collapse. Simultaneously, Miller foregrounds the nature of the literary speech act, which "is to find some way to speak this unspeakable, this wholly other of my private emotions" (161). Miller's is a paradigmatic deconstructionist reading insofar as it never confines itself to "destroying" the hierarchical order into which the jetty is thrown, but brings to the fore that which has been eclipsed by that which is now dismantled. Austin's vital distinctions were uncovered as inexplicable, whereas literature gives voice to what is beyond speech.

## Deconstruction Exemplified

Since literature speaks the unspeakable, we might take it as an illustration of the basic tenets of deconstruction. And so instead of theory showing us how literature "happens," here we can reverse the process, with literature showing us how deconstruction "happens." Of course literature as a whole will not lend itself to such an illustration, but the work of Beckett does, and in particular his *Texts for Nothing*.

The title of the piece already poses a problem, because it can mean two different things. The texts are just nothing, and hence unimportant, or they can be taken as a tribute to nothing, and hence important. The two significations turn out to be referential criteria, and instead of saying something about nothing, they provide an evaluation of it. The referential criteria, however, are opposites, which could mean that they either cancel each other out or that the issue has to be left undecided.

If one lays stress on either the "importance" or the "unimportance" of nothing, the initial meaning will shift accordingly: "nothing is important" will then get a negative slant, whereas "nothing is unimportant" a positive one. This apparent switch is due to the fact that the title of the piece suggests two readings in referential terms, which highlights the fact that "nothing" is beyond reference. Hence "nothing" can be neither important nor unimportant, and thus what it is turns out to be undecidable. Undecidability is one of the key terms of deconstruction. However, undecidability has repercussions on the meanings accorded to what eludes our grasp, and thus lays them open to deconstruction. In this respect the title gives a glimpse of what it could mean when Derrida says that deconstruction happens. If "nothing" cannot be conceived in referential terms, the question looms large as to what it *could* be. But this is exactly what has to be deconstructed, because if it were something, it would rest on an as yet undisclosed presupposition.

How, then, is "nothing" to be approached? As there can be no statements concerning "nothing," we are inclined to say that Beckett's text enacts "nothing," and in so doing it opens up a stage for illuminating deconstruction. Enactment may be the only prop left that allows us to grasp at nothing. However, enactment presupposes something that is to be staged, and is nothing such a something? If it were, then nothing would already have been grasped in some way. But if "nothing" is nothingness, the enactment has no anterior that is to be staged. Hence the enactment of nothing is bound to develop as an engendering of what is to be staged. If the text as an enactment has to bring forth what it enacts, and if what is to be enacted is nothing, then the text is bound to proceed as an incessant unscrambling of what the enactment exhibits. In other words, to "textualize" nothing makes itself felt by undoing the texture of the text. Thus the latter has to constitute its own undoing in order to render nothingness tangible. This is the blueprint of deconstruction, to which the text gives salience. How is this blueprint executed? To answer this question, we may single out certain levels of the text: the subject and the texture. These levels may be taken as "media" into which nothing, though never present, is inscribed.

The subject has shrunk to a disembodied personal pronoun, which more often than not assumes the character of a voice, though it is not a particular voice, but several voices. "What matter who's speaking [ . . . ] it won't be me, I'll be here, I'll say I'm far from here, it won't be me."[10] The more the voices cancel one another out, the more the personal pronouns begin to proliferate. The voices come from dislocated perspectives, and they appear as if they were observing one another. However, as they do so, what is voiced becomes dispersed. "And the voices, wherever they come from, have no life in them" (113), because they are cut off from the origin of their utterance. Thus the voices keep dwindling into murmurs, the "I exist in the pit of my inexistence" (114), and wants to be mute forever after all this loquaciousness.

What we are given to witness is a disembodied subject, the dispersal of voices, a carnivalization of stances that are momentarily adopted, a mutual silencing of voices, speaking and lapsing into murmurs, and the self-frustrating intentions of the pronouns, all of them signifying nothing. This ceaseless undoing makes it seem as if nothing were to be lured into presence. But as the undoing is intentional, the effort is without end, so that nothing will never become present. Hence it is the absence of the origin that powers these activities, which launch the subject on a trajectory of total dispersion that leads to nothing. The dual signification, however, can never be resolved: is it nothing which is signified, or does the undoing signify nothing? This difference is vital for deconstruction, as it highlights the inaccessibility of origins, which are forever deferred.

Thus *Texts for Nothing* can be read as an enactment of the deferral of origins that allows us to perceive how the basic idea of deconstruction operates. We can understand why the subject is scattered in an almost total fragmentation, since its disintegration points to the fact that its base is ungraspable and can never be penetrated. Moreover, these splintering pronouns and voices are forever on the point of vanishing, thus adumbrating the idea that the deferred origin may be nothing. At any rate deferral of origin destabilizes the notion of the subject, thus illustrating a general pursuit of deconstruction.

This feature is further illuminated by the texture of the text, which is pervaded by incessant denials, epitomized in phrases like "wipe it out, all you have to do is say you said nothing and so say nothing again [ ... ] And the yeses and the noes mean nothing in this mouth, no more than sighs it sighs in its toil [ ... ] No, something better must be found, a better reason, for this to stop, another word, a better idea, to put in the negative, a new no, to cancel all the others, all the old noes" (124, 136, 147). These old and new "noes" indicate that every negation is motivated by something that does the denying, and as long as one is involved in such a sequence one appears to have at least a certain knowledge why something has to be negated. But having such a knowledge would mean, in deconstructionist terms, providing supplements for whatever is irretrievably deferred and hence has to be exposed for what it seems to be. Beckett's text is pervaded by such awareness. The negations proliferate because each "no" harbors a motivation that is to be wiped out again. The more such an operation accelerates, the more the text turns into a vortex which annihilates all the "supplements" produced by the denials.

Beckett certainly did not intend to illustrate basic ideas of deconstruction, not least as his texts were at best contemporaneous with the development of deconstruction, if not *avant la lettre*. But he allows us to perceive what deferral of origin entails, and how it destabilizes totalizations by simultaneously exposing the claim to knowledge as a compensatory supplement. If Beckett's texts lend themselves to illuminating basic tenets of deconstruction, it is equally certain that they defy deconstructionist reading, because Beckett has already enacted what such a reading is meant to disclose.

## Notes

1  Jacques Derrida, "Some Statements and Truisms about Neologisms, Newisms, Postisms, Parasitisms, and other Small Seismisms," in David Carroll, ed., *The States of Theory: History, Art, and Discourse* (Irvine Studies in the Humanities), New York: Columbia University Press, 1990, p. 67.
2  Ibid., p. 79.
3  Ibid., p. 86.
4  Ibid., p. 85.
5  Ibid., p. 84.
6  Jacques Derrida, *Positions*, trans. Alan Bass, Chicago: Chicago University Press, 1981, p. 41.
7  Barbara Johnson, *The Critical Difference: Essays in the Contemporary Rhetoric of Reading*, Baltimore: Johns Hopkins University Press, 1980, p. 5.

8   J. L. Austin, *How to Do Things with Words*, ed. J. O. Urmson, Cambridge, Mass.: Harvard University Press, 1962, pp. 144f. The sources of all other quotations from this volume are given in the text with references to the appropriate pages.

9   J. Hillis Miller, *Speech Acts in Literature*, Stanford: Stanford University Press, 2001, p. 7. The sources of all other quotations from this volume are given in the text with references to the appropriate pages.

10  Samuel Beckett, *Texts for Nothing*, in *The Complete Short Prose 1929–1989*, ed. S. E. Gontarsky, New York: Grove Press, 1995, p. 109. The sources of all other quotations from this volume are given in the text with references to the appropriate pages.

# 10

# Anthropological Theory: Gans

Is there such a thing as an anthropological theory of art? The answer to this question requires a few preliminary remarks about what anthropology was in the past and what it appears to be today.

As long as the process of hominization was the objective of research, the evaluation of fossils was of paramount concern. These factual remains called for inferences, which were necessarily theory-laden, with evolution being the dominant explanatory model in modern times. Thus theoretical implications have always been a subconscious undercurrent in anthropology, though for a long time they did not attract any particular attention, since they were taken for realities, not very different in quality from those that can be observed. Evolution, however, does not present itself to observation, and equally ungraspable is the origin of humankind, which has given rise to all kinds of theories. But even if anthropology was a theory-laden enterprise right from its inception, a critical inspection of its explanatory procedures is of recent vintage.

The methodological scrutiny to which Darwinian anthropology has been subjected has resulted – according to different standpoints – in a departmentalization of what once seemed self-contained. We still have ethnography, which is basically what the practitioners of anthropology are concerned with, but we also have philosophical, social, cultural, historical, and even literary anthropology, distinguished by their respective objectives and their methodological presuppositions. Even ethnography has changed its focus, no longer dwelling exclusively on origins of hominization but also and especially on what happened after the hominids launched themselves. Clifford Geertz, for instance, made it his overriding concern to understand "what ethnography is, or more exactly *what doing ethnography is*,"[1] which he identified as a study of human culture becoming self-reflective. This spawned a multiplicity of approaches to assessing both the rise and the development of culture.

Consequently, "doing ethnography" is basically a two-tiered undertaking: it makes culture the prime focus of anthropology, and simultaneously initiates self-monitoring within all the operations involved in this study. Why should culture be so central? Because, as Geertz maintains, it is not something "added on, so to speak, to a finished or virtually finished animal" but is "ingredient, and centrally ingredient, in the production of the animal itself," which leads him to the conclusion that "[w]ithout men, no culture, certainly; but equally, and more significantly, without culture, no men."[2]

This is a common view, shared by a great many influential anthropologists today, irrespective of whether they regard the production of culture as a reparation undertaken by the "creature of deficiency,"[3] as Arnold Gehlen puts it, or as a result of the cortex expanding owing to the erect posture of humans, as André Leroi-Gourhan suggests. Whichever explanatory hypothesis one might be inclined to favor, all of them tend to conceive culture as the capstone in the rise of humankind. Furthermore, these divergent approaches share a common perspective. They view culture as a response to challenges, and this response as a revelation of what humans are. The double-sidedness of culture, as a product and as a record of human manifestation, has repercussions on humans themselves, insofar as they are molded by what they have externalized. As Geertz puts it, "men," in the final analysis, "every last one of them, are cultural artefacts."[4]

What remains noteworthy in these various theories of culture advanced by anthropologists is the fact that almost all of them end up discussing the role of the arts in the makeup of culture. Artistic elements emerge as important concomitant features right from the observable beginnings of humankind, providing indispensable "support" in the effort to meet challenges, for which Leroi-Gourhan's findings may serve as an example.

Artistic elements appear very early on in the evolution of culture, as evinced by the manufacturing of tools. The tool as an "exteriorization" of the hand does not exist for its own sake but has to fulfill a function. For this reason it has to have a form which will optimize the application for which it has been designed. Tools in prehistoric times already show marks of "decorative elements," which Leroi-Gourhan views as the "dialogue between the maker and the material employed."[5] Hence the three essential components are the tool's mechanical function, the form that facilitates it, and the style that configures the relationship of the maker to the product. The ornamental clothing of the tool indicates a "style, which is a matter of ethnic figurative value," and which accompanies "the mechanical function and the material solutions to the problem of functional approximation,"[6] thus "forging the tool" to its operable perfection.

"All art then is utilitarian," as Leroi-Gourhan contends, and the "gratuitousness of art does not lie in its motivation but in the flowering of the language of forms. [ . . . ] The twofold nature of art – collective and personal – makes it impossible to separate the functional completely from the gratuitous, to separate art for something's sake from art for art's sake, just as it makes impossible [ . . . ] a radical separation between figurative and decorative art."[7] Consequently, artistic figurations perform a prominent role in the system of human responsiveness to the challenges of an entropic environment; they are abstractions from reality in order "to reconstitute that reality's symbolic image."[8] Expressive features are isolated, like the phallus, vulva, bison's or horse's heads, and then reassembled in order to translate these features into a "mythogram." The selected elements are subjected to "schematization" and even "geometrization" – which highlights "an aspect of extreme schematization"[9] – and are thereby reduced to triangles, cubes, circles, and other geometric forms that reflect the effort to master something. Such efforts reveal that art is meant not to be a copy but a symbol that simultaneously structures "realities" and exhibits the structuring process.

Art, then, proves to be an indispensable element of human culture. If "its fundamental purpose is to signify,"[10] it appears already in prehistoric times as a laboratory of symbol-making, furnishing forms for controlling the environment, for establishing order, for representing realities, and for casting magic spells on what has to be coped with. What art bodies forth is a state of being ahead of what there is, and this aspiration in turn prefigures the human condition. Doing art seems to be deeply ingrained in human makeup as a representation of our relationship to a challenging environment. Hence there is no need to derive a special theory of art from the observable development of human culture, because "functional aesthetics" (Leroi-Gourhan) appears integral to humankind's externalization of its capabilities, for which symbolization provides essential guidance. What ethnography thus tells us is: without art no *Homo sapiens*. What, however, ethnography remains silent about is the particular function of literature in the process of cultural formation. And as culture has become – albeit only recently – the central concern of anthropology, literature as an integral feature of culture is bound to have an anthropological dimension of its own. Therefore we have to turn to generative anthropology as developed by Eric Gans, who has demonstrated the extent to which literature articulates the rhythm of culture, epitomizes its vicissitudes, and provides relief from what humans are subjected to.

## The Basics of Generative Anthropology

Eric Gans (b. 1941) breaks away from ethnographical research altogether and advances a construct of culture instead. In one sense, however, this construct meets the requirement for theories of culture that Geertz had already postulated, namely, that such theories should apply not only to past realities but also to realities to come,[11] which generative anthropology has convincingly accomplished.

Gans starts out from what he has called the "originary scene" through which human culture came into existence. Such a "scene," however, is nothing but a hypothesis which can only gain plausibility if its assumptions form a blueprint for the historical development of culture. This is one of the reasons why Gans tries to draw out the implications of the "originary scene" in order to accommodate the welter of occurrences between the inception of culture and the present. How, then, is this hypothetical "originary scene" envisaged?

A "band of hunters, armed with primitive weapons, face each other around the body of their victim,"[12] and all of them want to appropriate the kill, so that violence is imminent. The assumed details of the scene are not significant; what is important, however, is that the "hands reaching out toward the object hesitate in mid-course through the fear of each that he will fall victim to the reprisals of others. This hesitation turns the gesture of appropriation into a gesture of designation, and the locus of the body into the original scene of representation" (EC 14). The hesitation is effected through the "ostensive gesture"[13] by one of the group pointing toward what is at the center, and this designation inhibits the outbreak of violence. Two mutually interrelated features mark the "originary scene": an incipient conflict, and its abrogation by a gesture of representation. The interdiction of "appetitive satisfaction" caused by the ostensive gesture toward what is at the center converts the "originary scene" into an "originary event," which leads Gans to the conclusion that the act of representation as a deferral of conflict differentiates humankind from the animal kingdom. "In our anthropology, man is not distinguished from animals by his propensity to economic activity, but by his use of representation" (EC 88).

As long as representation is taken to effect the initial deferral of appetitive satisfaction, which opens up a difference between the individual and the appetitive object as well as a difference between the individuals themselves, the act of representation appears to be the explanatory pattern of this generative anthropology. Because the "designation of the object of contention does not leave the object as it was previously, a mere natural reality newly named, but transfigures it into a cultural object. What it was as a natural reality was something to appropriate for the satisfaction of the appetite; what it is now, as a result of the act of designation, is something that the collectivity surrounding it does not dare to appropriate immediately and individually, but only after the act of its designation and then only communally" (OT 88).

If conflict is prevented by the aborted gesture of appropriation turning into one of representation, how does the latter come to life? The answer is: through images formed by each individual facing the object from which they are all barred. The abrogation of appetitive satisfaction transforms the object into one of desire, indicating the impossibility of appropriation. "Esthetic contemplation is inevitably accompanied by desire. But the specifically esthetic moment is the contemplation itself, in which not the 'private' image of desired satisfaction but the 'public' image of the desire-object is perceived" (EC 31). The image of desire is therefore imaginary, and as representation – effecting the deferral of a real presence for the sake of avoiding conflict – it highlights the status of desire as unfulfilled satisfaction. Thus each individual entertains such an image, through which the inaccessibility of the central object translates itself into the mind. This is an initial step toward turning the representation of the inaccessible into productivity. The image that each individual has may be totally different from that of the others. However, impenetrable as these differences may be, the awareness prevails that each individual is bound to have an image, because what is made inaccessible prods the imagination into action. If having images is shared, a nascent sense of togetherness begins to emerge; a group is established. Representation of the inaccessible mobilizes the imagination, which transforms interdiction into a feeling of collectivity.

The originary event as a construct is not meant to mark the beginning of human evolution; it is, however, viewed as a mainspring of culture in all its diversifications and ramifications, from the ostensive gesture as the nascent institution of language through changing tribal organizations to the rich variations of art. Thus the originary event figures as a sort of retrospective image for the productive process that is to be observed in culture and that unfolds human history as a rhythmic alternation between restriction and derestriction. "At best such a scenario can be of heuristic value" (EC 99). In other words, Gans sees it as an illustration, not as an explanation.

If representation as deferral of violence or avoidance of conflict is the response to the "originary event," why is there no abolition of violence and conflict once and for all? What causes the established equilibrium within the social community to be disturbed again, so that new conflicts ensue? The answer to this question lies in organization. The interdiction of appetitive satisfaction – as we have seen – creates desire, and the eventual distribution of the desire-object creates an ethically organized community. Gans writes, "once the community exists in the mutual presence brought about by the sign, no particular act need be performed to preserve it. The first act to which we might attribute an ethical motivation is, rather, the distribution of the desire-object" (EC 47). Such a distribution contains an asymmetrical element insofar as, for instance, clan or totem feasts are presided over by a chief. In other words, the initially egalitarian group gives way to a hierarchically organized one, which divides the group into purveyor and consumer. But the unity of the social group is abandoned when one purveys and the others consume. Out of this asymmetry, originally meant to stabilize the group's organization, arose the most powerful drive for the development of culture: resentment. "We have seen that [ . . . ] the originary event is the moment in which the appetitive gesture is suspended [ . . . ] The sign at this point designates the center as the source of all potentialities. [ . . . ] But it is also the moment of the renunciation of appetitive satisfaction. The center denies its resources to the humans who require them. The denial is the source of desire as well as of originary resentment" (OT 109).

The submission required or enforced in hierarchically organized social bodies produces this resentment. There are no social organizations, from the totemistically structured clan to the elaborate stratifications of modern societies that are not based on and characterized by difference. And it is the contestation of this ineluctable difference that generates resentment. "The resentful imagination is a reaction against real perceptions that are painful in that they show another in the place that the self would like to occupy. Irrealizable desire is faced with the scandal of a humanly realized centrality. It is through resentment that the individual comes to feel his essential unfreedom within the social order, or, in other words, that he comes to exist fully as an individual, with the consciousness that his human capacities are not necessarily destined to receive their maximal satisfaction within the community" (EC 225). Thus resentment – in contesting difference – turns out to be the fuel that drives the life of culture, because the difference marks a blank that cannot be eliminated, and hence continually invites occupation. The impossibility of bridging the gap between center and periphery both generates and energizes human culture.

Although Gans demonstrates this continual relocation between center and periphery in ritual, social, and economic terms, it nevertheless finds its most tangible expression in literature which, for him, becomes the signature of high culture. This is primarily because it brings the original impulse of the sign to full fruition by allowing the inaccessible to be enacted, and in so doing it provides distance from the reality in which humans are otherwise so inextricably entangled. Conjuring the absent into presence makes literature into a fictitious occupation of the otherwise ineradicable gap between center and periphery. This is more than just an illustration of the cultural blueprint, as it also purveys a satisfaction not otherwise to be obtained, which elevates literature into a cultural need.

## An Anthropological View of Literature

The nature of satisfaction that literature provides is to be witnessed very early on in Greek tragedy, of which Euripides's *Iphigenia* and Sophocles's *Oedipus* are outstanding instances. Gans writes:

> Pentheus is like Oedipus a man of resentment, jealous of his authority and intolerant of the power exercised by his divine double over the women of his city. We identify both with his resentful centrality and with the periphery from which he is resented, just as we do with Oedipus; [ ... ] We both see ourselves in the place of the central protagonist and examine him from the safety of the periphery. The tragic hero is a figure of both self and other. [ ... ] The imaginary sacrifice of this central figure consoles us for lack of centrality; at the same time it teaches us through example the paradoxicality of our desire for centrality. (EC 299)

Thus Greek tragedy spotlights both difference and resentment as the constitutive components of human desire. Resentment, according to Gans

– and in this respect he joins hands with Nietzsche (EC 173 and 198) – energizes the generation of culture insofar as the position of the center is denied to those who find themselves on the periphery. Expressed resentment, however, turns into sublimation, which allows the spectators of these tragedies to entertain a relationship to their basically paradoxical desire: to be different from what they covet, but also to negotiate this difference. Hence literature produces something that is irrevocably absent from the life that humans lead, and at the same time, by presenting what is absent, it makes the workings of human culture transparent. "All culture," Gans contends, "is a defense of the social order against conflict, a deferral of violence through representation. What is at the center of the scene of representation is forbidden to the participants at the periphery" (EC 301). Greek tragedy appears to overcome this dichotomy, because the "origin of literature" arises out of "this degradation of the central figure to our own mortal level. [ ... ] We identify with the centrality we resent and are alienated from the centrality we desire. We suffer the hero's suffering while rejoicing in our distance from it" (OT 137). Such an experience strikes the spectators with fear and terror (Aristotle), and simultaneously purges them of their resentment, which is deferred, since the hero suffers from the crime of having occupied the center.

In this respect, literature provides an indispensable compensation for the lack of any transcendental stance, which by definition could only exist outside human culture and predicate what the latter is supposed to be. Instead of being beyond culture, literature is inside it, functioning as a monitoring "device," and allowing us to observe the driving forces out of which culture arises. As sublimation, literature appears to provide at least momentary satisfaction through its form of representation which, as avoidance of conflict, defers the real in favor of the unreal. While it does so, the disequilibrium inherent in desire is for a fleeting – though illusory – moment balanced out, so that a psychological equilibrium may be enjoyed. Thus literature does two things at once: it bridges the ineluctable difference between center and periphery, and at the same time allows detachment from all cultural constraints. Therefore, Gans accords a privileged status to literature and aesthetics in general. He writes: "The creation of independent esthetic institutions reflects the emergence of the esthetic as a discovery procedure for human self-understanding. The classical is the first historical esthetic because it opens up the history of art as an independent vehicle of anthropological knowledge" (OT 132). In other words, literature as an intracultural grandstand view allows us what is otherwise

impossible: the reading of culture. And as the latter keeps changing, literature spells out the way in which the life of culture proceeds. "The classical
esthetic requires that we as spectators know we have an imaginary but not
a real place in the central **agon**; this is its guarantee against resentment.
But the only way to insure that we remain on the periphery is to exclude
ordinary citizens from the central roles. [ ... ] This automatic exclusion
of the self from the center could not survive the coming of Christianity
with its foregrounding of the moral equality of all" (OT 148).

Because Christianity rejects the hierarchical separation of different
worlds, centrality is no longer the forbidden locus, the occupation of
which ends in disaster, and this is a consolation to those who are relegated
to the periphery. "The neoclassical work puts the scene itself on the stage"
(OT 160), to be witnessed in Renaissance tragedy, of which *Hamlet* is
a prominent example. "The most pregnant scene of modern tragedy is
Hamlet's first stage appearance. Dressed in black and showing con-
temptuous indifference to the worldly matters of the king's council, the young
prince distracts the spectators' attention by his eccentric strategy and
challenges to the central role of the king [ ... ] What is on stage is not a
simple center surrounded by the chorus as an extension of the audience;
the world of the stage has become a model of the originary scene as a whole,
with its periphery contrasted to its center" (OT 157f.). Thus the originary
scene turns into an exhibit, the enactment of which spells out a different
version of the otherwise hierarchical proclivity. Because staging the scene
is not meant as a mere replica of what happens in the life of culture, in
*Hamlet* centrality figures as a curse, as an injunction to take revenge, and
as usurpation, all of which are nothing but deficient modes of centrality.
Again, what the cultural interchangeability of center and periphery is unable
to reveal is displayed by putting the scene on stage. However, denigrating
the center results in Hamlet's establishing his own "private" centrality, the
assumption of which "poses a public threat that cannot go unnoticed" (157).
Centrality is tainted, and whoever tends to occupy it falls victim to its
degradation. The tragedy foregrounds the revaluation of the originary scene,
thus exhibiting what remains eclipsed in the life of culture.

Historicizing the pattern of center and periphery makes literature
into a procedure of discovery. Retaining this pattern allows Gans to
spotlight its subsequent historical rearrangements up to the point where it
becomes meaningless in postmodern market-driven society. "With Molière's
*Misanthrope* dependency on the public scene comes to appear comic rather
than tragic; when the stage is abandoned by the characters as the curtain

falls, the scene itself (rather than, as in tragedy, its occupants) has been liquidated by the force of the outsider's moral judgment. What remains for Rousseau is to openly deny the outsider's dependency. The public center has not yet lost its reality, but it has become a mere contingency from the standpoint of the self" (OT 162). Centrality, already disparaged in *Hamlet*, now becomes an empty husk which, however, calls for rearrangement as long as the constellation is not totally abolished.

The Romantics relocate the "heart of the originary scene" (OT 161f.) from center to periphery, which makes the self into the true center, so that centrality is no longer public but personal. Rivalry appears to be suspended, because the elevated self – instead of being resented – has to be emulated, thus indicating that resentment as the driving force of cultural change is on the wane.

Realism articulates another shift in this relationship. The imitation of ordinary life-experience destroys the last vestige of the sacred protection that separates the central figure from the rivalry of the periphery. Whatever occupies the "center" of Dickens's novels – be it domineering individuals, institutions, legal procedures, or authorities of different persuasions – is stripped of its aura, while the peripheral hero emerges victorious from the oppression to which he has been subjected by centrality.

The post-Romantics take another important step beyond their predecessors by splitting the self into two, because the "postromantic artist conceives of an authentic self different from the worldly, appetitive self. The higher self is revealed in art; it is the self of the creator and the self the artist appeals to in the audience. The anthropological significance of the 'two selves' doctrine will be better appreciated if we consider them as the subjects of rival originary hypotheses in which the 'high' and 'popular' interpretations of the originary scene are incarnated in interdependent personae. The opposition between the two selves is homologous with that between words and things. The higher self inhabits a world of pure representation that can only be reached by the transcendence of the world of appetite" (OT 182f.). To make the self into a work of art, as epitomized by Oscar Wilde, runs as a cultivation of subjectivity throughout the nineteenth century, and gains its centrality by relegating the consumer-oriented self to the margin. The question then arises whether the peripheral self is still driven by resentment or whether its marginalization is its own fault.

In modernism representation becomes an end itself insofar as literature turns into a representation of itself. What is now at the center is the realm of imagination, which is featureless, so that an "indefinite deferral of the sign" occurs (OT 197) that makes the language hermetic. The sign is stripped of its signifying function, as is to be witnessed in the poetry of Mallarmé. Thus the unmediated presence of the imagination becomes palpable by inhibiting the signification of signs.

With the dawn of postmodernism, representation is perceived as a form of repression, as it imposes constraints on an originally assumed freedom. Postmodern literature is no longer self-emulating but littered instead with quotations from literature of the past, creating the impression that our own current situation is undefinable. It reflects "the paradox of the subject who wishes both to consume the object [i.e., what he/she desires] and to withhold it indefinitely from consumption [ . . . ] the postmodern, who grasps the meaninglessness of the deferral of desire, sacred or not, contemplates the object 'undecidably'" (OT 218). The cultural pattern of center and periphery is liquidated, but its obsolescence does not mean the end of culture. If postmodern undecidability signals the exit from history "by demonstrating its boundedness within time, [it nevertheless] presupposes an originary entrance into the historical. The postmodern denial of the origin is ultimately a return to the origin, the inauguration of an originary anthropology" (OT 215). This means no less than that generative anthropology now maps and illuminates the whole range of the history of culture.

The prominent status accorded to literature and the aesthetic by Gans makes them appear two-faced. Do literature and the aesthetic serve as explanatory fictions for the generalizations necessary to a grasp of human culture, or are they already conceived as a literary anthropology exhibiting features of humans that are not brought out into the open anywhere else? If we read sentences like the following, we get the impression that the aesthetic is an indispensable prerequisite for human self-creation. "The esthetic offers an internal solution to resentment; the esthetic oscillation between representation and imaginary presence defers resentment by preventing the stabilization of the resentful opposition between center and periphery [ . . . ] Without the esthetic moment, the originary scene would collapse in conflict; the human would not have been preserved, for no knowledge of the center would have been acquired" (OT 125). The function exercised by the aesthetic in the originary scene is taken over by literature, which plays the interchange between center and periphery out into unforeseeable possibilities that with hindsight present themselves as the course of human history. What remains an open question, however, is why there is a need for the self-monitoring that literature appears to provide. Is the sublimation of resentment all that literature has to offer?

141

Human history, elucidated by the mirror of literature, serves in the final analysis as a visualization of what is "nonconstructible": namely, the originary event.[14] If the history of culture is an exegesis of the nonconstructible originary event from which it has ensued, then the underlying pattern of generative anthropology begins to emerge. As the originary event has generated the history of culture, the latter, in turn, lends plausibility to the positing of such an event. In other words, event and history are tied together by **recursive loops**. The "nonconstructibility" is made to loop into the history of culture, and the continual shifts of representation as deferral of conflict are made to loop into the originary event, whose nonconstructibility perpetuates itself in the unforeseeable turns taken by the rearranged relationships between center and periphery. Literature becomes the watch tower which allows us to monitor these unforeseeable turns, and hence reveals itself as the overall explanatory fiction. Since there is no stance outside the originary event or outside human culture, literature becomes an "innerworldly transcendence," permitting us to comprehend what otherwise exceeds all cognitive frameworks, whatever form they may take. The price to be paid, however, for this explanatory function of literature is the exclusion of all features of the human makeup other than the desire for centrality and the sublimation of resentment. For some this price will undoubtedly seem too high, but we have to take into consideration that Gans is using literature to elucidate conspicuous features of culture, just as ethnographers use prehistoric cave paintings (Altamira and Lascaux) for the same purpose. There is, however, also an exploratory side to this otherwise explanatory use of literature in Gans's approach: it comes to the fore in the construal of a cultural history. This seeks to find out what may have been the roots of culture, and how these roots have branched out into cultural patterns and institutions, thus making literature into a procedure of discovery.

## Notes

1  Clifford Geertz, *The Interpretation of Culture: Selected Essays*, New York: Basic Books, 1973, p. 5.
2  Ibid., pp. 47, 49.
3  See Arnold Gehlen, *Der Mensch: Seine Natur und seine Stellung in der Welt*, Bonn: Athenäum, ⁶1958, pp. 21, 35, 89, 383.
4  Geertz, *Interpretation of Culture*, p. 51.

5  André Leroi-Gourhan, *Gesture and Speech*, trans. Anna Bostock Berger, Cambridge, Mass.: MIT Press, 1993, pp. 306, 385.

6  Ibid., p. 308.

7  Ibid., p. 364.

8  Ibid., p. 365.

9  Ibid., p. 382.

10  Ibid., p. 364.

11  Geertz, *Interpretation of Culture*, p. 26.

12  Eric Gans, *The End of Culture: Towards a Generative Anthropology*, Berkeley and Los Angeles: California University Press, 1985, p. 99. The sources of all other quotations from this volume are given in the text with references to the appropriate pages, preceded by the letters EC.

13  Eric Gans, *Originary Thinking: Elements of Generative Anthropology*, Stanford: Stanford University Press, 1993, pp. 64–9 and 79–81. The sources of all other quotations from this volume are given in the text with references to the appropriate pages, preceded by the letters OT.

14  Gans, *End of Culture*, pp. 100f., writes: "Our hypothesis [ . . . ] posits its existence, not as a probabilistic result of a prior situation, but *because representation exists.* The nonconstructibility of the event is no proof of its non-existence. It is precisely the opposite that is the case. It is because the origin of representation is an event that is nonconstructible, just as any other historical occurrence is nonconstructible through positive hypotheses."

# 11

# Dewey's *Art as Experience*

Is it possible to arrive at a conception of art from the basic tenets of pragmatism? If the answer is yes, it will require a mode of theory-building that we have so far not encountered. Experience marks the boundaries of pragmatism, because there is no stance *beyond* it that would allow an assessment of it. If there were one, experience would only be the last thing before the last. But does this mean that it eludes comprehension altogether? Since there can be no theory of experience, and it cannot grasp itself either, how is it to be described? Obviously it is not a monolith, but exists in a variety of forms, and therefore the question arises as to whether there may be a form against which this variety can be measured.

In his book *Art as Experience* John Dewey (1859–1952) provided an answer to this problem by pinpointing features of aesthetic experience which, for him, highlight the nature of experience in general. He writes: "To esthetic experience [ . . . ] the philosopher must go to understand what experience is."[1] Furthermore, the title of his work points to a relationship between art and experience, the elucidation of which reveals a different type of theory-building hitherto not observed in our discussion. We shall be looking more closely at this later on. Dewey starts out by saying that it is his "task to restore continuity between the refined and intensified forms of experience that are works of art and the everyday events, doings, and sufferings that are universally recognized to constitute experience" (3). Hence an aesthetic experience provided by the work of art is not something different from ordinary experiences, though it is one that reaches what Dewey calls "fulfilment." And he continues: "*If* artistic and esthetic quality is implicit in every normal experience, how shall we explain how and why it so generally fails to become explicit? Why is it that to multitudes art seems to be an importation into experience from a foreign country and the esthetic to be a synonym for something artificial?" (12f.). If aesthetic experience is not an intruder from outside, it is bound to be inherent in all experience, because "experience is the result, the sign, the reward of that interaction of organism and environment which, when it is carried to the full, is a transformation of interaction into participation and communication" (22).

Interaction is the key term for Dewey's whole approach, which he specifies insofar as experience "has pattern and structure, because it is not just doing and undergoing in alternation, but consists of them in relationship" (44). "EXPERIENCE occurs continuously, because the interaction of live creature and environing conditions is involved in the very process of living" (35). If the interaction between doing and undergoing produces experience, then the latter will assume its salience according to the conditions from which it has arisen. Obviously – since a work of art has form which the ordinary environment lacks – the doing and undergoing in an aesthetic context engender an experience which is different from those experiences that are governed by pragmatic needs in our day-to-day living. Hence the aesthetic experience is to be distinguished from other experiences, though all of them emerge from the same relationship through which "live creatures" sustain themselves.

## Aesthetic Experience

As doing and undergoing designate the matrix out of which all experience arises, how do they work in relation to art? Does the form of the work bar the recipient from doing? Dewey's answer is no, of course, for a

> perceiver [ ... ] must *create* his own experience. And his creation must include relations comparable to those which the original producer underwent. They are not the same in any literal sense. But with the perceiver, as with the artist, there must be an ordering of the elements of the whole that is in form – although not in details – the same as the process of organization the creator of the work consciously experienced. Without an act of recreation the object is not perceived as a work of art. (54)

Thus doing and undergoing still apply to the acquisition of experience, and the very recreation of the work through the recipient results in the participation that gives rise to the aesthetic experience. In this respect Dewey is in line with the phenomenological theory, which also stresses the distinction between the artistic and the aesthetic pole, the interrelation of which brings the work to life. "The process of art in production," he contends, "is related to the esthetic in perception" (49).

To simplify analysis, we shall have a separate look at aesthetic experience and the work of art in order to spotlight the nature of this dovetailing, which is the most conspicuous feature of the pragmatist "theory of esthetics" (144) that Dewey laid out in his book.

What are the distinctive features of aesthetic experience, and to what extent is the latter paradigmatic for the plurality of experiences? "Experience," Dewey maintains,

> in the degree in which it *is* experience is heightened vitality. Instead of signifying being shut up within one's own private feelings and sensations, it signifies active and alert commerce with the world; at its height it signifies complete interpenetration of self and the world of objects and events. Instead of signifying surrender to caprice and disorder, it affords our sole demonstration of a stability that is not stagnation but is rhythmic and developing. Because experience is the fulfilment of an organism in its struggles and achievements in a world of things, it is art in germ. (19)

If common experience results from our interaction with the environment, realizing itself through the fundamental rhythm of doing and undergoing, it is a product, and hence contains an artistic impulse. Since all experience is a budding form of art, aesthetic experience is bound to be experience par excellence, which elevates it into a measuring rod for the nature of experience in general.

What does a work of art make its recipient do in order to engender an aesthetic experience? According to Dewey, "what counts is what we *do*, not what we receive. The essential thing esthetically is our own mental activity of starting, traveling, returning to a starting point, holding on to the past, carrying it along; the movement of attention backwards and forwards, as these acts are executed by the mechanism of motor imagery. The resulting relations define *shape* and shape is *wholly* a matter of relation" (102). Perception, then, becomes an aesthetic experience to the degree in which the heterogeneous operations the recipient is made to perform achieve a final balance. The latter is an indication that the multifaceted aspects of the work have been fused into a shape, thus transforming the recipient's perception into an aesthetic experience. For this to happen, the basic structure of experience still obtains, as Dewey constantly reminds us:

> The rhythm peculiar to different relations between doing and undergoing is the source of the distribution and apportionment of elements that concludes the directness and unity of perception. Lack of proper relationship and distribution produces a confusion that blocks singleness of perception. Just relationship produces the experience by virtue of which a work of art both excites and composes. The doing stirs while, [*sic*] undergone consequences bring a phase of tranquillity. A thorough and related undergoing effects an accumulation of energy that is the source of further discharge in activity. The resulting perception is ordered and clear and at the same time emotionally toned. (160)

If the doing means working out the different interactions to be spotted in the work itself, the undergoing, though a relief from activity, marks the stage at which the recipient internalizes what the doing has yielded, and hence perception gains form.

These two quotations show how Dewey keeps refining the phases through which perception of the work of art turns into aesthetic experience. The main reason for this procedure is the fact that aesthetic experience cannot be assessed from a vantage point outside itself. Hence Dewey resorts to a methodological procedure that is somewhat akin to Clifford Geertz's **thick description**. This means that only features of what is under investigation can be detailed, as there are no umbrella concepts to theorize what is to be ascertained, and positing one would lead to "thin description," i.e., subjecting the phenomena under observation to preconceived ideas. Whatever components are registered, they have to be interrelated, thus allowing us to sense what they adumbrate – namely, how aesthetic experience evolves. Giving salience to the latter is bound to proceed in terms of thick description, which is meant to unfold distinctive markers that will permit experience to be grasped.

If form is such a crucial quality for aesthetic experience, what are its basic components? Dewey writes, "cumulation, tension, conservation, anticipation, and fulfilment [are] formal characteristics of an esthetic experience" (145), and these keep acting upon one another through the basic rhythm of doing and undergoing. Rhythm, however, is not only confined to regulating the interaction of these components, but is, according to Dewey, "rooted deep in the world itself [ ... ] There is rhythm in nature before poetry, painting, architecture and music exist. Were it not so, rhythm as an essential property of form would be merely superimposed upon material, not an operation through which material effects its own culmination in experience" (147). Thus rhythm accounts for the inherent dynamism of aesthetic experience that makes its components continually interact with one another; but although it is a primordial signature of our world, it must operate in a special way with aesthetic experience. "There is, of course, no rhythm without recurrence," Dewey writes, but what distinguishes "esthetic recurrence" from a "[m]echanical recurrence [ ... ] of material units [ ... ] is that of *relationships* that sum up and carry forward. Recurring units as such call attention to themselves as isolated parts, and thus away from the whole. Hence they lessen esthetic effect. Recurring *relationships* serve to define and delimit parts, giving them individuality of their own. But they also connect; the individual entities they mark off demand, *because* of the relations, association and interaction with other individuals. Thus the parts vitally serve in the construction of an expanded whole" (166).

The recurrent rhythm fans out aesthetic experience into ever-expanding connections, because each relationship established between components is subjected to rhythmic variation, which in turn engenders new and unforeseeable linkages, thus generating a graduated sequence of relationships. The components tend to become differently connected with one another, and assume kaleidoscopically shifting features which fuel the drive toward fulfillment. The question then arises: in what way is such a rhythmically articulated experience fulfillment? According to Dewey, the latter does away with the subject/object split. "For the uniquely distinguishing feature of esthetic experience is exactly the fact that no such distinction of self and object exists in it, since it is esthetic in the degree in which organism and environment coöperate to institute an experience in which the two are so fully integrated that each disappears" (249).

The immersion of the self in the object does not mean that it vanishes altogether. If it did, one would have to ask whose experience it is that thus emerges. Therefore Dewey feels compelled to qualify what it means to the subject to be enveloped in aesthetic experience, and he makes some far-reaching statements about the work of art in order to keep the subject from dissolving. He contends:

> A work of art elicits and accentuates [the] quality of being a whole and of belonging to the larger, all-inclusive, whole which is the universe in which we live. This fact, I think, is the explanation of that feeling of exquisite

intelligibility and clarity we have in the presence of an object that is experienced with esthetic intensity. It explains also the religious feeling that accompanies intense esthetic perception. We are, as it were, introduced into a world beyond this world which is nevertheless the deeper reality of the world in which we live in our ordinary experiences. We are carried out beyond ourselves to find ourselves. I can see no psychological ground for such properties of an experience save that, somehow, the work of art operates to deepen and to raise to great clarity that sense of an enveloping undefined whole that accompanies every normal experience. This whole is then felt as an expansion of ourselves. (195)

Thus, having an aesthetic experience does not mean that the subject evaporates, as the elimination of the subject/object split might intimate, but rather that the subject is both with itself and outside itself – a duality that appears mutually exclusive, but whose interfusion is accomplished by the results of the encounter with the work of art.

In order to explain this extraordinary experience, Dewey has to define the work of art, which at first glance appears highly problematic for a pragmatist view, as the act of defining implies a stance outside art. We must therefore take a look at the definitions advanced by Dewey in order to spell out his solution to an apparent dilemma. He contends that "esthetic art [ . . . ] does something different from leading to an experience. It constitutes one" (85). For this to happen the artist "must remake his past experiences so that they can enter integrally into a new pattern. He cannot dismiss his past experiences nor can he dwell among them as they have been in the past" (138). This indicates already the drift of Dewey's argument: the artist's diversified experiences become the work's blueprint. "When the structure of the object is such that its force interacts happily (but not easily) with the energies that issue from the experience itself; when their mutual affinities and antagonisms work together to bring about a substance that develops cumulatively and surely (but not too steadily) toward a fulfilling of impulsions and tensions, then indeed there is a work of art" (162).

This makes the definition of the work of art pretty homologous to that of aesthetic experience, and Dewey continues in this vein, even when accounting for the transformation of external material through the artist's imagination. Thus he writes:

The work of art [ . . . ] unlike the machine, is not only the outcome of the imagination, but operates imaginatively rather than in the realm of physical existences. What it does is to concentrate and enlarge an immediate

149

experience. The formed matter of esthetic experience directly *expresses*, in other words, the meanings that are imaginatively evoked [ ... ] And yet the meanings imaginatively summoned, assembled, and integrated are embodied in material existence that here and now interacts with the self. The work of art is thus a challenge to the performance of a like act of evocation and organization, through imagination, on the part of the one who experiences it. (273f.)

What all these qualifications – perhaps we should call them properties of the work of art – add up to is neatly summarized in the following statement: "The *product* of art – temple, painting, statue, poem – is not the *work* of art. The work takes place when a human being coöperates with the product so that the outcome is an experience that is enjoyed because of its liberating and ordered properties" (214).

## Circularity

Dewey's argument has now come full circle. On the one hand the work of art triggers an aesthetic experience in the perceiver, and on the other this very experience allows us to grasp what the work consists of – namely, a range of diversified experiences. Dewey refrains from saying what art is which, as an ontological statement, would be impossible from a pragmatist angle. Hence he discriminates between art as a product and a work, and the latter "is complete only as it works in the experience of others than the one who created it. [ ... ] The enduring art-product may have been, and probably was, called forth by something occasional, something having its own date and place. But *what* was evoked is a substance so formed that it can enter into the experience of others and enable them to have more intense and more fully rounded out experiences of their own" (106, 109). Consequently, "[p]erfection in execution cannot be measured or defined in terms of execution; it implies those who perceive and enjoy the product executed" (47). And this is so because the "artist embodies in himself the attitude of the perceiver while he works" (48). Anticipating the perceiver's dispositions and transmitting the artist's own experiences make up the substance of a work. "Since the work of art is the subject-matter of experiences heightened and intensified, the purpose that determines what is esthetically essential is precisely the formation of an experience *as* an experience" (294).

Here the strategy behind Dewey's theory-building comes fully into focus. If the work of art is the fountainhead that purveys aesthetic experience, the work itself can only be fathomed in terms of what is obtained from it. This makes the theory operate in circles. Artists interact with their environment from which there ensues an experience . The latter, in turn, interacts with the assumed disposition of the recipient, through which it is shaped so that it can enter into the recipient's experience. The aesthetic experience thus engendered is made to loop back into the work of art in order to determine what it is – the purveyor of aesthetic experience which itself is a source that is generated by the artist's experience.

Thus circularity is the blueprint of a pragmatist theory of art. It arises out of a minimalistic presupposition that there is an interaction between environment and organism, which unfolds through the rhythm of doing and undergoing that generates experience. Conceiving aesthetic experience as a special outcome of this basic assumption poses the problem of explaining its nature. Dewey articulates this nature in terms of multiple circles, and this circularity allows him to theorize *art as experience* within the pragmatist boundaries of the notion of experience.

## An Example

Looking at a poem in terms of the aesthetic experience engendered by it, we can only highlight formal features, because the experience will register differently with every individual. However, we can show how it develops and engages the recipient. T. S. Eliot's "Fire Sermon" from *The Waste Land* (Appendix C) may serve as an illustration for what Dewey has mapped out in his "esthetic theory." In this poem we encounter a great many allusions to other literary texts, social systems, and existing conventions, all of which make up the environment with which the poet interacted. The selection could be described as the "doing," and the segments imported into the text as the "undergoing," because they provide a set of shapes for the poem. The allusions thus assembled are to Marvell ("But at my back in a cold blast I hear"), to Spenser ("Sweet Thames, run softly till I end my song"), to Shakespeare ("Musing upon the king my brother's wreck"), to Verlaine ("*Et O ces voix d'enfants, chantant dans la coupole!*"), to Eliot's own poetry ("The sound of horns and motors, which shall bring / Sweeney to Mrs. Porter in the spring"), all of which alternate with segments from ordinary reality, such as promiscuous scenes ("The nymphs are departed. / And their friends, the loitering heirs of city directors; / Departed, have left no addresses"). We thus obtain from the poet's experience, which has arisen out of his interaction with the environment, a string of broken images, and these appear to cast the phenomenon of love into ever-changing shapes.

Such a montage of poetic fragments, glimpses of ordinary life, truncated references to history, Greek mythology, Wagner's Rhine-daughters, and Buddhism, sparks off an aesthetic experience in the sense in which Dewey conceived it. "The essential thing esthetically is our own mental activity of starting, traveling, returning to a starting point, holding on to the past, carrying it along; the movement of attention backwards and forwards, as these acts are executed by the mechanism of motor imagery. The resulting relations define *shape* and shape is *wholly* a matter of relation" (102). Thus the recipient is spurred into figuring relationships within this kaleidoscopically shifting imagery, and out of this activity an aesthetic experience begins to develop. What unleashes this aesthetically intriguing activity is the disconnected sequence of images; the interactive "doing" consists in sorting out the puzzles with which the perceiver is confronted; and the "undergoing" results in the patterns to be obtained from the intervention. There are a great many countervailing movements the perceiver feels called upon to make in view of the gaps to be bridged, the obstacles to be overcome, the ideas to be tested, but all of them aim to discover the relationship that makes the disconnected items fall into a pattern.

As the segments are thrown into relief against one another, so a theme and horizon structure begins to emerge. This means that each of the segments is to be viewed from the standpoint of another, thus becoming the theme which, in turn, becomes the horizon for what is to follow. For instance, something different is spotlighted when the promiscuous scene is viewed from the Spenserian allusion, and vice versa. In this respect each fragment imprints itself on another one, thereby splitting it up into a two-tiered reference: what it originally meant is contrasted by a superimposed reference that begins to play against it. Hence a reciprocal spotlighting occurs that endows the relationship with form. The latter makes each of the segments chosen by the poet – be it a Spenserian playfulness, a Marvellian winning of the world, a scene of promiscuity – reveal its limitations in relation to what it is meant to encompass, namely, love. The more the recipient becomes engaged in trying to unravel this tangle, the more intense will be the aesthetic experience purveyed by the work.

What further enhances the aesthetic experience triggered by Eliot's poem is the graduated sequence of experiences that shade off into one another. This tallies with the basic requirement for an aesthetic experience as outlined by Dewey: "The scope of a work of art is measured by the number and variety of elements coming from past experiences that are organically absorbed into the perception had here and now: They give it its body and its suggestiveness. They often come from sources too obscure to be identified in any conscious memorial way, and thus they create the aura and penumbra in which a work of art swims" (123). Eliot's string of references to love ranging from the sixteenth to the twentieth centuries telescopes highly diversified representations into one another, and so love emerges as a phenomenon to be transmitted as an experience only through a perpetual transcending of the modes through which it has been represented. This makes the actual form important, because representation freezes love into a definitive shape, which has to be outstripped if an experience of love is to be communicated to a recipient.

Moreover, each of the broken images appears to indicate that representation has to be ruptured for it to be faithful to what it is meant to represent. They all reveal that they are historically conditioned concepts of love, which still function as regulators in the production of an experience that develops by overstepping demarcations. In their metamorphoses, the images outstrip one another, as none of them could claim to be an adequate, let alone comprehensive, rendering of love. For this reason the shading of different experiences into one another is pertinent, because it allows the phenomenon of love to be enacted in the mirror of its history. The idea of love which now emerges is orchestrated for and by the recipients who, in interacting with it, will develop an aesthetic experience that carries them beyond themselves, thus fulfilling what Dewey considered to be the hallmark of aesthetic experience.

Eliot's poem contains two further steering devices to thrust its recipients beyond themselves: the title section which is an allusion to Buddha, and Tiresias, "in whom the two sexes meet" (72). Buddha preached the sermon invoked by the title "against the fires of lust and other passions,"[2] and Tiresias, as Eliot explains in his notes, "although a mere spectator and not indeed a 'character,' is yet the most important personage in the poem. [ ... ] What Tiresias *sees*, is in fact, the substance of the poem."[3] Everyday notions of love are thus annihilated, and only the mind's eye can perceive what ordinarily cannot be seen. Shedding what one is used to is a prerequisite for ordinary experience, but the aesthetic experience is extraordinary

153

in that the recipients must leave themselves in order to make the experience their own. This is the circularity through which Dewey captures "Art as Experience."

## Notes

1   John Dewey, *Art as Experience*, New York: Capricorn Books, [12]1958, p. 274. The sources of all other quotations from this volume are given in the text with references to the appropriate pages.
2   Frank Kermode, "Explanatory Notes," in T. S. Eliot, *The Waste Land and Other Poems*, ed. Frank Kermode, New York: Penguin Books, 1998, p. 101.
3   T. S. Eliot, *The Waste Land and Other Poems*, ed. Frank Kermode, New York: Penguin Books, 1998, pp. 72f.

# 12

# Showalter's "Toward a Feminist Poetics"

The title of Elaine Showalter's (b. 1941) essay indicates that there is no fully fledged feminist theory of the arts, and this is confirmed in the essay itself. "The anatomy, the rhetoric, the poetics, the history, await our writing. [ . . . ] The task of feminist critics is to find a new language, a new way of reading that can integrate our intelligence and our experience, our reason and our suffering, our scepticism and our vision. This enterprise should not be confined to women."[1] Why is the objective so hard to achieve, and what are the obstacles that have to be cleared?

The "current theoretical impasse in feminist criticism," Showalter believes,

> is more than a problem of finding "exacting definitions and a suitable terminology," or "theorizing in the midst of a struggle." It comes from our own divided consciousness, the split in each of us. We are both the daughters of the male tradition, of our teachers, our professors, our dissertation advisers, and our publishers – a tradition which asks us to be rational, marginal, and grateful; and sisters in a new women's movement which engenders another kind of awareness and commitment, which demands that we renounce the pseudo-success of token womanhood and the ironic masks of academic debate. How much easier, how less lonely it is not to awaken [ . . . ] Yet we cannot will ourselves to go back to sleep. (141)

The predicament thus outlined seems crippling when it comes to developing a feminist theory of art and literature, since the parameters for feminist theorizing cannot be discovered by dismantling what female scholars have been subjected to, although this is an indispensable preparatory task for revealing genuine differences, since "[f]eminist criticism cannot go around forever in men's ill-fitting hand-me-downs" (139). However, in the male-dominated marketplace of criticism, self-assertion of womanhood appears to be hedged in by the current states of theory. Thus the

> experience of women can easily disappear, become mute, invalid, and invisible, lost in the diagrams of the structuralist or the class conflict of the Marxists. Experience is not emotion; we must protest now as in the nineteenth century against the equation of the feminine with the irrational. But we must also recognize that the questions we most need to ask go beyond those that science can answer. We must seek the repressed messages of women in history, in anthropology, in psychology, and in ourselves, before we can locate the feminine not-said. (141)

Thus the dilemma outlined is twofold: (1) female experience cannot be articulated in purely formalist or political terms, although it requires structuring in order to be objectified, and political vindication in order to be acknowledged. The armory, however, provided by both structuralism and the class struggle tends to vitiate this experience. (2) Since female experience cannot be voiced through these available channels, it is prone to be dubbed as the other of what is rational. Can there be another way of reading and writing through which this female experience were able to reveal itself?

## Women as Readers

Elaine Showalter gives an example of a feminist critic's reading by referring to Irving Howe's interpretation of the opening scene of Thomas Hardy's *The Mayor of Casterbridge*, "which begins with the famous scene of the drunken Michael Henchard selling his wife and infant daughter for five guineas at a country fair." She quotes Howe's interpretation at some length in order to point out the salient features of a male reading: "To shake loose," Howe writes, "from one's wife; to discard the drooping rag of a woman, with her mute complaint and maddening passivity; to escape not by a slinking abandonment but through the public sale of her body to a stranger, as horses are sold at the fair; and thus to wrest, through sheer amoral wilfulness, a second chance out of life" (129). A woman, Showalter contends, "will have a different experience of this scene." The fantasies of the male critic distort the text insofar as Susan Henchard does not appear to be drooping, complaining, or passive. Furthermore, Howe appears to overlook the fact "that Henchard sells not only his wife but his child, a child who can only be a female. Patriarchal societies do not readily sell their sons, but daughters are all for sale sooner or later," when given away for marriage. According to Showalter, Howe also glosses over the fact that Hardy presented Henchard as a "self-proclaimed 'woman-hater,' a man who has felt at best a 'supercilious pity' for womankind," who is, however, "humbled and 'unmanned' by the collapse of his own virile façade, the loss of the mayor's chain, his master's authority, his father's rights" (130).

This is a deconstructionist reading of a paternalistic view, and indicates a trend to be observed in feminist criticism, which uncovers and condemns the **phallogocentric** attitude that informs a great deal of male criticism. However, Showalter is aware of the trap such a deconstructionist reading entails. Just as deconstruction tends to become captive to the position whose hidden assumptions it uncovers, she maintains that in "this analysis" of Hardy's novel "one of the problems of the feminist critique is that it is male-oriented. If we study stereotypes of women, the sexism of male critics, and the limited roles women play in literary history, we are not learning what women have felt and experienced, but only what men have thought women should be" (130). Thus a feminist reading has to be twofold. It must dismantle a phallogocentric reading, and simultaneously search for what a feminist reading can spotlight, which is summed up as follows: "Hardy's female characters in *The Mayor of Casterbridge*, as in his other novels, are somewhat idealized and melancholy projections of a repressed male self" (130). What this dual countering of male criticism and Hardy's novel reveals is the difficulty of voicing the genuinely female experience that a feminist poetics strives for. Jonathan Culler has pinpointed this as the inherent problem of reading like a woman: "The appeal to the experience of the reader provides leverage for displacing or undoing the system of concepts or procedures of male criticism, but 'experience' always has this divided, duplicitous character: it has always already occurred and yet is still to be produced – an indispensable point of reference, yet never simply there."[2]

In an important essay on "Representing Ophelia," Showalter tries to meet the challenge that poses itself to feminist reading. She runs through the gamut of Ophelia's various representations during the last four centuries up to the present, in which Ophelia has been used as a paradigm for prevailing ideologies ranging from the fallen woman to the specifications of psychiatric findings. "But since the 1970s," Showalter writes, "we have had a feminist discourse which has offered a new perspective on Ophelia's

157

madness as protest and rebellion. For many feminist theorists, the madwoman is a heroine, a powerful figure who rebels against the family and the social order; and the hysteric who refuses to speak the language of the patriarchal order, who speaks otherwise, is a sister."[3] This assessment, however, is not just a straightforward assertion but emerges as a result of the contextuality that Showalter has scrutinized. She therefore contends that when

> feminist criticism chooses to deal with representation, [ ... ] it must aim for a maximum interdisciplinary contextualism, in which the complexity of attitudes towards the feminine can be analyzed in their fullest cultural and historical frame [ ... ] There is no "true" Ophelia for whom feminist criticism must unambiguously speak, but perhaps only a Cubist Ophelia of multiple perspectives, more than the sum of all her parts.[4]

It is this rootedness in different historical settings that generates a multi-faceted experience, arising out of the reactions to what women have been subjected to. Yet, simultaneously, a "Cubist Ophelia" reveals that the very diversity of such an experience is difficult to encompass in critical discourse.

## Women as Writers

In her essay "Woman and Fiction" (1929) Virginia Woolf describes the situation of a woman writer, spotlighting the obstacles when it comes to conveying a female experience in creative writing. The title of her essay, she maintains, is meant to suggest an ambiguity, "for in dealing with women as writers, as much elasticity as possible is desirable; it is necessary to leave oneself room to deal with other things besides their work, so much has that work been influenced by conditions that have nothing whatever to do with art."[5]

> The extraordinary woman depends on the ordinary woman. It is only when we know what were the conditions of the average woman's life – the number of her children, whether she had money of her own, if she had a room to herself, whether she had help in bringing up her family, if she had servants, whether part of the housework was her task – it is only when we can measure the way of life and the experience of life made possible to the ordinary woman that we can account for the success or failure of the extraordinary woman as a writer. (77)

It is the woman's burden of daily routine that conditions not only her writing habits but also the topics she writes about. This is one of the reasons why her experiences have frequently been locked away in diaries, memoirs, and autobiographies, a great many of which have only recently seen the light of day.

When the first breakthrough of women writers occurred in the nineteenth century, it is significant to note that the four great novelists – Jane Austen, Emily Brontë, Charlotte Brontë, and George Eliot – had no children, and only two of them were married. But even after upper-class women writers eventually had "a room of their own," the environment still hedged them in, allowing at best a critical response. "Thus, when a woman comes to write a novel," Virginia Woolf maintains, "she will find that she is perpetually wishing to alter the established values – to make serious what appears insignificant to a man, and trivial what is to him important. And for that, of course, she will be criticized; for the critic of the opposite sex will be genuinely puzzled and surprised by an attempt to alter the current scale of values, and will see in it not merely a difference of view, but a view that is weak, or trivial, or sentimental, because it differs from his own" (81). Relating herself to a male-dominated world, the scope of a female writer becomes proportionately narrow, and leaves little else for her to do but to undermine the standards of this world. Hence the actual life of the woman shrinks to anonymity, and it is only recently "that this dark country is beginning to be explored in fiction" (82).

Now we can see, as Showalter has indicated, why it is so difficult to spell out a female experience, because female writers have only recently come into focus through the change of circumstances. Thus Virginia Woolf writes: "The aloofness that was once within the reach of genius and originality is only now coming within the reach of ordinary women" (80). This advance – under way since the 1920s – begins to reveal, in Showalter's words, the "feminist content of feminine art [which] is typically oblique, displaced, ironic, and subversive; one has to read between the lines, in the missed possibilities of the text" ("Poetics," 138). And even though a male-dominated culture no longer overshadows women's writings, still "in Woolf's famous definition of life: 'a luminous halo, a semi-transparent envelope surrounding us from the beginning of consciousness to the end,' there is a submerged metaphor of uterine withdrawal and containment" (139).

A feminist theory does not seem to have come into its own as yet, because it is impeded by what it has to react to. When Edith Wharton speaks of her childhood occupations, she says: "My imagination lay there, coiled and sleeping, a mute hibernating creature, and at the least touch of common things – flowers, animals, words, especially the sound of words, apart from their meaning – it already stirred in its sleep, and then sank back into its own rich dream, which needed so little feeding from the outside that it instinctively rejected whatever another imagination had already adorned and completed."[6] What is implied in this statement is the fact that the imagination is not a self-activating human potential but has to be prodded into action – albeit very lightly – by a stimulus from outside. What quickens Wharton's childhood fantasies are things of nature and bodily sensations, which enrich the dreamy atmosphere in which she feels immersed. Such a situation is bound to change whenever the imagination is activated by the challenges of a patriarchically organized society. Quite apart from the question whether there are biologically rooted differences between a woman's imagination and a man's, the former is inevitably exposed to what is foreign to it, and hence is fettered in its unfolding.

## Revisions and Additions

The state of feminist poetics has been succinctly outlined by Annette Kolodny, who suggests "that the current hostilities might be transformed into a true dialogue with our critics if we at last made explicit what appear, to this observer, to constitute three crucial propositions to which our special interest inevitably gives rise."[7] The three propositions are as follows: "(1) literary history (and with that, the historicity of literature) is a fiction; (2) insofar as we are taught how to read, what we engage are not texts but paradigms; and finally, (3) since the grounds upon which we assign aesthetic value to texts are never infallible, unchangeable, or universal, we must examine not only our aesthetics but, as well, the inherent biases and assumptions informing the critical methods which (in part) shape our aesthetic responses" (151). Literary history is a fiction insofar as there is no definitive understanding of the past as the canon appears to suggest, because the past is called up and utilized "on behalf of a better understanding of the present" (151). Thus the past is continually reinterpreted, and this goes hand in hand with a reinterpretation of the present. And it is the introduction of choices and observations by "feminist literary theorists" that effects a "reshaping [of] our sense of the past" (152). The second proposition follows from the first. Instead of being guided by the paradigms of the canon, we should read the texts women have composed in order to get acquainted with "the lying-in room, the parlor, the nursery, the kitchen, the laundry, and so on – [whereas the usually male reader] will necessarily lack the capacity to fully interpret the dialogue or action embedded therein; for, as every good novelist knows, the meaning of any character's action or statement is inescapably a function of the specific situation in which it is embedded" (155). "Males ignorant of women's 'values' or conceptions of the world will, necessarily, be poor readers of works that in any sense recapitulate their codes" (156). Thus an unbiased reading of women's texts will remove the blinkers set by paradigms and instead enrich the canon. Again the third proposition follows from the second. It "calls into question that recurrent tendency in criticism to establish norms for the evaluation of literary works when we might better serve the cause of literature by developing standards for evaluating the adequacy of our critical methods. [ ... ] The choice [ ... ] is not between retaining or discarding aesthetic values; rather, the choice is between having some awareness of what constitutes (at least in part) the bases of our aesthetic responses and going without such an awareness" (157).

The propositions advanced intend to revise certain entrenched conceptions in literary criticism, such as the idea of the canon as an unalterable assembly of artistic achievements. Since the canon also represents "cultural capital," it is more than ever opportune to augment this capital through the addition of what women writers are able to contribute to it. The canon will no longer be a monolith but will be reshaped by new additions, giving the cultural capital a revitalized currency. Thus the canon will tend to become global, as the articulation of categorically different experiences furnishes a broadening of guidance in a world in which we have to rely on our last subsidy: the imagination bodied forth in the wide range of human experiences.

If feminist criticism sets out in this direction, it is only natural that its procedures should be open to inspection. Whenever this happens, a confrontational attitude will be replaced by a commitment to self-clarification, which in the end will be more persuasive for those who still have reservations about feminist aesthetics at a time when self-defense is no longer necessary. In spite of a still prevailing diversity, Kolodny contends that this "would finally place us securely where, all along, we should have been: camped out, on the far side of the minefield, with the other pluralists and pluralisms" (159). But she also sounds a warning: "just because we will no longer tolerate the specifically sexist omissions and oversights of earlier critical schools and methods does not mean that, in their stead, we must establish our own 'party line'" (161).

## Notes

1 Elaine Showalter, "Toward a Feminist Poetics," in Elaine Showalter, ed., *The New Feminist Criticism: Essays on Women, Literature, and Theory*, New York: Pantheon Books, 1985, pp. 141f. The sources of all other quotations from this essay are given in the text with references to the appropriate pages.

2 Jonathan Culler, *On Deconstruction: Theory and Criticism after Structuralism*, Ithaca: Cornell University Press, 1982, p. 63.

3 Elaine Showalter, "Representing Ophelia: Women, Madness, and the Responsibilities of Feminist Criticism," in Charles Kaplan and William Anderson, eds., *Criticism: Major Statements*, New York: St. Martin's Press, [3]1991, p. 709.

4 Ibid., pp. 709f.

5 Virginia Woolf, *Granite and Rainbow*, New York: Harcourt, Brace, 1958, p. 76. The sources of all other quotations from this volume are given in the text with references to the appropriate pages.

6 Edith Wharton, *A Backward Glance*, New York: Appleton-Century, 1934, p. 4.

7 Annette Kolodny, "Dancing Through the Minefield: Some Observations on the Theory, Practice, and Politics of a Feminist Literary Criticism," in Showalter, ed., *New Feminist Criticism*, p. 151. The sources of all other quotations from this essay are given in the text with references to the appropriate pages.

# 13

# Theory in Perspective

The approaches that we have outlined reveal the multifaceted nature of art, which distinguishes theory from aesthetics as developed by the prominent philosophical systems of the nineteenth century. If art can mean so many different things when grasped in cognitive terms, the theories bear eloquent witness to the fact that there is no definitive determination of what it is. In other words, an ontological definition of art is now out of the question. But that was exactly what nineteenth-century aesthetics endeavored to provide, albeit with a range of changing "ontologies," from Hegel's conception of art as a vehicle for the appearance of truth to Adorno's view of it as the foreshadowing of perfection in a depraved world.

In contradistinction to aesthetics, the various modern theories allow us to perceive that art cannot be explained ontologically, but only in terms of how it functions. Even statements about form and structure are a means of grasping function, and preconceived notions of the nature of art have given way to multiple pathways of exploration. Hence the emphasis on function not only marks a break away from classical aesthetics, but also alerts us to important twentieth-century trends that are brought into focus by the theories concerned. Their different objectives give rise to contours of an intellectual landscape.

## An Intellectual Landscape

The phenomenological theory conceives the work of art as an intentional object to be distinguished from real and ideal objects. An intentional object is not given, but has to be built, and this requires elucidation of the phases through which it comes into being. The work of art creates a specific form of intentionality, and simultaneously exhibits the basic features of the latter. While intention is an act that directs itself to something in order to grasp it, the intentional object points to "metaphysical qualities" without, however, being able to control its intended impact. The theory, which presents an anatomy of the intentional object, throws light on a basic issue of twentieth-century thought – namely, how objects are given to consciousness and how this approaches and grasps what is given to it.

The hermeneutical theory sees the work of art as a means of enhancing self-understanding. An investigation of understanding is guided by awareness that there is a gap between what is to be understood and the subject who is supposed to understand it. Owing to this gap, all normative concepts that might guide or even determine understanding have to be deconstructed, since the gap has to be negotiated. This makes understanding into two-way traffic, because in comprehending what is alien, the self is simultaneously alerted to its own dispositions. Consequently, an encounter with the works of art that have accumulated through human history makes self-understanding into an ongoing process of ever-growing self-awareness.

Gestalt theory is based on the idea that ordinary perception is already a creative act through which we group data into percepts. We lure into presence something that is out there, though not in the form in which we grasp it. Hence the work of art is no longer conceived as an imitation of a given object, as in the Aristotelian tradition; instead, representation is a performative act by means of which something is given presence. What is represented is not in the nature of an object but of a schema. Into this have been inserted corrections that arise out of "making," which is guided by being "matched" to what the artist may have seen in the mind's eye. Such a representation can only take place because performance gives presence to something which, as an object, did not exist before the operation that produced it.

Reception theory is concerned with the impact exercised by the work of art, which is dual by nature: it impacts both upon reality and upon the reader. Making inroads into the reality within which it was produced, the work rearranges the structures and the semantics of the social and cultural systems in which it intervenes. These rearrangements move the systems themselves into focus, and hold them up for observation. Such a reaction to realities brings something into the world that did not exist before, and this has the character of a virtual reality which the reader is given to process, thereby allowing reception theory to spotlight what the work of art makes the reader do.

Semiotic theory points to the fact that the world cannot be determined or defined, but only read. Reading signs is the basic objective of semiotics in order to spell out what is observed. The sign as a signifier denotes a signified which, however, requires a commonly shared code in order to fix the meaning of what it designates. But where codes come from, and "who" created them, remains an open question. The work of art, however, makes the signs ambiguous and self-focusing, thereby violating codes, and code violation in turn becomes a matrix for code production.

The life of the psyche proceeds, according to the psychoanalytical theory, as a multiple interlocking of primary with secondary processes. Exposition of the creative process focuses on the basic operation of these complex interrelationships. The work of art produced through the creative process illuminates the phases of its emergence in a sequence ranging from ego decomposition to reintrojection, thus revealing the ego rhythm as the minimum content of art. This rhythm, pulsating between oceanic dedifferentiation and structured focusing, features the subject in its continual restructuring of itself.

Marxist theory in all its variants has been concerned with the self-production of human life. Initially, the work of art was regarded as a superstructural phenomenon conditioned by the material base out of which it arose. As this qualification revealed nothing about the nature of the relationship between work and base, it triggered attempts to specify the connection. The concept of the work as a reflection held sway for quite some time, until it was replaced by a view of art as a paradigm of creative practice. Instead of reflecting material reality, it forms reality, which almost reverses the initial base/superstructure relationship, because the creative practice cannot be reduced to representation or reflection. What makes the work of art paradigmatic is the triadic relationship between its components, i.e., the dominant, the residual, and the emergent, which sets the productive process in motion. Out of this dynamic interrelationship arises the complexity of material reality in all its social, cultural, and artistic diversity. Thus art becomes the hallmark of the formative process through which human beings create both their world and themselves.

In deconstruction difference looms large. Whatever there is, is marked by difference both internally and externally, because phenomena have a differential structure, and each one is different from others. This is due to the fact that phenomena do not originate out of themselves. Thus the origin is forever deferred, because every phenomenon is inhabited by its own other. Deconstruction is basically a reading that tries to open up what has been eclipsed. Uncovering the absent leads to an insight into the open-ended dependence of every phenomenon.

Generative anthropology conceives of culture as the deferral of violence by means of representation. Initially, representation arose out of a gesture that inhibited humans from getting what they wished to appropriate. This interdiction resulted in a division of human life into center and periphery, which became the frame of human culture. The center was always something coveted by those on the periphery, whose growing resentment at being excluded from centrality fueled the life of culture, which developed through the center and periphery constantly changing places. Literature assumes a dual function in this ongoing alternation: it operates as a procedure of discovery by acting out what the prevailing structure of center and periphery has made inaccessible, and by representing this cultural frame it monitors the course of events, thus providing distance.

For pragmatism, experience is the be-all and end-all. But such a bounded horizon raised the question of how experience could be assessed if there was no stance beyond it. Hence aesthetic experience as purveyed by the work of art was considered to be of a special kind, and it was elevated into a measuring rod in terms of which all other experiences could be distinguished from one another and qualified accordingly.

Feminism tries to develop a gender-specific poetics by undermining the prevalent male hegemony. In doing so, feminist critics have explored the political potential of the work of art, which they have sought to exploit. However, the politics of the aesthetic – significant though it may be – has proved difficult to focus on, let alone to formulate.

The salient features of an intellectual landscape now begin to emerge, offering a panorama of twentieth-century thought. The work of art, approached from different angles and grasped in terms of these approaches, lends itself to charting this landscape. By elucidating the formation of the intentional object, art is made to reflect on intentionality as an operation of mapping. Through its encounter with the subject, it figures the process of self-understanding. In freeing representation from imitating a given object, it highlights performance as an activity that brings into presence something hitherto nonexisting. By intervening in reality, it is made to rearrange that which does exist, and which the recipient is given to process. Through code violation, it turns into a code-producing matrix, the reading of which allows us to monitor communication. By revealing the workings and the

166

function of the ego rhythm, it is made to depict the subject as continually restructuring itself. Through its creative practice, it projects modes of human self-production. By uncovering what has been excluded, it exhibits the way in which every phenomenon is inhabited by something other. By enacting the basic cultural fabric of center and periphery, it stages what is otherwise inaccessible. When it provides an aesthetic experience, it opens up an horizon that makes it possible to assess all kinds of experience. And when it goes against the grain, it releases an armory for subversion.

The specific elaborations of intentionality, self-understanding, performance, intervention, communication, ego rhythm, absence, inaccessibility, experience, and politics which these theories are concerned with, elevate the work of art into an illumination of central twentieth-century concerns.

In charting this landscape, the theories provide a comprehensive frame for a method of interpretation. However, as all of them are abstractions from concrete encounters with the works, they also conceive art as a prism that allows the mapping of intellectual issues such as we have seen. Finally, they open up an insight into the human condition by answering the question why humans need art. On the one hand, the theory functions as a tool, and on the other, it makes a general statement about how art functions in human life.

## The Fabric of Theory

The theories presented model their framework according to the task they set out to accomplish. Approaching the work of art from different angles results in a diversity of structural components, and these work differently together in each of the theories concerned. What we can observe is an array of architectural and operational models. If the framework of a theory is architectural, it is basically a grid superimposed on the work for the purpose of cognition; if it is operational, it is basically a networking structure for the purpose of elucidating how something emerges.

The exposition of the intentional object, as demonstrated by the phenomenological theory, requires a scaffolding that allows us to perceive how the levels of the work are geared to one another for the intentional object to arise. Thus the layered structure constitutes the architecture for pre-aesthetic cognition of the work of art. An architecturally conceived framework is a fairly stable one, within which everything is more or less under control.

This also applies to an architectural frame that allows for certain movements, as in the anthropological theory, in which the duality between center and periphery permits the mobility of changing places. Thus binarism is the architectural blueprint for the rise and life of culture, and whenever theories are architecturally structured, they are permeated by an epistemological concern.

It is different with operational theories, which highlight what the work of art is potentially able to reveal. Cognition becomes subservient to the display of art as an experiential reality. Conceiving of representation in terms of performance, as gestalt theory does, means illuminating something that hitherto did not exist. Indeterminacies begin to arise, and whenever these are to be coped with, the components of theories are bound to assume a networking structure, because indeterminacies have to be narrowed down. Schema and correction are the identifiable components, allowing us to read the otherwise unfathomable making and matching.

Viewing the work of art in terms of the inroads made into contextual realities, whose structure and semantics are broken up, gives rise to a different kind of indeterminacy. The work appears to be punctured by blanks and negations on both its syntactical and its paradigmatic axis, which means not only bringing order to a disconnected sequence, but also fathoming what might have caused the referential reality to break up. Reception theory structures indeterminacies insofar as blanks and negations specify authorial strategies, and mark what the reader is given to resolve.

In its attempt to grasp the rise of art through a rhythmically shifting, decomposing ego realized by splintering, subconscious scanning and reintrojection, the psychoanalytical theory teems with negative terminology. The ego rhythm swings between oceanic dedifferentiation and structured focusing, exhibiting the minimum content of art in upheavals and threats that are to be mastered. The deeper one digs into the origins of art, the more handicapped the conceptual language tends to become.

In deconstruction stable constituents appear to vanish altogether, as evinced by the dual countering between the devastating and the stating "jetty." The one disrupts hierarchies by exposing their supplementarity, and the other states what is hidden by pointing up what is absent. The operation proceeds as a play movement, adumbrating an artistic element of a transgression of boundaries.

There is a dual inference to be derived from our observations so far. Translating the work of art into cognitive terms is bound to produce indeterminacies that arise out of what a conceptual language is unable to grasp. Tackling indeterminacies, however, leads to art being inscribed into the cognitive terminology by giving it a negative slant.

Another variant of theory formation is to be discerned in semiotics. Initial assumptions concerning the work of art triggered a host of differing definitions of the iconic sign. Obviously, the original concept of the latter proved to be no longer tenable, and its ensuing repairs revealed a desire to preserve it by providing alternative definitions. This eventually reached a point where iconicity had to be jettisoned as a designation of the work of art. Such a development resembles the process which Thomas Kuhn has described, in which "normal science" – i.e., working within and adhering to a paradigm – runs up against persistent anomalies, so that the paradigm can no longer be defended, and hence has to be given up. When the iconic sign was discarded, it was replaced by an operation which realized itself in a countervailing movement. Violations of code-governed sign functioning made it possible to delineate the workings of art as a code-producing matrix, but the cognitive terms employed for grasping art, such as ambiguity or violation, again have a negative slant, indicating how art inscribes itself into a cognitive grasp.

A Marxist-inspired theory developed along the same lines as semiotics. The initial presupposition of base and superstructure as a means of defining art had to be abandoned, and so did the many attempts to repair the initial definition. This was replaced by the idea of developing multiple stances, such as signs, notations, conventions, genres, forms, and author-ship, whose interrelation made it possible to ascertain the operations that set the creative practice in motion. In Marxist terms, then, art spawned an array of viewpoints when subjected to comprehension.

Finally, the pragmatist theory is conditioned by the fact that the work of art cannot be investigated independently of the experience obtained from it. But as the work of art engenders the experience, it is itself to be considered in terms of what it makes possible. Thus a circular operation gets under way, which meant not only to negotiate the gap between the aesthetic experi-ence of the recipient and the work of art, but also to ascertain whether the work purveys the experience or merely triggers it. Purveying is content-laden, whereas triggering leaves the recipient to provide the content. But as the recipient could hardly produce the content, circularity is bound to operate between purveying and triggering. Circularity is not an act of comprehension but of bridging gaps between what can and cannot be ascertained.

What are the inferences to be drawn from the structural inscription of the work of art into the various operations outlined? Grasping a work of art in theoretical terms appears to have different effects on respective approaches. It plunges initial presuppositions into a sequence of revisions (semiotics and Marxism). It gives a negative slant to the conceptual languages employed (gestalt, reception, deconstruction, psychoanalytical theory). It inscribes itself into the reasoning through indeterminacies (gestalt and pragmatism) that range from blanks and negations (reception) through a maze of multiple pathways (psychoanalytical theory) to free play (deconstruction). They are all markers through which the work of art imprints itself on every operational attempt to capture it cognitively. This situation is different with an architecturally conceived theory (phenomenological, anthropological theory), whose epistemological concern subjects art to a preconceived thought system for the purpose of obtaining the knowledge that can be derived from art.

## What Does the Multiplicity of Theories Tell Us?

Art, so it seems, does not carry its own determination within itself. Yet it provokes determinations of the kind outlined by the theories presented. At the same time, it appears to make allowances for different conceptualizations, all of which – insofar as they are theories – require closure, thus making the work of art seem open-ended, because the theory is unable to encompass it in its entirety. However, our experiences suggest that the work of art is not open-ended but only gives this impression when theories try to capture it.

Whenever art is theorized, the framework of the theory involuntarily reveals the historicity of the basic decisions that have fashioned it. Each theory, we may conclude, functions as a divining-rod for the historical need that it is called upon to cope with. Thus the referentially inexhaustible reservoir can be tapped and utilized according to historical exigencies. Basically, then, a theory negotiates between the prevailing exigencies and the arts, and whenever this happens, the arts are integrated into a sociocultural context to serve whatever purpose.

This may also account for the reductions to which a work of art is subjected whenever it is grasped in cognitive terms, and in this sense theory also produces what it is unable to encompass. Although it cannot be said that theories sequentially take up what appears to have been sacrificed by their predecessors, all of them operate according to the same principle of reduction, and so the sequence is bound to grasp other aspects of art's potential. This may be one of the reasons why we have such a multiplicity of theories. Furthermore, just as the dominant philosophical systems of the nineteenth century developed an aesthetics in order to conceive of art in terms of their own tenets, so basic disciplines in the humanities feel equally called upon to provide an exposition of art.

The diversity of theories gives rise to the question whether there is a general undercurrent operative in all of them. In fact most of them assert that art comes to fruition in the recipient. In phenomenological theory it is the concretization of the work by the reading process that brings the layered structure to life. In hermeneutical theory it is the self which, in encountering the work of art, gains in self-understanding. In gestalt theory the beholder's active participation brings the work to fruition. In semiotic theory it is the reading of the idiolect that unfolds the deviational matrix. In psychoanalytical theory the work of art is anchored in the ego rhythm. In deconstruction it is the reading of the "postcard" which the author has sent into the world that creates dissemination of reception. In anthropological theory it is the basic cultural frame that is staged, allowing readers to gain distance from what they are otherwise entangled in. And in pragmatist theory the work of art provides aesthetic experience for its recipients.

What does this pervasive trend indicate? The work of art, once embedded in a sacred, religious, or secular setting and then uprooted and carried into the museum – meant to celebrate its autonomy – has found a new location in the recipient as beholder, spectator, and reader. The array of theories thus highlights an important shift in the localization of the arts, which are taken out of the museum and transferred into the recipient's "mind and soul" as their new home and habitation.

This leaves a final question, which, however, can only be tentatively answered. Why is there such an urge to translate the work of art into cognition? There are two possible answers: we want to know what it is that we ourselves have experienced, or we want to comprehend the unfamiliarity witnessed in the work of art. In the one instance we strive to obtain knowledge of experience, and in the other to grasp what exceeds referentiality and crosses boundaries. In both cases theory confronts us with the paradoxical urge to capture in cognitive terms something which by nature eludes cognition.

# 14

# Postscript

## *Postcolonial Discourse: Said*

Let us conclude by casting a glance at a contrasting foil to theory, which is of equal importance in the humanities today: discourse. Theory is of fairly recent vintage, whereas discourse has a comparatively long history. Theory explores a given subject matter, which it translates into cognitive terms, thus systematically opening up access to whatever is under scrutiny. Discourse maps a territory and determines the features of what it charts, thus projecting a domain to be lived in. There are a great many current discourses, such as hegemonic, oppositional, feminist, minority, ethnic, colonial, anticolonial, and postcolonial, to name only the most prominent forms. Each individual one claims to pattern the world by equating it with a ground plan. We shall now focus on the postcolonial discourse developed by Edward Said (1935–2003), the exposition of which will be twofold: to exhibit the structural features of discourse, and to highlight what its mapping is meant to achieve.

## Basic Features of Discourse

Before discussing postcolonial discourse, let us remind ourselves of the constituents of discourse formation. This is all the more pertinent since the field of postcolonial studies appears to be "thoroughly riven with disciplinary self-doubt and mutual suspicion,"[1] which turns "postcolonialism" into "a portmanteau word – an umbrella thrown up over many heads, against a great deal of rain. Confusion necessarily abounds in the area."[2] Among the different attempts to clear up this confusion, discourse analysis plays a significant role. Those who advocate a postcolonial discourse take their cue

> from Michel Foucault's dismissal of a Marxist theory of ideology in favor of a notion of "discourse": at heart, a notion that considers social subjects, social consciousness, to be formed not through ideologies that have their base in economic or class relations but through a form of power that circulates in and around the social fabric, framing social subjects through strategies of regulation and exclusion, and constructing forms of "knowledge" which make possible that which can be said and that which cannot.[3]

For Edward Said, Foucault's contention "that the fact of writing itself is a systematic conversion of the power relationship between controller and controlled into mere 'written' words"[4] becomes the overriding guideline for the postcolonial discourse that he unfolds in his *Culture and Imperialism*.

*L'Ordre du discours*[5] carries a double meaning: it is both order and command. We "should not imagine," Foucault contends, "that the world presents us with a legible face, leaving us merely to decipher it; it does not work hand in glove with what we already know; there is no prediscursive fate disposing the world in our favor. We must conceive discourse as a violence that we do to things, or, at all events, as a practice we impose on them; it is in this practice that the events of discourse find the principle of their regularity."[6] This regularity organizes what "things" are meant to be, and discourse as an imposition is not a form of cognition but a practice, which distinguishes it from theory. There is no prior signification within what has to be arranged, and hence "we must not imagine some unsaid thing, or an unthought, floating about the world, interlacing with all its forms and events. Discourse must be treated as a discontinuous activity, its different manifestations sometimes coming together, but just as easily unaware of, or excluding each other" (AK 229). This is to be witnessed, for instance, in the encounter between postcolonial, colonial, and anticolonial discourses, whose conflicts involuntarily reveal what has been intentionally excluded in the process of mapping. It is their collision which generates a critical potential that appears all the more expedient as the discursive order not only structures the domain charted, but also preordains its practice. If discourse has "the power of constituting domains of objects, in relation to which one can affirm or deny true or false propositions" (AK 234), then the components are of vital concern.

Outlining these constituents, Foucault starts out from the supposition "that in every society the production of discourse is at once controlled, selected, organized and redistributed to a certain number of procedures, whose role is to avert its powers and its dangers, to cope with chance events, and to evade its ponderous, awesome materiality" (AK 216). Hence discourse is governed by rules, of which the all-pervasive one, operative in all forms, is that of exclusion; it marks what is prohibited. The principles of exclusion are manifold. Discourse is not free to say just anything but is basically confined to the division between true and false, and is simultaneously driven to assert what is taken for truth. "[W]e are unaware of the prodigious machinery of the will to truth, with its vocation of exclusion" (AK 220).

Foucault continually details the mechanisms of exclusion, summed up under the umbrella concept of "rarefaction," which indicates the control and the confinement that shape the discourse. But rarefaction also points to what the discourse is silent about, owing to the principle of exclusion which always invokes "the rules of some discursive 'policy'" (AK 224). Prohibition and the division between truth and falsehood are external procedures that police the discourse, and this is internally controlled by what Foucault calls the commentary, the author, and the discipline. All of them are pertinent to colonial and anticolonial discourse in the broadest sense. The commentary is meant to complete what the text says, the "author function" is the controlling reference for what the reading is intended to convey, and the discipline is "defined by groups of objects, methods, and their corpus of propositions considered to be true, the interplay of rules and definitions, of techniques and tools: all these constitute a sort of anonymous system, freely available to whoever wishes, or whoever is able to make use of them" (AK 222). As we shall see, all three internal retrenchments function as basic constituents of colonial discourse. The commentary glosses over what colonials think of themselves, the author brings his own culture to bear, and the discipline of narrative literature casts the natives in terms of diversified "propositions." The rarefaction of discourse thus becomes manifest.

However, the order of discourse is not fully covered by this mechanism of exclusion and control, because rarefaction is brought about not only by the external and internal retrenchments but also, as Foucault maintains, by "a third group of rules serving to control the discourse. Here, we are no longer dealing with the mastery of the power contained within discourse [ ... ] it is more a question of determining the conditions under which it may be employed, of imposing a certain number of rules upon those individuals who employ it, thus denying access to everyone else. This amounts to a rarefaction among speaking subjects: none may enter into discourse on a specific subject unless he has satisfied certain conditions or if he is not, from the outset, qualified to do so" (AK 224f.). This makes it obvious that discourse not only charts a world, but is also a practice that guides the way we live within this world. Hence there are rituals of initiation, which the subject has to undergo in order to become a participant in "the fellowships of discourse [les 'sociétés de discours'[7]]" (AK 225). The rituals are regulations of admittance, similar to those required by every system of education, the outcome of which is again dual: the individual – for instance the colonizer – is subjected to the power of discourse, but is simultaneously enabled to wield it.

There is a final duality that marks the order of discourse, which becomes all the more obvious when we realize that the "reality" we live in consists of a welter of discourses, which are bound to enter into multiple relationships. Rarefaction as the hallmark tends to become ambivalent, and this ambivalence is engendered through the very constituents of discourse. According to Foucault, we "tend to see, in an author's fertility, in the multiplicity of commentaries and in the development of a discipline so many infinite resources available for the creation of discourse. Perhaps so, but they are nonetheless principles of constraint, and it is probably impossible to appreciate their positive, multiplicatory role without first taking into consideration their restrictive, constraining role" (AK 224). Thus the positive side of rarefaction is stressed. "But, once we have distinguished these principles of rarefaction, once we have ceased considering them as a fundamental and creative action, what do we discover behind them?" (AK 229). Certainly "not any continuous outpouring of meaning, and certainly not any monarchy of the signifier" (AK 234). What they reveal instead are the conditions responsible for the imposition of constraints. The latter, however, are principles of exclusion, and what has been excluded is brought to the fore whenever discourses become antagonistic.

## Strategies of Postcolonial Discourse

Edward Said's postcolonial discourse, as developed in his book *Culture and Imperialism*,[8] works as an imposition in the Foucauldian sense on both colonial and anticolonial discourses. These are the "objects" to be charted, and it is this tripartite relationship through which postcolonial discourse gains salience. Hence the latter assumes a critical position toward what it operates upon, although it has the same structure as the discourses on which it focuses its power. It is also marked by the same rarefaction that distinguishes all discourses, which are only differentiated from one another by the motivation that causes their respective restrictions. Said outlines his objective as follows:

> I want first to consider the actualities of the intellectual terrains both common and discrepant in post-imperial public discourse, especially concentrating on what in this discourse gives rise to and encourages the rhetoric and politics of blame. Then, using the perspectives and methods of what might be called a comparative literature of imperialism, I shall consider the ways in which a reconsidered or revised notion of how [*sic*] a post-imperial intellectual attitude might expand the overlapping community between metropolitan and formerly colonized societies. By looking at the different experiences contrapuntally, as making up a set of what I call intertwined and overlapping histories, I shall try to formulate an alternative both to a politics of blame and to the even more destructive politics of confrontation and hostility. (18)

What makes Said's approach particularly appealing within the framework of a book dealing with theory formation in the realm of art is the prominence he accords to narrative literature as the shaping force of imperial discourse. Thus literature assumes a completely different function under the auspices of colonialism because, as Said contends, "cultural forms like the novel [ ... ] were immensely important in the formation of imperial attitudes, references, and experiences" (xii). As "narrative plays such a remarkable part in the imperial quest" (xxii), colonialism cannot be confined to economic exploitation, or political hegemony, but is driven by the mighty propellant of culture that molds imperial discourse. The national culture of the metropolitan center becomes the overall imposition, and literature conditions this discourse with the narrative component as commentary, which is bound, in Foucault's words, to say "what has already been said, and repeat tirelessly what was, nevertheless, never said" (221).

This complicity between literature and imperialism brings to light the intimate connection between culture and politics, which is hardly admitted by the self-understanding of culture. Therefore Said focuses on "how the processes of imperialism occurred beyond the level of economic laws and political decisions, and – by predisposition, by the authority of recognizable cultural formations, by continuing consolidation within education, literature, and the visual and musical arts – were manifested at another significant level, that of the national culture, which we have tended to sanitize as a realm of unchanging intellectual monuments, free from worldly affiliations" (12f.). A certain duality thus becomes apparent: the realm of imagination turns out to be a political weapon, the employment of which becomes instrumental in justifying imperial domination.

The very observation that metropolitan culture energizes Western imperialism constitutes the operational drive of postcolonial discourse, which functions primarily as discourse analysis, i.e., laying bare how knowledge and fantasy are superimposed on distant lands that are ruled by the metropolitan center. This discursive practice is different from Marxism, deconstruction, and new historicism which, according to Said, "have avoided the major [ ... ] determining, political horizon of modern Western culture, namely imperialism" (62). Hence it is the task of postcolonial discourse to highlight this interrelation between culture and imperialism, which is to be achieved by contrapuntal reading. "The point is that contrapuntal reading must take account of both processes, that of imperialism and that of resistance to it, which can be done by extending our reading of the texts to include what was once forcibly excluded" (66f.). The thrust of such a procedure is multifaceted. First of all contrapuntal reading strives to articulate what the imperial discourse has concealed or excluded, and it brings to light why this has remained unexplored or deliberately ignored. Such a disclosure naturally rebounds on the assertions of imperial discourse, and so disclosure is the operational constraint of postcolonial discourse. But as resistance to colonialism is also two-sided, postcolonial discourse has to ferret out what has motivated the opposition. The overall disclosure of contrapuntal reading, however, is meant to lay open "how culture participates in imperialism [and] yet is somehow excused for its role" (107), although there are no reasons why it should be excused. Since Kant we have believed in the isolation of cultural and aesthetic realms from the worldly domain, but now it is time to link them again in order to discover what culture-inspired imperialism has shut out. This focus on what hegemonic discourses have suppressed is the hallmark of postcolonial discourse guided by the strategy of contrapuntal reading. Such a discourse, therefore, is not a theory, because charting the consequences of and resistance to imperialism aims to reveal what has hitherto been eclipsed, and this cannot be mistaken for the transcendental vantage point that structures a theoretical framework.

## The Novel as Imperial Discourse

Literature is permeated with references to Europe's overseas expansion, and continually maps its affiliations with the empire. "Nearly everywhere in nineteenth- and early twentieth-century British and French culture we find allusions to the fact of empire, but perhaps nowhere with more regularity and frequency than in the British novel" (62). From the countless instances in which the empire is a crucial setting, we shall single out Jane Austen, Joseph Conrad, and Rudyard Kipling.

It may come as a surprise to read Jane Austen's *Mansfield Park*, at least in parts, as a colonial discourse. And yet the insulated English setting of Mansfield Park draws its sustenance from Sir Thomas's Caribbean sugar plantation, "maintained by slave labor (not abolished until the 1830s); these are not dead historical facts but, as Austen certainly knew, evident historical realities" (89). There is a complete subordination of the colony to the metropolitan center. Whatever it lacks is provided by a West Indian plantation. Moreover, the positive ideas of home, nation, language, proper order, good behavior, and moral values, so obviously cherished in the social world of Mansfield Park, "tend to devalue other worlds, and perhaps more significantly from a retrospective point of view, they do not prevent or inhibit or give resistance to horrendously unattractive imperial practices" (81). This does not mean that the novel sets out to imperialize, but what is troubling is "how little Britain's great humanistic ideas [ . . . ] stand in the way of the accelerating imperial process" (82). Instead, Austen lets us observe how Sir Thomas transplants the ideas of ordination, law, and propriety that guide him at home to the administration of his plantation, thus foisting his attitudes on the colonials.

Imperialism shied away from even addressing the exploitation, let alone the life, of those who provided sustenance for the metropolitan center. This leads Said to the conclusion "that the novel, as a cultural artefact of bourgeois society, and imperialism are unthinkable without each other" (70f.). Jane Austen, Said indicates, takes imperialism for granted, which makes it appear as if it were just another British institution, and therefore she glosses over the intertwined histories of the overlapping territories, which a contrapuntal reading of the postcolonial discourse tries to bring to the fore.

Within the history of imperialism Joseph Conrad marks an important step, as he reflects on the divide between the experience of the dominant society and its impact on the subordinate realm. Such a dual perspective may have something to do with Conrad's position as an outsider, which allows him a fresh insight into a situation that the imperial culture has created. Thus the overlapping of territories and intertwining of histories, which Jane Austen ignored completely, now moves into focus. Yet there is neither synchrony nor correspondence between the two domains, so that the relationship between the imperial culture and the "civilization" that is brought to the distant lands remains unquestioned.

Conrad's *Heart of Darkness* is a telling example of how the imperialist divide is handled. Although the world-conquering attitude of Kurtz is exposed as just a form of looting, the listeners to Marlow's tale on the deck of the *Nellie* are not offered a full view of what Kurtz's exploitation may have meant to those who were its victims. There is no attempt to look for a non-imperialist alternative to the power the white man wields in the jungle, or the one Marlow wields as narrator.

> Thus Conrad encapsulates two quite different but intimately related aspects of imperialism: the idea that is based on power to take over territory, an idea utterly clear in its force and unmistakable consequences; and the practice that essentially disguises or obscures this by developing a justificatory regime of self-aggrandizing, self-originating authority interposed between the victim of imperialism and its perpetrator. We would completely miss the tremendous power of this argument if we were merely to lift it out of *Heart of Darkness*, like a message out of a bottle. (69)

Kurtz's ivory-trading empire and Marlow's narrative reveal a common theme: "Europeans performing acts of imperial mastery and will in (or about) Africa" (23). They fail, however, to understand what they call disablingly and disparagingly the "darkness." Whether Conrad himself had understood it remains in doubt; but even if he had, he did not articulate it, because "as a non-European 'darkness' [it is] in fact a non-European world *resisting* imperialism" (30).

Spotlighting this two-sidedness does not mean for Conrad that he must strike a balance. The exposure of Kurtz's looting and the intermittent garrulousness of Marlow when relating his experiences to an audience are at best threaded with traces of irony, but this never subverts the imperialist attitude. Hence it becomes the task of postcolonial discourse to represent what has been excluded by the colonial discourse. "Being on the inside shuts out the full experience of imperialism, edits it and subordinates it to the dominance of one Eurocentric and totalizing view" (28). What has been omitted, i.e., the suffering of people subjected to the greed-driven violence, and the hidden motivation that shapes Marlow's narrative of his journey along the river, has to be focused on as a counterbalance to Conrad's rather elaborate form of colonialism, whose sophistication tends to blind us to the "horror."

Rudyard Kipling's *Kim* gives the imperial discourse another turn by presenting the protagonist of the novel as a "liminal figure." Kim O'Hara is an Irish outcast boy who later becomes a player in the British Secret Service Great Game.

His duality is doubled up by Colonel Creighton, who is both an ethnographer, in charge of the "survey of India," and head of British Intelligence, thus representing "the almost insuperable contradiction between a political actuality based on force, and a scientific and humane desire to understand the Other hermeneutically and sympathetically in modes not influenced by force" (56). Creighton embodies the intimate relationship between knowledge and power, because "you cannot govern India unless you know India, and to know India means to understand the way it operates" (153). This knowledge, however, is never disinterested but is used to buttress power, following the principles of order and control. Creighton prefigures the Foucauldian discourse, and Kipling takes him to be "an ideal Indian official" (154). Although an awareness of otherness prevails, the "Other" is never engaged in its own right. Kipling refrains from viewing India in terms of the domineering white man who is in possession of the empire, but leaves no doubt that he accepts the "massive colonial system whose economy, functioning, and history has acquired the status of a virtual fact of nature" (134).

This is strikingly borne out by his treatment of the Indian mutiny of 1857 which, in spite of the horrendous reprisals by white men, Kipling considered a " 'calling' [of] the Indian mutineers 'to strict account' "(148). Hence Said can say: "So far is Kipling from showing two worlds in conflict that he has studiously given us only one, and eliminated any chance of conflict appearing altogether" (148). It was simply India's destiny to be ruled by Britain.

And yet *Kim* is teeming with minute and lovingly described features of Indian life, which had never previously occurred in colonial discourse. "To be able to see all India from the vantage of controlled observation: this is one great satisfaction. Another is to have at one's fingertips a character who can sportingly cross lines and invade territories, a little Friend of all the World – Kim O'Hara himself. It is by holding Kim at the center of the novel (just as Creighton the spy master holds the boy in the Great Game)

Kipling can *have* and enjoy India in a way that even imperialism never dreamed of" (155).

Kipling was not a neutral figure in the Anglo-Indian relationship but a prominent actor in it. Imperialism and the suffering it had caused were not on his agenda. However, he was fully aware that India was an "Other" offering a multifaceted and exotic life, which provided intense excitement. "The overlap between the political hold of the one and the aesthetic and psychological pleasure of the other is made possible by British imperialism itself: Kipling understood this, yet many of his later readers refuse to accept this troubling, even embarrassing truth" (161). India, for all her vastness and multifariousness, allowed the colonizer inconceivable pleasures, never available anywhere else. However, in order for these pleasures to be enjoyed, it was essential that India should be ruled by Britain. Colonialism, as a cloak for protecting the enchantment to be derived from the "Other," reveals the complicity between culture and imperialism.

When imperialism was on the wane, a debate about culture and empire began in both France and Britain. Albert Camus's narratives, for instance, became concerned with the actual state of Franco-Algerian affairs. However, he did not focus on their history and on any of the dramatic changes, because for him there was no such thing as an Algerian nation. Instead, he hailed Algeria as a new France that had to be communicated to the metropolitan audience in order to make it experience the life of the *colon*. This switch of perspectives, however, is still an imperial gesture, since Algeria was considered to be a part of French geography.

Said regards William Butler Yeats as the first prominent Western advocate of decolonization, "who during a period of anti-imperialist resistance articulates the experiences, aspirations, and restorative vision of a people suffering under the domination of an offshore power" (220). This is tellingly expressed in *The Tower* (1928), in which Yeats advances the prophetic perception that colonial violence has to be counteracted by a politics of reason, which Said takes as "the first important announcement in the context of decolonization of the need to balance violent force with an exigent political and organizational process" (235).

Yeats and Camus, however, were not concerned with distant lands dominated by colonial powers but with what was nearest to them: Ireland and Algeria, the one subjugated by the British, the other a French province. These writers and their ilk were voices inside imperialist nations that tried to turn the colonizing impact of culture against this culture itself, thus anticipating the strategy of postcolonial discourse.

## Modes of Resistance

The developments within imperialistic nations did not give rise to resistance, though they marked a turning point insofar as these nations were confronted with "crimes of violence, crimes of suppression, crimes of conscience" (195). Manifestations of resistance by colonized nations were manifold, depending on time, location, opportunity, and objective. Yet all of them are discourses meant to impinge on imperial hegemony, driven by the intention to remap the very realities that were disfigured by colonialism. Hence they are patterned according to the Foucauldian order of discourse. Their main objective is to imagine a culture and a past independent of colonialism, and to conceive an anti-imperialistic type of nationalism. In view of its different pursuits, anticolonial discourse is also marked by rarefaction, and it becomes the task of postcolonial discourse to highlight the conditionality responsible for the retrenchments.

> Three great topics emerge in decolonizing cultural resistance [ . . . ] One, of course, is the insistence on the right to see the community's history whole, coherently, integrally. Restore the imprisoned nation to itself. [ . . . ] Local slave narratives, spiritual autobiographies, prison memoirs form a counter-point to the Western powers' monumental histories, official discourses, and panoptic quasi-scientific viewpoint. [ . . . ] Second is the idea that resistance, far from being merely a reaction to imperialism, is an alternative way of conceiving human history. [ . . . ] Third is a noticeable pull away from separatist nationalism toward a more integrative view of human community and human liberation. (215f.)

The struggle to achieve these objectives is continually threatened by their dependence on what has to be overcome. Resistance to colonialism cannot help being conditioned by what it opposes. Hence there are anti-colonial discourses which, in spite of their understandable preoccupations, tend to go awry. Nativism is a case in point, which elevates the tribe to a be-all and end-all, and thus reveals by its backward movement that "Imperialism courses on" (230). Equally problematic is an orthodox nationalism that "followed along the same track hewn out by imperialism" (273). In these two instances, resistance is shaped in terms of what it wants to abolish. Therefore Frantz Fanon, the first major proponent of anti-imperialism, maintains that a "rapid step" is to be taken "from national consciousness to political and social consciousness."[9] If advocating nativism and nationalism turns out to be a dead end, it still highlights the power of domination that converts resistance into imitation.

The extent to which metropolitan culture spearheaded imperialism can be gauged from the mimetic reversals of Western literature through which anticolonial discourse gains its salience. Tayeb Salih's *Seasons of Migrations to the North* is a direct inversion of Conrad's *Heart of Darkness*. We have Conrad's river, which evokes a voyage into darkness but this time leads from a Sudanese village into the heart of Europe, where the protagonist – being a mirror image of Kurtz – unleashes the same kind of violence, which for Salih results in the following conclusion: "Over there is like here, neither better nor worse. [ ... ] The fact that they came to our land I know not why, does that mean that we should poison our present and our future? Sooner or later they will leave our country, just as many people throughout history left many countries. [ ... ] Once again we shall be as we were – ordinary people – and if we were lies we shall be lies of our own making."[10]

Equally crucial is the recasting of Shakespeare's *Tempest* by Caribbean writers, who show that Caliban has a history of his own emerging out of his exploitation for the purpose of someone else's development, and hence we must "explode Prospero's old myth" (George Lamming). Moreover, Caliban "is true to the Creole, or *mestizo* composite of the new America," thus being preferred to Ariel, since Caliban is the true symbol of hybridity, as articulated by the Cuban critic Roberto Fernández Retamar (213). Such reinscriptions into paradigms of Western literature illuminate two important aspects of anticolonial discourse. On the one hand, familiar patterns of Western literature are deliberately taken up in order to communicate the agenda of decolonization, but this in itself is a confirmation of Western forms of articulation. On the other hand, however, the hybrid discourse constitutes a massive infusion of non-European cultures into the metropolitan heartland, signaled by what has since been called *The Empire Writes Back*.[11] "Moreover, what Foucault has called the subjugated knowledges," Said contends, "have erupted across the field once controlled, so to speak, by the Judeo-Christian tradition; and those of us who live in the West have been deeply affected by the remarkable outpouring of first-rate literature and scholarship emanating from the post-colonial world, a locale no longer 'one of the dark places of the earth' in Conrad's famous description, but once again the site of vigorous cultural effort" (243).

Thus colonial impingement on the metropolitan heartland has created new configurations of culture, which Said takes pains to illuminate. But what all of them allow us to perceive is the hybridity of culture, which the age of imperialism eclipsed, because the hegemonic culture was taken as indisputably superior to the primitive tribal organization of the colonized. Such an attitude ignored the stratification of culture in the imperialist nations themselves, implicitly assuming that culture has an identity. What in the classical imperial hegemony was an intertwining of power and legitimacy has now changed into a growing awareness of the intertwining of cultures.

## The Order of Postcolonial Discourse

We "should begin by acknowledging that the map of the world has no divinely or dogmatically sanctioned spaces, essences, or privileges" (311). Hence post-colonial discourse imposes itself on those discourses that have charted the world in terms of their own agenda, thus exposing what has powered them and what they have remained silent about. This applies equally to deplorable features of third world discourses, criticism of which prevents postcolonial discourse from becoming merely anticolonial, though it still supports the principles of the latter. Thus postcolonial discourse is primarily an attempt to remap the world charted by imperialism.

The critical thrust of this discourse is to bring to light the important role played by culture in the process of colonization. "At the heart of European culture during the many decades of imperial expansion," Said writes, "lay an undeterred and unrelenting Eurocentrism. This accumulated experiences, territories, peoples, histories; it studied them, it classified them, it verified them [ . . . ] but above all, it subordinated them by banishing their identities, except at a lower order of being, from the culture and indeed the very idea of white Christian Europe. This cultural process has to be seen as a vital, informing, and invigorating counterpoint to the economic and political machinery at the material center of imperialism" (221f.).

Having revealed what powered imperialism, postcolonial discourse takes up basic strands of the order of discourse, as outlined by Foucault: "It is thus that critical and genealogical descriptions are to alternate, support and complete each other. The critical side of the analysis deals with the systems enveloping discourse; attempting to mark out and distinguish the principles of ordering, exclusion and rarity in discourse" (AK 234). However, if contrapuntal reading reveals what has been eclipsed, it functions as a presupposition of what discourse is meant to perform. Dwelling on culture as the energizing force of imperialism is bound to bring culture under close scrutiny. This is all the more pertinent as decolonized peoples assert their own cultures, and in confronting these with the hegemonic one they drive home the fact that culture is never a unified system. It consists instead of a great many "anti-systemic hints and practices for collective human existence" (335), marked by diversity of components, critical energies, and antithetical characteristics. This becomes all the more obvious after the infusion of non-European cultures into the metropolitan center. Instead of taking on an assumed identity, culture is now characterized by hybridity, out of which the ultimate objective of postcolonial discourse arises. Western and third world cultures can no longer be treated separately, as they are inextricably interwoven. Center and periphery have now to be telescoped, so that each becomes the backdrop of the other, and charting this process brings postcolonial discourse to full fruition:

> First, by a new integrative or contrapuntal orientation in history that sees Western and non-Western experiences as belonging together because they are connected by imperialism. Second, by an imaginative, even utopian vision which reconceives emancipatory (as opposed to confining) theory and performance. Third, by an investment neither in new authorities, doctrines, and encoded orthodoxies, nor in established institutions and causes, but in a particular sort of nomadic, migratory, and anti-narrative energy. (279)

Once again this is in line with what the order of discourse, according to Foucault, is meant to achieve. "The genealogical side of discourse, by way of contrast, deals with a series of effective formation of discourse: it attempts to grasp it in its power of affirmation, by which I do not mean a power opposed to that of negation, but the power of constituting domains of objects, in relation to which one can affirm or deny true or false propositions" (AK 234). In remapping a world distorted by imperialism, and enabling us to discriminate between truth and falsehood, postcolonial discourse has become an indispensable aid in our quest to grasp the essence of human culture.[12]

## Notes

1   Stephen Slemon, "Post-Colonial Critical Theories," in Gregory Castle, ed., *Postcolonial Discourses: An Anthology*, Oxford: Blackwell, 2001, p. 100. ("I do not

think that there is a 'postcolonial theory,' because a set of assumptions from which to view colonialism is the basis for a discourse, but not the framework of a theory.")

2  Ibid., p. 104.

3  Ibid., p. 111.

4  Edward W. Said, *The World, the Text, and the Critic*, Cambridge, Mass.: Harvard University Press, 1983, p. 47.

5  Michel Foucault, *L'Ordre du discours*, Paris: Gallimard, 1971.

6  Michel Foucault, *The Archaeology of Knowledge*, trans. A. M. Sheridan Smith, New York: Pantheon Books, 1972, p. 229. The Appendix contains the translation of *L'Ordre du discours* under the title "The Discourse on Language." The sources of all other quotations from this volume are given in the text with references to the appropriate pages, preceded by the letters AK.

7  Foucault, *L'Ordre du discours*, p. 41.

8  Edward W. Said, *Culture and Imperialism*, New York: Vintage Books, 1994. The sources of all quotations from this volume are given in the text with references to the appropriate pages.

9  Quoted in ibid., p. 273.

10  Quoted in ibid., p. 212.

11  See Bill Ashcroft, Gareth Griffiths, and Helen Tiffin, eds., *The Empire Writes Back*, London: Routledge, 1989.

12  Robert J. C. Young, "Colonialism and the Desiring Machine," in Castle, ed., *Postcolonial Discourses*, p. 77, writes: "it would be true to say that Said, Bhabha, and Spivak constitute the Holy Trinity of colonial discourse-analysis, and have to be acknowledged as central to the field."

# Glossary

**Aesthetic idiolect**     "The rule governing all deviations at work at every level of a work of art, the unique diagram which makes all deviations mutually functional" (Umberto Eco, *A Theory of Semiotics*, Bloomington: Indiana University Press, 1976, p. 272).

**Agon**     Contest. In literature the referential realities of the text and intratextual positions are arranged antagonistically.

**Apperception**     Consciousness of having a perception. Perception in terms of past perceptions. The process of understanding by which newly observed qualities of an object are related to past experiences.

**Concretization**     The actualization/realization of a literary work in the act of reading. We are usually not conscious of the difference between the work of art and our own reading of it.

**Correlate**     An individual meaning unit projected by the work and realized as an idea by the reader in the reading process.

**Denotatum**     "Anything that would permit the completion of the response sequence to which an interpreter is disposed because of a sign" (Charles Morris, *Signs, Language and Behavior*, New York: Braziller, 1955, p. 349). That which is signified by the signifier.

**Différance**     "The verb *différer* means to differ and to defer. *Différance* sounds exactly the same as *difference*, but the ending *ance*, which is used to produce the verbal nouns, makes a new form of meaning 'difference-differing-deferring.' Différance thus designates both a 'passive' difference already in place as the condition of signification and an act of differing which produces differences" (Jonathan Culler, *On Deconstruction*, Ithaca: Cornell University Press, 1982, p. 97).

Derrida himself gave the following definition in an interview: "*Différance* is the systematic play of differences, or the traces of differences, of the *spacing* by means of which elements are related to each other. This spacing is the simultaneously active and passive [ ... ] production of the intervals without which the 'full' terms would not signify, would not function" (Jacques Derrida, *Positions*, trans. Alan Bass, Chicago: Chicago University Press, 1981, p. 27).

**Goal-object**     "An object that partially or completely removes the state of an organism (the need) which motivates response-sequences" (Charles Morris, *Signs, Language and Behavior*, New York: Braziller, 1955, p. 349).

**Heuristics/heuristic**     A method of finding something out. In education it means that pupils are trained to find things out for themselves. In aesthetics, it indicates that a certain set of assumptions (gestalt psychology) serves to find out basic features of art.

***Jouissance***     "There is no adequate translation in English of this word. 'Enjoyment' conveys the sense, contained in *jouissance*, of enjoyment of rights, of property etc. [ ... ] in modern English, the word has lost the sexual connotations it still retains in French" ("Translator's note," in Jacques Lacan, *The Four Fundamental Concepts of Psycho-Analysis*, ed. Jacques-Alain Miller, trans. Alan Sheridan, New York and London: Norton, 1981, p. 281).

**Oceanic dedifferentiation/scanning**     "Freud spoke of an 'oceanic' feeling of religious experience; the mystic feels at one with the universe, his individual existence lost like a drop in the ocean [ ... ] Dedifferentiation suspends many kinds of boundaries and distinctions; at an extreme limit it may remove the boundaries of individual existence and so produce a mystic oceanic feeling that is distinctly manic in quality. [ ... ] The artist must not rely on the conventional distinction between 'good' and 'bad' if he attempts truly original work. Instead he must rely on lower undifferentiated types of perception which allow him to grasp the total indivisible structure of the work of art. [ .... ]

The scanning of the total structure enables him to revalue details that initially appeared good or bad. [ ... ] The scanning of the total structure often occurs during a temporary absence of mind. [ ... ] Oceanic dedifferentiation usually occurs only in deeply unconscious levels and so escapes attention; if made conscious, or rather, if the results of unconscious undifferentiated scanning rise to consciousness, we may experience feelings of manic ecstasy. The swing between manic and depressive states may be a direct outcome of the rhythmical alternation between differentiated and undifferentiated types of perception which all creative work entails" (Anton Ehrenzweig, *The Hidden Order of Art*, Berkeley and Los Angeles: California University Press, 1967, pp. 294f.).

**Paradigmatic axis of reading**    Negations in the text point to a hidden motivation, which may adumbrate a positive equivalent. The sequence of these equivalents causes the imaginary object of the text to emerge during the reading process. The object could be an overall meaning, an experience to be transmitted, a communication to be achieved.

**Phallologocentrism**    Phallogocentrism "mercilessly suppresses the uncontrollable multiplicity of ambiguities, the disseminating play of *writing*, which irreducibly transgresses any unequivocal reading" (Barbara Johnson, *The Critical Difference: Essays in the Contemporary Rhetoric of Reading*, Baltimore: Johns Hopkins University Press, 1980, p. 124). It designates the patriarchal structure that organizes the reading of text and the cultural order in general, and is a symbol of power.

**Purposive without purposiveness**    A concept developed by Kant in his *Critique of Judgment*, indicating that the idea of beauty whose features are purposefully organized is without a purpose.

**Recursive loop**    A constructive circularity, in which something is fed forward that triggers a backward feed, either confirming what has been projected or fine-tuning it. Gans's originary scene is fed forward into human history, which appears to have developed according to the assumption of the originary scene, thus confirming the original hypothesis.

**Scanning** (*see* **oceanic dedifferentiation**)

**Speech act theory**    This concerns itself with the actions brought about by linguistic utterances. It distinguishes between two main types of utterance: those which are true in any circumstances, called locutionary speech acts, and those which cause something to happen, called performative speech acts – for instance, saying "I do" in a wedding ceremony.

**Splintering/splitting** (*see also* **structured focusing**)    "The dissociation of the ego's undifferentiated bottom levels from its highly differentiated top

189

levels" (Anton Ehrenzweig, *The Hidden Order of Art: A Study in the Psychology of Artistic Imagination*, Berkeley and Los Angeles: California University Press, 1967, pp. 295f.).

**Structured focusing** (*see also* **splintering**)    The opposite of splintering. The operation in which the surface ego interacts with the undifferentiated levels of the unconscious.

**Supplement**    "The supplement is an inessential extra, added to something complete in itself, but the supplement is added in order to complete, to compensate for a lack in what was supposed to be complete in itself. These two different meanings of *supplement* are linked in a powerful logic, and in both meanings the supplement is presented as exterior, foreign to the 'essential' nature of that to which it is added on or in which it is substituted" (Jonathan Culler, *On Deconstruction*, Ithaca: Cornell University Press, 1982, p. 103).

**Syntagmatic axis of reading**    Sequential linking of heterogeneous sections of the text, which are separated by blanks that transform the text into a sequence of ideas in the reader's mind. Unlike expository writing, which becomes more and more predictable, the literary text enhances its unpredictability by means of this sequence.

**Thick description**    A method proposed and developed by Clifford Geertz for the analysis of culture, roughly defined as follows: "Cultural analysis is (or should be) guessing at meanings, assessing the guesses, and drawing explanatory conclusions from the better guesses" (Clifford Geertz, *The Interpretation of Culture: Selected Essays*, New York: Basic Books, 1973, p. 20). This process cannot appeal for verification to any given frame of reference, unlike "thin description," which is primarily a reification of abstract concepts that are superimposed on cultural phenomena.

**Trichotomy**    Designates a triadic sign relationship, such as sign/object/interpretant, and types of signs such as iconic/indexical/symbolic.

# Appendix A: John Keats, *Ode on a Grecian Urn*

### I

| | | |
|---|---|---|
| | Thou still unravish'd bride of quietness, | a |
| | Thou foster-child of silence and slow time, | b |
| | Sylvan historian, who canst thus express | a |
| | A flowery tale more sweetly than our rhyme: | b |
| 5 | What leaf-fring'd legend haunts about thy shape | c |
| | Of deities or mortals, or of both, | d |
| | In Tempe or the dales of Arcady? | e |
| | What men or gods are these? What maidens loth? | d |
| | What mad pursuit? What struggle to escape? | c |
| 10 | What pipes and timbrels? What wild ecstasy? | e |

### II

| | | |
|---|---|---|
| | Heard melodies are sweet, but those unheard | a |
| | Are sweeter; therefore, ye soft pipes, play on; | b |
| | Not to the sensual ear, but, more endear'd, | a |
| | Pipe to the spirit ditties of no tone: | b |
| 15 | Fair youth, beneath the trees, thou canst not leave | c |
| | Thy song, nor ever can those trees be bare; | d |
| | Bold Lover, never, never canst thou kiss, | e |
| | Though winning near the goal – yet, do not grieve; | c |
| | She cannot fade, though thou hast not thy bliss, | e |
| 20 | For ever wilt thou love, and she be fair! | d |

### III

| | |
|---|---|
| Ah, happy, happy boughs! that cannot shed | a |
|    Your leaves, nor ever bid the Spring adieu; | b |
| And, happy melodist, unwearied, | a |
|    For ever piping songs for ever new; | b |
| More happy love! more happy, happy love! | c |
|    For ever warm and still to be enjoy'd, | d |
|       For ever panting, and for ever young; | e |
| All breathing human passion far above, | c |
|    That leaves a heart high-sorrowful and cloy'd, | d |
|       A burning forehead, and a parching tongue. | e |

25 at line "More happy love! more happy, happy love!"
30 at line "A burning forehead, and a parching tongue."

### IV

| | |
|---|---|
| Who are these coming to the sacrifice? | a |
|    To what green altar, O mysterious priest, | b |
| Lead'st thou that heifer lowing at the skies, | a |
|    And all her silken flanks with garlands drest? | b |
| What little town by river or sea shore, | c |
|    Or mountain-built with peaceful citadel, | d |
|       Is emptied of this folk, this pious morn? | e |
| And, little town, thy streets for evermore | c |
|    Will silent be; and not a soul to tell | d |
|       Why thou art desolate, can e'er return. | e |

35 at line "What little town by river or sea shore,"
40 at line "Why thou art desolate, can e'er return."

### V

| | |
|---|---|
| O Attic shape! Fair attitude! with brede | a |
|    Of marble men and maidens overwrought, | b |
| With forest branches and the trodden weed; | a |
|    Thou, silent form, dost tease us out of thought | b |
| As doth eternity: Cold Pastoral! | c |
|    When old age shall this generation waste, | d |
|       Thou shalt remain, in midst of other woe | e |
| Than ours, a friend to man, to whom thou say'st, | d |
|    Beauty is truth, truth beauty, – that is all | c |
|       Ye know on earth, and all ye need to know. | e |

45 at line "As doth eternity: Cold Pastoral!"
50 at line "Ye know on earth, and all ye need to know."

# Appendix B: Edmund Spenser, "Februarie: Aegloga Secunda" from *The Shepheardes Calender*

ARGUMENT.

THIS ÆGLOGUE is rather morall and generall, then bent to any secrete or particular purpose. It specially conteyneth a discourse of old age, in the persone of *Thenot* an olde Shepheard, who for his crookednesse and unlustinesse, is scorned of *Cuddie* an unhappy Heardmans boye. The matter very well accordeth with the season of the moneth, the yeare now drouping, & as it were, drawing to his last age. For as in this time of yeare, so then in our bodies there is a dry & withering cold, which congealeth the crudled blood, & frieseth the wetherbeaten flesh, with stormes of Fortune, and hoare frosts of Care. To which purpose the olde man telleth a tale of the Oake and the Bryer, so lively and so feelingly, as if the thing were set forth in some Picture before our eyes, more plainly could not appeare.

CUDDIE.   THENOT.

AH for pittie, wil rancke Winters rage,
These bitter blasts never ginne tasswage?
The kene cold blowes through my beathen hyde,
All as I were through the body gryde.
My ragged rontes all shiver and shake,
As doen high Towers in an earthquake:
They wont in the wind wagge their wrigle tailes,
Perke as Peacock: but nowe it avales.

THENOT.

Lewdly complainest thou laesie ladde,
Of Winters wracke, for making thee sadde.
Must not the world wend in his commun course
From good to badd, and from badde to worse,
From worse unto that is worst of all,
And then returne to his former fall?
Who will not suffer the stormy time,
Where will he live tyll the lusty prime?
Selfe have I worne out thrise threttie yeares,
Some in much joy, many in many teares:
Yet never complained of cold nor heate,
Of Sommers flame, nor of Winters threat:
Ne ever was to Fortune foeman,
But gently tooke, that ungently came.
And ever my flocke was my chiefe care,
Winter or Sommer they mought well fare.

CUDDIE.

No marveile *Thenot*, if thou can beare
Cherefully the Winters wrathfull cheare:

For Age and Winter accord full nie,
This chill, that cold, this crooked, that wrye.
And as the lowring Wether lookes downe,
So semest thou like good fryday to frowne.
But my flowring youth is foe to frost,
My shippe unwont in stormes to be tost.

### THENOT.

The soveraigne of seas he blames in vaine,
That once seabeate, will to sea againe.
So loytring live you little heardgroomes,
Keeping your beastes in the budded broomes:
And when the shining sunne laugheth once,
You deemen, the Spring is come attonce.
Tho gynne you, fond flyes, the cold to scorne,
And crowing in pypes made of greene corne,
You thinken to be Lords of the yeare.
But eft, when ye count you freed from feare,
Comes the breme winter with chamfred browes,
Full of wrinckles and frostie furrowes:
Drerily shooting his stormy darte,
Which cruddles the blood, and pricks the harte.
Then is your carelesse corage accoied,
Your carefull heards with cold bene annoied.
Then paye you the price of your surquedrie,
With weeping, and wayling, and misery.

### CUDDIE.

Ah foolish old man, I scorne thy skill,
That wouldest me, my springing youngth to spil.
I deeme, thy braine emperished bee
Through rusty elde, that hath rotted thee:
Or sicker thy head veray tottie is,
So on thy corbe shoulder it leanes amisse.
Now thy selfe hast lost both lopp and topp,
Als my budding braunch thou wouldest cropp:
But were thy yeares greene, as now bene myne,
To other delights they would encline.
Tho wouldest thou learne to caroll of Love,

And hery with hymnes thy lasses glove.
Tho wouldest thou pype of *Phyllis* prayse:
But *Phyllis* is myne for many dayes:
I wonne her with a gyrdle of gelt,
Embost with buegle about the belt.
Such an one shepeheards woulde make full faine:
Such an one would make thee younge againe.


THENOT.
Thou art a fon, of thy love to boste,
All that is lent to love, wyll be lost.


CUDDIE.
Seest, howe brag yond Bullocke beares,
So smirke, so smoothe, his pricked eares?
His hornes bene as broade, as Rainebowe bent,
His dewelap as lythe, as lasse of Kent.
See howe he venteth into the wynd.
Weenest of love is not his mynd?
Seemeth thy flocke thy counsell can,
So lustlesse bene they, so weake so wan,
Clothed with cold, and hoary wyth frost.
Thy flocks father his corage hath lost:
Thy Ewes, that wont to have blowen bags,
Like wailefull widdowes hangen their crags:
The rather Lambes bene starved with cold,
All for their Maister is lustlesse and old.


THENOT.
*Cuddie,* I wote thou kenst little good,
So vainely tadvaunce thy headlesse hood.
For Youngth is a bubble blown up with breath,
Whose witt is weakenesse, whose wage is death,
Whose way is wildernesse, whose ynne Penaunce,
And stoopegallaunt Age the hoste of Greevaunce.
But shall I tel thee a tale of truth,
Which I cond of *Tityrus* in my youth,
Keeping his sheepe on the hils of Kent?

CUDDIE.

To nought more *Thenot*, my mind is bent,
Then to heare novells of his devise:
They bene so well thewed, and so wise,
What ever that good old man bespake.

THENOT.

Many meete tales of youth did he make,
And some of love, and some of chevalrie:
But none fitter then this to applie.
Now listen a while, and hearken the end.

THERE grewe an aged Tree on the greene,
A goodly Oake sometime had it bene,
With armes full strong and largely displayd,
But of their leaves they were disarayde:
The bodie bigge, and mightely pight,
Throughly rooted, and of wonderous hight:
Whilome had bene the King of the field,
And mochell mast to the husband did yielde,
And with his nuts larded many swine.
But now the gray mosse marred his rine,
His bared boughes were beaten with stormes,
His toppe was bald, and wasted with wormes,
His honor decayed, his braunches sere.
   Hard by his side grewe a bragging brere,
Which proudly thrust into Thelement,
And seemed to threat the Firmament.
Yt was embellisht with blossomes fayre,
And thereto aye wonned to repayre
The shepheards daughters, to gather flowres,
To peinct their girlonds with his colowres.
And in his small bushes used to shrowde
The sweete Nightingale singing so lowde:
Which made this foolish Brere wexe so bold,
That on a time he cast him to scold,
And snebbe the good Oake, for he was old.
   Why standst there (quoth he) thou brutish blocke?
Nor for fruict, nor for shadow serves thy stocke:

Seest, how fresh my flowers bene spredde,
Dyed in Lilly white, and Cremsin redde,
With Leaves engrained in lusty greene,
Colours meete to clothe a mayden Queene.
Thy wast bignes but combers the grownd,
And dirks the beauty of my blossomes rownd.
The mouldie mosse, which thee accloieth,
My Sinamon smell too much annoieth.
Wherefore soone I rede thee, hence remove,
Least thou the price of my displeasure prove.
So spake this bold brere with great disdaine:
Little him answered the Oake againe,
But yielded, with shame and greefe adawed,
That of a weede he was overawed.

   Yt chaunced after upon a day,
The Husbandman selfe to come that way,
Of custome for to servewe his grownd,
And his trees of state in compasse rownd.
Him when the spitefull brere had espyed,
Causlesse complained, and lowdly cryed
Unto his Lord, stirring up sterne strife:
O my liege Lord, the God of my life,
Pleaseth you ponder your Suppliants plaint,
Caused of wrong, and cruell constraint,
Which I your poore Vassall dayly endure:
And but your goodnes the same recure,
Am like for desperate doole to dye,
Through felonous force of mine enemie.

   Greatly aghast with this piteous plea,
Him rested the goodman on the lea,
And badde the Brere in his plaint proceede.
With painted words tho gan this proude weede,
(As most usen Ambitious folke:)
His colowred crime with craft to cloke.

   Ah my soveraigne, Lord of creatures all,
Thou placer of plants both humble and tall,
Was not I planted of thine owne hand,
To be the primrose of all thy land.
With flowring blossomes, to furnish the prime,

And scarlot berries in Sommer time?
How falls it then, that this faded Oake,
Whose bodie is sere, whose braunches broke,
Whose naked Armes stretch unto the fyre,
Unto such tyrannie doth aspire:
Hindering with his shade my lovely light,
And robbing me of the swete sonnes sight?
So beate his old boughes my tender side,
That oft the bloud springeth from wounds wyde:
Untimely my flowres forced to fall,
That bene the honor of your Coronall.
And oft he lets his cancker wormes light
Upon my braunches, to worke me more spight:
And oft his hoarie locks downe doth cast,
Where with my fresh flowretts bene defast.
For this, and many more such outrage,
Craving your goodlihead to as wage
The ranckorous rigour of his might,
Nought aske I, but onely to hold my right:
Submitting me to your good sufferance,
And praying to be garded from greevance.
   To this the Oake cast him to replie
Well as he couth: but his enemie
Had kindled such coles of displeasure,
That the good man noulde stay his leasure,
But home him hasted with furious heate,
Encreasing his wrath with many a threate.
His harmefull Hatchet he hent in hand,
(Alas, that it so ready should stand)
And to the field alone he speedeth.
(Ay little helpe to harme there needeth)
Anger nould let him speake to the tree,
Enaunter his rage mought cooled bee:
But to the roote bent his sturdy stroke,
And made many wounds in the wast Oake.
The Axes edge did oft turne againe,
As halfe unwilling to cutte the graine:
Semed, the sencelesse yron dyd feare,
Or to wrong holy eld did for beare.

For it had bene an auncient tree,
Sacred with many a mysteree,
And often crost with the priestes crewe,
And often halowed with holy water dewe.
But sike fancies weren foolerie,
And broughten this Oake to this miserye.
For nought mought they quitten him from decay:
For fiercely the good man at him did laye.
The blocke oft groned under the blow,
And sighed to see his neare overthrow.
In fine the steele had pierced his pitth,
Tho downe to the earth he fell forth with:
HIs wonderous weight made the grounde to quake,
Thearth shronke under him, and seemed to shake.
There lyeth the Oake, pitied of none.
    Now stands the Brere like a Lord alone,
Puffed up with pryde and vaine pleasaunce:
But all this glee had no continuance.
For eftsones Winter gan to approche,
The blustring Boreas did encroche,
And beate upon the solitarie Brere:
For nowe no succoure was seene him nere.
Now gan he repent his pryde to late:
For naked left and disconsolate,
The byting frost nipt his stalke dead,
The watrie wette weighed downe his head,
And heaped snowe burdned him so sore,
That nowe upright he can stand no more:
And being downe, is trodde in the durt
Of cattell, and brouzed, and sorely hurt.
Such was thend of this Ambitious brere,
For scorning Eld.

CUDDIE.

    Now I pray thee shepheard, tel it not forth:
Here is a long tale, and little worth.
So longe have I listened to thy speche,
That graffed to the ground is my breche:
My hartblood is welnigh frorne I feele,

And my galage growne fast to my heele:
But little ease of thy lewd tale I tasted.
Hye thee home shepheard, the day is nigh wasted.

THENOTS EMBLEME.

*Iddio perche è vecchio,*
*Fa suoi al suo essempio.*

CUDDIES EMBLEME.

*Niuno vecchio,*
*Spaventa Iddio.*

GLOSSE.

KENE) sharpe.
Gride) perced: an olde word much used of Lidgate, but not found (that I know of) in Chaucer.
❧Ronts) young bullockes.

❧Wracke) ruine or Violence, whence commeth ship-wracke: & not wreake, that is vengeaunce or wrath.
❧Foeman) a foe.
❧Thenot) the name of a shepheard in Marot his Æglogues.
❧The soveraigne of Seas) is Neptune the God of the seas. The saying is borowed of Mimus Publianus, which used this proverb in a verse.
Improbè Neptunum accusat, qui iterum naufragium facit.
❧Heardgromes) Chaucers verse almost whole.
❧Fond Flyes) He compareth carelesse sluggardes or ill husbandmen to flyes, that so soone as the sunne shineth, or yt wexeth any thing warme, begin to flye abroade, when sodeinly they be over-taken with cold.
❧But eft when) A verye excellent and lively description of Winter, so as may

bee indifferently taken, eyther for old Age, or for Winter season.
❧Breme) chill, bitter.
❧Chamfred) chapt, or wrinckled.
❧Accoied) plucked downe and daunted.
❧Surquedrie) pryde.
❧Elde) olde age.
❧Sicker) sure.
❧Tottie) wavering.
❧Corbe) crooked.
❧Herie) worshippe.
❧Phyllis) the name of some mayde unknowen, whom Cuddie, whose person is secrete, loved. The name is usuall in Theocritus, Virgile, and Mantuane.
❧Belte) a girdle or wast band.
❧A fon) a foole.
❧lythe) soft and gentile.
❧Venteth) snuffeth in the wind.
❧Thy flocks Father) the Ramme.
❧Crags) neckes.
❧Rather Lambes) that be ewed early in the beginning of the yeare.
❧Youth is) A verye moral and pitthy Allegorie of youth, and the lustes thereof, compared to a wearie wayfaring man.
❧Tityrus) I suppose he meane Chaucer, whose prayse for pleasaunt tales cannot

dye, so long as the memorie of hys name shal live, and the name of Poetrie shal endure.

¶Well thewed) that is, Bene moratæ, full of morall wisenesse.

¶There grew) This tale of the Oake and the Brere, he telleth as learned of Chaucer, but it is cleane in another kind, and rather like to Æsopes fables. It is very excellente for pleasaunt descriptions, being altogether a certaine Icon or Hypotyposis of disainfull younkers.

¶Embellisht) beautified and adorned.

¶To wonne) to haunt or frequent.

¶Sneb) checke.

¶Why standst) The speach is scornefull and very presumptuous.

¶Engrained) dyed in grain.

¶Accloieth) encombreth.

¶Adawed) daunted and confounded.

¶Trees of state) taller trees fitte for timber wood.

¶Sterne strife) said Chaucer .s. fell and sturdy.

¶O my liege) a maner of supplication, wherein is kindly coloured the affection and speache of Ambitious men.

¶Coronall) Garlande.

¶Flourets) young blossomes.

¶The Primrose) The chiefe and worthiest.

¶Naked armes) metaphorically ment of the bare boughes, spoyled of leaves. This colourably he speaketh, as adjudging hym to the fyre.

¶The blood) spoken of a blocke, as it were of a living creature, figuratively, and (as they saye) κατ᾽ εἰκασμόν.

¶Hoarie lockes) metaphorically for withered leaves.

¶Hent) caught.

¶Nould) for would not.

¶Ay) evermore.

¶Wounds) gashes.

¶Enaunter) least that.

¶The priestes crewe) holy water pott, wherewith the popishe priest used to sprinckle and hallowe the trees from mischaunce. Such blindnesse was in those times, which the Poete supposeth, to have bene the finall decay of this auncient Oake.

¶The blocke oft groned) A livelye figure, whiche geveth sence and feeling to unsensible creatures, as Virgile also sayeth: Saxa gemunt gravido &c.

¶Boreas) The Northerne wynd, that bringeth the moste stormie weather.

¶Glee) chere and jollitie.

¶For scorning Eld) And minding (as shoulde seme) to have made ryme to the former verse, he is conningly cutte of by Cuddye, as disdayning to here any more.

¶Galage) a startuppe or clownish shoe.

EMBLEME

¶This embleme is spoken of Thenot, as a moral of his former tale: namelye, that God, which is himselfe most aged, being before al ages, and without beginninge, maketh those, whom he loveth like to himselfe, in heaping yeares unto theyre dayes, and blessing them wyth longe lyfe. For the blessing of age is not given to all, but unto those, whome God will so blesse: and albeit hat many evil men reache unto such fulnesse of yeares, and some also wexe olde in myserie and thraldome, yet therefore is not age ever the lesse blessing. For even to such evill men such number of yeares is added, that they may in their last dayes repent, and come to their first home. So the old man check-eth the rashheaded boy, for despysing his gray and frostye heares.

❡Whom Cuddye doth counterbuff with a byting and bitter proverbe, spoken indeede at the first in contempt of old age generally, for it was an old opinion, and yet is continued in some mens conceipt, that men of yeares have no feare of god at al, or not so much as younger folke. For that being rypened with long experience, and having passed many bitter brunts and blastes of vengeaunce, they dread no stormes of Fortune, nor wrathe of Gods, nor daunger of menne, as being eyther by longe and ripe wisedome armed against all mischaunces and adversitie, or with much trouble hardened against all troublesome tydes: lyke unto the Ape, of which is sayd in Æsops fables, that oftentimes meeting the Lyon, he was at first sore aghast and dismayed at the grimnes and austeritie of hys countenance, but at last being acquainted with his lookes, he was so furre from fearing him, that he would familiarly gybe and jest with him: Suche longe experience breedeth in some men securitie. Although it please Erasmus a great clerke and good old father, more fatherly and favourablye to construe it in his Adages for his own behoofe, That by the proverbe Nemo Senex metuit Jovem, is not meant, that old men have no feare of God at al, but that they be furre from superstition and Idolatrous regard of false Gods, as is Jupiter. But his greate learning notwithstanding, it is to plaine, to be gainsayd, that olde men are muche more enclined to such fond fooleries, then younger heades.

# Appendix C: T. S. Eliot, "The Fire Sermon" from *The Waste Land*

The river's tent is broken: the last fingers of leaf
Clutch and sink into the wet bank. The wind
Crosses the brown land, unheard. The nymphs are departed.
Sweet Thames, run softly, till I end my song.
The river bears no empty bottles, sandwich papers,
Silk handkerchiefs, cardboard boxes, cigarette ends
Or other testimony of summer nights. The nymphs are departed.
And their friends, the loitering heirs of city directors;
Departed, have left no addresses.
By the waters of Leman I sat down and wept . . .                                    10
Sweet Thames, run softly till I end my song,
Sweet Thames, run softly, for I speak not loud or long.
But at my back in a cold blast I hear
The rattle of the bones, and chuckle spread from ear to ear.
A rat crept softly through the vegetation
Dragging its slimy belly on the bank
While I was fishing in the dull canal
On a winter evening round behind the gashouse
Musing upon the king my brother's wreck
And on the king my father's death before him.                                       20
White bodies naked on the low damp ground
And bones cast in a little low dry garret,
Rattled by the rat's foot only, year to year.
But at my back from time to time I hear
The sound of horns and motors, which shall bring
Sweeney to Mrs. Porter in the spring.

O the moon shone bright on Mrs. Porter
And on her daughter
They wash their feet in soda water
*Et O ces voix d'enfants, chantant dans la coupole!*                    30

Twit twit twit
Jug jug jug jug jug jug
So rudely forc'd.
Tereu

Unreal City
Under the brown fog of a winter noon
Mr. Eugenides, the Smyrna merchant
Unshaven, with a pocket full of currants
C.i.f. London: documents at sight,
Asked me in demotic French                                             40
To luncheon at the Cannon Street Hotel
Followed by a weekend at the Metropole.

At the violet hour, when the eyes and back
Turn upward from the desk, when the human engine waits
Like a taxi throbbing waiting,
I Tiresias, though blind, throbbing between two lives,
Old man with wrinkled female breasts, can see
At the violet hour, the evening hour that strives
Homeward, and brings the sailor home from sea,
The typist home at teatime, clears her breakfast, lights            50
Her stove, and lays out food in tins.
Out of the window perilously spread
Her drying combinations touched by the sun's last rays,
On the divan are piled (at night her bed)
Stockings, slippers, camisoles, and stays.
I Tiresias, old man with wrinkled dugs
Perceived the scene, and foretold the rest –
I too awaited the expected guest.
He, the young man carbuncular, arrives,
A small house agent's clerk, with one bold stare,                   60
One of the low on whom assurance sits
As a silk hat on a Bradford millionaire.
The time is now propitious, as he guesses,

The meal is ended, she is bored and tired,
Endeavours to engage her in caresses
Which still are unreproved, if undesired.
Flushed and decided, he assaults at once;
Exploring hands encounter no defence;
His vanity requires no response,
And makes a welcome of indifference.                    70
(And I Tiresias have foresuffered all
Enacted on this same divan or bed;
I who have sat by Thebes below the wall
And walked among the lowest of the dead.)
Bestows one final patronising kiss,
And gropes his way, finding the stairs unlit . . .

She turns and looks a moment in the glass,
Hardly aware of her departed lover;
Her brain allows one half-formed thought to pass:
"Well now that's done: and I'm glad it's over."          80
When lovely woman stoops to folly and
Paces about her room again, alone,
She smoothes her hair with automatic hand,
And puts a record on the gramophone.

"This music crept by me upon the waters"
And along the Strand, up Queen Victoria Street.
O City city, I can sometimes hear
Beside a public bar in Lower Thames Street,
The pleasant whining of a mandoline
And a clatter and a chatter from within                  90
Where fishmen lounge at noon: where the walls
Of Magnus Martyr hold
Inexplicable splendour of Ionian white and gold.

                    The river sweats
                    Oil and tar
                    The barges drift
                    With the turning tide
                    Red sails
                    Wide
                    To leeward, swing on the heavy spar.   100

The barges wash
Drifting logs
Down Greenwich reach
Past the Isle of Dogs.
                    Weialala leia
                    Wallala leialala

Elizabeth and Leicester
Beating oars
The stern was formed
A gilded shell                                              110
Red and gold
The brisk swell
Rippled both shores
Southwest wind
Carried down stream
The peal of bells
White towers
                    Weialala leia
                    Wallala leialala

"Trams and dusty trees.                                     120
Highbury bore me. Richmond and Kew
Undid me. By Richmond I raised my knees
Supine on the floor of a narrow canoe."

"My feet are at Moorgate, and my heart
Under my feet. After the event
He wept. He promised 'a new start.'
I made no comment. What should I resent?"

"On Margate Sands.
I can connect
Nothing with nothing.                                       130
The broken fingernails of dirty hands.
My people humble people who expect
Nothing."
                    la la

To Carthage then I came

Burning burning burning burning
O Lord Thou pluckest me out
O Lord Thou pluckest

burning

# Index